GROUPS IN GUIDANCE

ALLYN AND BACON, INC.   BOSTON, 1962

GROUPS IN GUIDANCE

THE DYNAMICS OF GROUPS
AND THE APPLICATION OF GROUPS IN GUIDANCE

Pages 323 through 354 are missing.

EDWARD C. GLANZ

Professor and Chairman, Psychology and Guidance Division
College of Basic Studies, Boston University

24374

PREFACE

Groups provide a basic tool for all counselors, guidance personnel, and teachers. Counseling and testing have long been major approaches within guidance and personnel programs; groups and group techniques offer a third major strategy.

Administrators, teachers, and guidance personnel are all aware of the need for a thorough understanding of the rationale, applications, advantages, and dangers of testing and counseling as they are used with students. Group approaches demand a similarly rigorous adherence to total understanding of the dynamics of the group in guidance.

The use of groups in a guidance program can help to provide a deeper and broader concept of learning and living in school. Successful application, however, depends upon an acceptance of group approaches based upon scientific knowledge and research. *Groups in Guidance* is based upon three assumptions:

1. Group techniques can provide a fundamental approach in guidance, counseling, and education.
2. Group approaches have arisen from a body of basic scientific research and study; group techniques must be understood as

tools useful in patterning social interaction and learning climates.

3. Specific applications of group techniques in guidance and personnel programs are possible and desirable.

Three major sections are included in *Groups in Guidance;* each part is an outgrowth of one of the foregoing assumptions.

E.C.G.

ACKNOWLEDGEMENTS

Many persons help an author to complete a book. Reviews of outlines, chapters, and even brief sections were offered by counselors, group workers, and guidance persons. Groups and guidance were first joined for the author by Professor Kenneth Herrold of Teachers College, Columbia University. Boston University offered a supporting and flexible environment for experimentation. An alert peer group in the Psychology and Guidance Division of the College of Basic Studies offered constant sharpening and testing of all ideas.

Judith Dennis, Sandra Myers, and Mary Beth Wells all aided in the preparation and typing of the manuscript. Delores Getchell prepared the illustrative sketches. The editorial and administrative staff at Allyn and Bacon guided and nurtured ideas and specifics.

Other authors and publishers have graciously permitted many short and long quotations. Credits are indicated by authors' names and references to the bibliography.

A family always shares in the writing of a book. Shirley, Erich, and Gary have accepted the step of a husband and father to a drummer they do not hear. They have made it possible for Thoreau's words to live.

CONTENTS

If a man does not keep pace with his companions,
perhaps it is because he hears a different drummer.
Let him step to the music which he hears,
however measured or far away.

HENRY DAVID THOREAU

PART ONE

Group techniques, psychological testing, and individual counseling form the three conceptual tools that aid guidance workers in individualizing the goals of education. Part 1 defines the basic elements of a group, illustrates how groups relate to guidance and education, and offers a philosophy of the use of groups in guidance.

1. GROUPS, GROUPWORK, AND GROUP GUIDANCE

The time has come . . . to talk of many things: of shoes—and ships—and sealing wax—of cabbages—and kings . . . . This conversation from the walrus and the carpenter in *Alice in Wonderland* is appropriate to many situations. It is particularly apt whenever guidance workers, counselors, or college personnel workers attempt to organize their ideas and feelings about groups, groupwork, and "group guidance." Instead of shoes, cabbages, and kings, the terms *cohesiveness, process observers,* and *functional leadership* can easily be substituted; and the sea has become "boiling hot"; and pigs do have wings.

The crowded, tortuous history of groups of all types in guidance has cast a cloud of uncertainty and distortion over a collection of specific and useful guidance tools which can be applied effectively by personnel workers and guidance counselors on all educational levels. A brief review of ideas, concepts, and approaches can bring order to what may at first appear to be chaos. An examination of the relationship between counseling and group activities, and a brief view of the philosophical basis in guidance for group activities will also aid in obtaining a meaningful perspective of groups in guidance.

GROUPS IN PERSPECTIVE

Groups can be used effectively and conveniently in many settings. The family is a primary group, and much can be learned within the intimate setting of the family about the dynamics of interpersonal relations. Community groups, church groups, government organizations, recreation groups, and sports teams have historically and purposely used group procedures. However, the classroom, from kindergarten to graduate seminar, is the primary environment in which guidance workers function. Common examples of groups in operation are illustrated in the following situations:

> . . . and the children were playing "colors." They were all seated in a circle on the floor and there were five large discs of different colors. One child would remove a disc while all the other children covered their eyes. In turn, each child would attempt to state which disc had been removed. If the child succeeded in this task, he was permitted to remove the next disc. (Kindergarten teacher)

> The class, restricted to twenty registrations, was organized on the first day very arbitrarily by the professor. There were four tables which formed a square, and five of the students were requested to sit at each of the tables. The professor said that this would allow each of us to see the other members of the class. We filled out a seating chart, and he promised to have it mimeographed for us for the next class meeting. He sat outside the square and made us discuss the reasons why we had registered for the course. He would not participate in the discussion; but, rather, told us that we would have to learn to discuss ideas among ourselves. He summarized at the end of the hour and gave us a "whopping" big assignment for the next class meeting. (Graduate student in political economy)

> We are going to discuss the Case of Mary today. She has applied for entrance into the state teachers' college. You all have the mimeographed case study with Mary's grades here at Central High School. The second page lists all of the results of guidance tests that Mary took while she was a student at this high school. At the close of our group discussions, the recorder for each group will report the conclusions of each group to the class. After all seven groups have reported, I will review with you what actually happened to Mary and

what she is doing now. (Group guidance teacher to sophomore guidance class of 62 students)

She gave us a slip of paper with our test scores on it. We had to draw a "graph" and color it in. She said we would talk about the test scores tomorrow. (Seventh grade student)

Each of these situations reveals a different group in operation within a school setting. Each of the group situations concerns a task. There is a specific assignment for each member of the group, and the group as a whole has an objective. The group sizes vary from approximately six to thirty. The first two groups are regular classes in a standard school situation: kindergarten and graduate school. The other two groups illustrate groups in guidance activities. One wonders what growth the future holds for the members in each group.

Elementary school groups

The creative use of small groups is traditional in the early grades of a school system. Groups are necessary in the first few grades; they are the foundation of good teaching. The elementary school teacher has been recognized as an important guidance resource along with others who are specialists (Cottingham, 1956; Martinson and Smallenberg, 1958). The child in the lower grades is unable to verbalize his counseling problems, and varying guidance skills are mandatory for the teacher at this level. The elementary school teacher is called upon not only to teach skillfully, but also to aid in the diagnostic study of the child and to assist in the follow-through with recommendations for treatment and action.

Daily experiences in the early grades involve teachers in reading groups, while a coloring group strives to keep crayon marks within the lines of drawings. Games and singing exercises are introduced through group organization. Occupational activities and mental health efforts are often the responsibility of the classroom teacher in the upper grades in elementary schools. Some achievement and aptitude test results may be used in guidance of groups and individuals. Group procedures may also be used in helping parents to understand their children.

The more formal guidance activities in the elementary school are the responsibilities of speech therapists, remedial reading specialists, school psychologists and psychometrists, school social workers, and the health staff. Diagnostic data are often gathered on the basis of pupil performance in group situations such as peer adjustments in play and school-work groups.

These group behaviors are a child's responses to his school affiliations. Treatment procedures also are often undertaken through group structures. Reading and speech groups, and even the manipulation of environmental forces and group pressures are all standard approaches of specialists in the elementary system (Rosecrance and Hayden, 1960; Newman, 1956).

Junior high school groups

Group guidance, orientation, occupations, or life adjustment classes usually make their first appearance in the school system at the junior high school level. The beginning of occupational exploration on a more formal basis is frequently required in these grades. Aptitude batteries, such as the Differential Aptitude Tests and the California Aptitude Tests, are often administered to students. Interest inventories may be given, and continued testing in the achievement areas provides guidance personnel with a wide range of guidance data on individual students.

School psychologists or well-trained school counselors are capable of handling many of the problems which occur among students in the junior high schools. However, an overwhelming number of students in this group need to be introduced to problems of self-analysis through an understanding of the data that has been collected about them in the guidance program. Guidance workers must provide service and assistance to the child who does not have serious problems, since this type of child predominates. Newer programs designed to aid in this process of self-understanding through group effort have recently been developed.

The junior high school years, transition years in which the student is becoming capable of symbolizing and verbalizing his problems, are a fertile period for effective mental health learning. Students are able to examine themselves, their group relationships, their family structures, their future plans, and other important areas of education and learning. Groups can provide a pathway for teachers, counselors and guidance workers to assist students facing these problems (Marsolf, 1956, pp. 356–81; Redl and Wattenberg, 1959, pp. 262–96).

Groups in high school

Traditionally, it has been at the high school level that guidance and counseling activities have been emphasized, and this continues to be so. Group activities are involved in virtually every phase of guidance. More specifically, groups can be used effectively and conveniently in all these areas:

1. School organization and program
2. Student orientation
3. School publications
4. The curriculum
5. Life adjustment courses
6. Psychology courses
7. Educational planning
8. Vocational planning
9. Occupations courses
10. Pre-counseling units
11. Multiple counseling
12. Psychological testing
13. College planning
14. Student activities
15. Reading courses
16. Speech therapy
17. Self-appraisal
18. Placement

The dimensions of group activities on the high school level are limited only by the creativity of the guidance personnel in charge of the program.

Groups in higher education

Junior colleges, teachers' colleges, liberal arts colleges, professional and technical schools, as well as graduate schools, provide settings for the use of groups. All secondary school program areas are generally present on a higher education level. Additional environments, not found in secondary schools, also provide an opportunity for the creative use of groups. Such resources include dormitories, houses, dining facilities, fraternities, sororities, graduate seminars, and faculty homes. Private schools on either a secondary or post-secondary school level offer opportunities for creative groupwork, routinely. Many institutions stress such possibilities in their advertising and public relations programs.

WHAT IS A GROUP

A group may be a three-member subcommittee for the senior prom, a sixteen-member occupational study group, a six-member group psychotherapy session, a two-member speech therapy conference, or even a class of one hundred and fifty students. These illustrations demonstrate reasons for the confused feelings many guidance counselors and teachers have towards groups and groupwork ideas. The meaning of a word varies with the user and with the situation.

Group practices are so different that only complex and abstract definitions can encompass most types of groups (Homans, 1950; Cooley, 1909; Sherif and Sherif, 1953). Some authors simply state that a group is "several persons," or "a collection of individuals" doing things co-operatively. "Group guidance" is defined in many ways; an inclusive definition is "any phase" of a program of guidance carried on with "groups of individuals" (Bennett, 1955, p. 2).

Interaction, size, and *function* are three concepts in group theory which can aid in clarifying the meaning and use of the term "group." These ideas are basic to an understanding of the use of group procedures in varying environments, such as guidance programs, counseling, and classrooms.

Interaction

An interdependent effect of group members' activities is a mandatory condition in a group.

Several women in a large department store watching a demonstration of a new hair-curling device may be referred to as a group. Yet it is obvious that the women are not members of a true group. There is no interaction. Outside of physical contiguity, there is no meaning when the word group is used in this context.

An example of a distant, but meaningful interaction relationship in a group is three people swimming together in an isolated cove. They are dependent upon each other, and each derives a tentative feeling of safety from the mere presence of the others. Cattell (1951) speaks of this situation as a "true group."

Definitions often seem to involve extreme examples, but the degree of the interrelatedness of the members in a group can help to differentiate among mobs, crowds, collections, lectures, classes and other groups. The idea of interaction among the members of a group is incorporated in the term "group dynamics" as used by Kurt Lewin (Bach, 1954, p. 340).

A different meaning of the term "interaction" exists when interaction is associated with the idea of the group "field." This group field is greater than the sum of its interacting parts, the members of the group. This concept is an outgrowth of the "Gestalt" psychologists and the writings of Lewin (1951), Cartwright (1951), and others.

Interaction of members (group dynamics) and interaction between the group and its members (group field) are essential to the existence of a group.

Size

Disagreement exists about the minimum and maximum number of persons for a group. The minimum is sometimes set at two persons, sometimes at three. Two persons are regarded as a special unit such as a dyad, couple, or pair. Counseling, therapy, tutoring and many other activities of two persons have not usually been considered as group activities. Certain principles of group theory frequently apply in the two-person unit, but three persons is a more useful and meaningful minimum for a group.

A maximum figure for group size is even more difficult to determine. Authorities and research have established maximums for various types of groups, but never in a total or gross sense. Classes of one hundred or more are referred to as groups in reports of case study discussions at the Harvard Business School. These groups are interactive in every sense of the word, yet it is difficult to think of other interacting groups of this size.

School groups can be small, medium, or large. Let us consider a small group as having 3–6 members; a medium group, 5–18; and a large group, over 18. Let us also recognize that this breakdown is relative and would be inappropriate under unusual circumstances. The interpretation of size as a variable in groups is related to the purpose of the group and the biases and attitudes of those in charge of it. The issue of exact size for a group is often a spurious concern.

The hapless teacher, skilled in her own field, but not knowledgeable about group procedures, who has been summarily assigned to a class of sixty-five active youngsters and told to "give 'em group guidance," is understandably hostile to group guidance and group procedures. However, her anger should be directed toward the uncritical and undesirable administrative decision, rather than toward "group guidance." The capable American history teacher might more effectively teach a street corner gang in a large American city how to play cricket than attempt to lead a large class in group procedures in guidance, about which he knows nothing. There are techniques and approaches for accomplishing such a task, but success depends upon the judicious use of many sophisticated group skills.

Function

Function, or purpose, is a third concept in the theory of groups that can bring order to conflicting claims and research results in the area of groups. A simple classification of three categories can include most groups and still differentiate among diverse concepts of action in groups. Groups are usually organized for three reasons: (1) to accomplish a task, (2) to develop or change the participants, or (3) to provide a structured learning situation (class). Purists will immediately cry that the third classification must include the first two categories; all groups provide a learning situation. However, much has been accomplished by teachers in a classroom structure in school or non-school situations with no reference to group procedures as such. The class is a group and many of the techniques, approaches, and skills of groupwork are appropriately used in classroom situations. (N.S.S.E., 1960). The puddle only becomes muddled as age-old teaching devices are equated with group procedures.

Task groups and growth groups are two clearly recognizable concepts. *Task-centered groups* are organized to do specific jobs. Committees are appointed to prepare a report, an occupational group is organized to complete a field trip to an electronics assembly plant, or a small group of students is charged with the task of discussing a case study and making action recommendations. The job of the group is assumed to be accomplishable.

Growth-centered groups are concerned primarily with aiding members to gain skills, to develop insights, to socialize, or even to change their personalities or achieve a therapeutic experience. PeeWee and Little League games involve groups designed to develop baseball skills, social behavior, and sportsmanship. It doesn't really matter (or should not matter) who wins the baseball game. Some adults confuse the issues and feel that the team must be task-centered (win the game); however, at least in the Pee Wee Leagues, this is not the group's primary purpose.

Function is a significant aspect of the operation of groups. Further examples of the differences and similarities between task-centered and growth-centered groups can clarify the interrelationships of these concepts. A remedial speech group may decide to study the many varieties of flowers as a subject for a later discussion meeting. The knowledge of flowers in this group is incidental, the *talking* is vital. The group could have decided to study the many styles of painting or the habits of turtles. The members must have something about which they can talk. The selection of the topic is a function of the interests and ages of the group, and it is incidental to the group's main purpose. Such a speech therapy group is growth-centered.

Growth-centered groups are very common in all types of treatment areas. Moreno (1934) developed "psychodrama" as a therapeutic group experience. Individuals "role-play" or act out parts in a re-enactment of real or hypothetical life experiences. Dramatic talent, missed lines, or the quality of the performance are not of primary concern to the members; patient growth, emotional clarification, and maturity are the goals of the group which is growth-centered. Many varieties of group therapy experiences are found in the literature of groups (Powdermaker and Frank, 1953; Corsini, 1957). Educational groups designed to discuss family relations, to take field trips, to read faster and better, as well as to study a subject, are also primarily designed as growth-centered groups rather than task-centered groups.

"Primarily designed . . ." is a key phrase revealing the dual nature of many groups. A social service study group in the guidance program of a high school is organized to collect and to order the facts about the many occupations in the social service field. The group may be charged with the responsibility of inviting speakers for the "Career Day" to be held later in the year. The director of guidance in this school has assigned a task to the group which he hopes it will carry out responsibly. The task nature of the group's charge (study the field and invite certain speakers) is uppermost in the minds of the students as they complete the assignment. The director of guidance knows that the decision to invite certain people is one of the minor outcomes of the group's efforts. He hopes for growth, knowledge, and maturity on the part of the members of the group. The students view the group as primarily task-centered; the director of guidance views the group as primarily growth-centered.

Confusion is always present in group activity when the members and the group organizers do not have a clear idea of how the purpose of the group is related to task or growth goals. Conflict and confusion are not involved if the joint nature of the activity is recognized by the appropriate persons. The social matron who has hoped to become the president of the local flower association in the community is concerned with her own prestige and recognition. From the group she hopes to achieve something which is essentially a status (growth) goal. She may resign when her hope is frustrated, though her task goal of learning about flowers be still operative. The matron has revealed that her "growth goals" were stronger than the so-called point of the group—to learn about flowers, a task goal.

School classes are primarily growth-centered, but they always have an intermediate goal of a task nature. Pure task groups are present in industry, business, government, and community life. In every case of group action, one or another, or a combination, of these task or growth purposes of the group may be ascertained through an analysis of its objectives and operation.

Groupwork

When groups are organized and used, groupwork techniques are being used. A teacher may separate a class of thirty-five students into three discussion groups, each of 10–12 students. These smaller groups provide for detailed examination of specific aspects of the subject under study. The teacher may be said to be using group dynamics. She is using the tools of the group specialist. A lecturer in a large hall may interrupt his presentation and organize "buzz groups" or "66 groups." These special techniques permit a group of 4–8 persons sitting contiguously, to turn their heads and to discuss together a question or issue raised by the speaker.

Many diverse academic situations can involve groupwork. Faculty members may meet on the campus lawn with a group of freshmen and discuss the coming years of college life. A guidance counselor and a teacher may co-operate to construct a sociogram of the relationships among the students in a particular class. Career study groups may be organized among college-bound seniors. A high school psychology class may assign specific roles to class members and act out a particularly distressing situation in the family structure. A sixth grade science class may undertake to explore a museum and planetarium and, later, in small groups, discuss the vocational implications as well as the scientific facts learned.

Groupwork or group dynamics has a history which can be traced to the work of early sociologists, psychologists, industrial specialists, and other social scientists, such as Simmel (1951), Wolff (1950), Cooley (1909), Thrasher (1927), and Terman (1904). Significant impetus resulted from the detailed study of human relations at the Hawthorne Electric Works. A comprehensive summary of these findings was first published by Roethlisberger and Dickson, under the title, *Management and the Worker* (1939). The "social climates" study of Lewin, Lippitt, and White (1939) was another monumental study that revealed the effects of varied types of leadership on group members. Many individual research efforts and program developments preceded the approaches and techniques now used in group situations in education, industry, and the community.

The National Training Laboratory was established in 1946, following World War II, with the assistance of the U.S. Navy. Yearly training sessions in Bethel, Maine, and in workshops across the country, have been held in order to make group procedures an effective tool for persons from all walks of life working with others.

All of these diverse, but related roots underlie the current use of organized, unorganized, formal, informal, or spontaneously developed groups. Differing methods and purposes have characterized such applications. All of these human interactions are groups in action, groupwork, or even "group dynamics."

"GROUP GUIDANCE"

Guidance has been a potent force in education since the turn of the century (Barry and Wolf, 1957; Hutson, 1958). Attempts were made early in the history of guidance to apply techniques and principles within the structure of a group. The term "group guidance" was thus originated. These early efforts were frequently attempted by ill-trained, though sincere counselors or guidance workers. Classes of 35 to 100 were organized for guidance purposes, and for want of a better term, "group guidance" was employed. Regular classroom teachers were told to do "group guidance." Counselors and guidance workers with no knowledge of the dynamics of groups, also attempted to apply regular teaching devices that were poorly suited to the newer problems of guidance.

The results of many early "group guidance" efforts were catastrophic. Teachers rebelled and guidance workers were intellectually stoned by their peers in the school community. Students joined the fray and hurled cat-calls at "group guidance" and "group guidance" workers. "Group guidance" became "dirty work" in many quarters. The guidance worker or counselor was removed from the conflict as greater counseling emphasis was introduced into the guidance and personnel fields. Many counselors found refuge in one-to-one counseling relationships. "Group guidance" was banished from the scene in many schools. The counseling issue was real, and aided guidance to mature and to become professionally oriented. However, even as counseling and other skills of the guidance worker became available, many guidance workers continued to avoid "group guidance" at all costs. Those in the field of guidance had been burned badly; and, as a burned child would, they feared and still fear newer conflagrations.

Educational theory, economic and social pressures of the decades following World War II, and the pressure of numbers in the 1960's have forced guidance workers to reassess their position. Individual significant forces creating a new climate for groups have included the writings of James Conant on the American high school (1959), stressing guidance needs; the National Defense Education Act of 1958, establishing guidance training institutes throughout the country; and the inexorable march of more and more students into school classes. Guidance workers now need to be capable of working with larger numbers of students. "Group guidance" is tentatively entering the swirl of activity again. The toes of guidance workers, even their legs, are getting wet again. It is to be hoped that the painful lesson of history has been effectively learned. Tools, techniques, ideas, and concepts of groups are now available.

Guidance workers must become more efficient as well as more effective. The research and techniques of the many related disciplines studying the dynamics of groups have provided resources which can be used by all guidance persons. Group techniques are specific and capable of being misapplied, as well as effectively used. Perhaps, guidance workers can avoid the trap of damning the future because of the past, not "backing into the future with eyes on the past," but learning from the past and using knowledge and skill as weapons for the future.

Groups and (or versus?) counseling

Occasional counselors and groupwork specialists have stated that counseling and group activities are unrelated, and inappropriate for combined use in a given school or community. This attempt to separate the two tools is found less frequently at the present time. Combined use of such techniques can be found in mental hospitals (Powdermaker and Frank, 1953); mental hygiene centers (Samler, 1959); industries (Thelen, 1954); schools, colleges, and junior high schools (Strang, 1958a; Bennett, 1955); and even elementary schools (Martinson and Smallenberg, 1958).

Many skilled counselors are serving as group leaders and vice versa. On occasion, individual counselors or guidance persons may take the position that although the techniques of counseling and group activities are related, it is undesirable for the same person to attempt to use both approaches. Most specialists, however, feel that a good group leader needs to be skilled in techniques of counseling. Most guidance authorities also include group skills as a standard tool for counselors and guidance persons.

The issue of counseling or groupwork with students is not totally a straw man. Many writers in the fields of psychology, counseling, and guidance are not predisposed towards interest in group procedures. These persons are most concerned with counseling and counseling techniques. They seem to feel that counseling is the primary tool of the guidance worker and are only vaguely interested in the non-counseling type of guidance activity. Counselors in this tradition (counseling is the "basic tool" of guidance) may be from a client-centered or clinical methodological position. They are frequently not "anti-groupwork," but, rather, "pro-counseling." This view of guidance restricts the opportunity for counselors to be trained in group activities as well as in counseling. Counseling and group activities are two major tools; it would seem desirable that guidance persons be equally skilled in individual *and* group approaches.

Reports of counseling and groupwork programs and some beginning research findings would seem to be pointing in the direction of joint operation (Calia, 1957; Driver, 1958; Trueblood, 1960). Trueblood, a counselor trainer, is concerned because training experiences in group activities are neglected in guidance and counseling training. He goes further, and after an analysis of group leaders' responses, states, ". . . the activities [group] advisor needs to develop counseling skills and attitudes . . ." (Trueblood, 1960, p. 17).

Other research workers in both the counseling and groupwork fields have reported that use of both techniques by the same person is profitable (Richards, 1958; Brewer, 1958; Driver, 1958). Driver's book, *Small Groups in Counseling and Guidance* (1958), is devoted to this principle. The second part of the book contains descriptions of how small group procedures can be combined with other guidance and counseling techniques.

"Multiple" or group counseling is a term which has grown up as attempts have been made to counsel with a group rather than with one person. This term was probably first used by Clifford Froehlich in California and by Helen Driver in Kansas. They and other proponents have used counseling techniques with small groups of students or clients. Three to twelve persons usually have been involved. The developments in multiple counseling were preceded and accompanied by many efforts at group therapy. Early writers and research in this approach include Slavson (1937), and Moreno (1934).

The multiple counseling approaches and the group therapists have merged counseling and groupwork. Many problems are associated with the mixture of two different approaches. Extreme skill in both areas is mandatory for any person attempting to combine them. The group counselors are wrestling with difficult tasks. The road has been difficult and success is by no means yet assured, although recent research findings are promising.

Multiple or group counselors are coming to grips with serious counseling problems. The best practices of each field are necessary to solve such issues. "Group guidance" techniques have been concerned with occupational data collection, educational collection, test interpretation, case study discussion, mental health and human relations. Certainly these are also counseling issues. Newer skills and program designs can bring counseling and group guidance closer together.

A multiple approach to guidance

The semantic issue of multiple counseling or "group guidance" versus counseling seems to be a fruitless concern on the part of guidance persons. Rather it is better that guidance workers, counselors, and all personnel workers adopt a broad view of guidance. The time is past when a white-jacketed guidance worker can ensconce himself in a small corner in a large school and do only psychotherapy with fifteen or twenty students per year. Although psychotherapy is a vital and valuable tool for properly trained counselors, psychologists, guidance workers or group workers, guidance workers need to be prepared to use counseling, interviewing, groupwork, teaching, and many other techniques. Guidance cannot be equated with any single technique (Lloyd-Jones and Smith, 1954). A director of guidance or pupil personnel needs to utilize and to program the approaches and techniques of many specialists. Specialists are, of course, always needed; however, only confusion can occur when any one service is said to be guidance or a guidance program.

Groupwork has become a major tool in the kit of the guidance worker. Rightfully so, group activities seem to be rejoining the "big two" of counseling and testing as techniques of guidance. The deeply held prejudices of the past against "group guidance" are passing. Many persons have continued to work for group procedures through the years. Lloyd-Jones, Hoppock, Strang, Wrenn, and Bennett are all names that have stood for the best practice and professional concern for all students through individual and group approaches. Research, though slow to follow theory, has begun to support the philosophical position of the multiple philosophy and multiple approach in guidance. Major research contributions in all group areas will be examined throughout the chapters to follow.

The guidance or personnel worker needs to examine his own attitudes and feelings of security. Extreme specialism brings strong feelings of adequacy in a professional jungle. Guidance, however, with its broad aim of helping students to learn and to profit from education, demands that every useful approach be given a reasonable and appropriate opportunity in the daily programs of schools at all levels.

GROUPS IN GUIDANCE

Group activities, counseling, testing, occupational and educational planning, interviewing, advising and many other techniques are all parts of guidance. Each of these approaches is useful and appropriate at various times. Guidance workers need to assess carefully the methods, applications, changes and advantages of each technique. Group procedures appear deceptively simple and many people have been drawn by their "Lorelei-like" attraction without carefully assessing their rigorous demands upon the user.

Counseling may appear simple to a casual observer. Yet, the demands upon a counselor are many if subjects are to be helped. Group techniques are equally complex and, in like fashion, are based on a thorough knowledge of psychological, sociological, and human relations disciplines, as well as on research findings in these areas.

"Group Guidance" can exist, as can "Individual Guidance." The assumption that anything taking place in groups may be classified as "group guidance" has damaged the concept of groups in guidance. Specific techniques and appropriate training are vital to success in the use of groups. Imprecise meanings and confusion of terms have made it difficult for guidance workers to assess the importance of groupwork. A large body of literature exists which describes theory and research in group techniques. Few specialists in guidance are willing to state that groups are unnecessary to the success of a guidance program. Many writers are uncertain about the role of groups (Gunderson, 1950; Koile, 1955; Cupp, 1958). Some workers object strongly to groups (Barnes, 1958).

The historical situation suggests the attitude of the carpenter who assumes that he must build the house with *either* a hammer *or* a saw. Common sense demands that both the hammer and saw be used, although for different purposes. It is debatable whether every guidance worker should be trained in both counseling and groupwork, but it seems desirable. Training in group procedures can help to meet student needs with whichever procedure is most effective and efficient: teaching, counseling, or groupwork.

All personnel who use groupwork approaches need to be able to serve as group leaders, to train others as group leaders, to organize student groups, to train students in leadership and membership techniques, to serve as resource consultants to presently operating groups, and to take advantage of available approaches and skills in all areas of group dynamics. The training of a group specialist is closely related to the training of a counselor. The objectives and emotions of the participants are similar in both processes; but techniques, procedures, and skills used in counseling are different from those used in groupwork. Theory and practice must be properly blended so as to produce adequate results.

The remainder of this book will attempt to present to guidance workers the facts, concepts and procedures which are basic to the use of group and group dynamics approaches in guidance. Hopefully, like Alice, if it is possible to "Take care of the sense, the sounds will take care of themselves."

SUMMARY

Groups have been viewed and described at all educational levels. Elementary school practices, junior and senior high school programs, and group elements in higher education have been illustrated.

A group has been defined in terms of interaction, size, and purpose. Groups were sub-divided into 3 categories: (a) small, 3–6; (b) medium, 5–18; and (c) large, over 18. Interaction is outlined as interdependence. The purposes or functions of groups are (1) task-centered; (2) growth-centered; and (3) learning-centered (usual classes).

Groupwork or group dynamics is a general term which applies to the use of groups in many different fashions in variable environments. The use of groups serves as the identifying factor within groupwork. Group-guidance history includes early failures, as well as more recent ideas of developing the many uses of groups in guidance. Group guidance and group counseling are vital contemporary issues.

Multiple approaches to guidance as well as a multiple philosophy of guidance provide a receptive environment for skilled and professionally oriented use of groups in guidance.

SUGGESTED READINGS

Association for Supervision and Curriculum Development, *Fostering Mental Health in Our Schools*. Washington, D. C.: National Education Association, 1950.

———, *Preparation of Core Teachers for Secondary Schools*. Washington, D. C.: National Education Association, 1953.

———, *Guidance in the Curriculum*. Washington, D. C.: National Education Association, 1955.

National Society for the Study of Education, *Mental Health in Modern Education*, Fifty-Fourth Yearbook. Chicago: University of Chicago Press, 1955.

———, *Personnel Services in Education*, Fifty-Eighth Yearbook. Chicago: University of Chicago Press, 1959.

———, *The Dynamics of Instructional Groups*, Fifty-Ninth Yearbook. Chicago: The University of Chicago Press, 1960.

Strang, Ruth, *Group Work in Education*. New York: Harper & Bros., 1958.

Thelen, Herbert A., *Education and the Human Quest*. New York: Harper & Bros., 1960.

Warters, Jane, *Group Guidance*. New York: McGraw-Hill Book Co., 1960.

Willey, R. D., and W. M. Strong, *Group Procedures in Guidance*. New York: Harper & Bros., 1957.

Wrenn, C. Gilbert, *Student Personnel Work in College*. New York: The Ronald Press Co., 1951.

———, "Philosophical and Psychological Bases of Personnel Services in Education," in National Society for the Study of Education, *Personnel Services in Education*, Fifty-Eighth Yearbook. Chicago: University of Chicago Press, 1959, 41–81.

2. ANATOMY OF A GROUP

An efficiently functioning group appears to be a simple social form to the participants as well as to any outside observers. Similarly, a glass clock with all of its works in sight, looks like a simple mechanism, as it runs smoothly and strikes correctly. Many tinkerers, both young and old, have found that seeming simplicity can be frustratingly complex. Groups need to be examined and their components exposed for all to see.

How do groups function? What content or subject matter is usable in group situations? What factors can explain why some groups succeed in accomplishing a particular task, while similar groups fail miserably? What are the views and reactions of faculty members and students as they participate in group procedures and learn from them? How can guidance workers serve large numbers of students through group approaches? The answers to these questions can help guidance workers to understand the importance of groups and the dimensions of service to students that are possible when group procedures are added to the usual techniques of a guidance or personnel program.

In Chapter 1, groups were analyzed in terms of size and purpose. While these aspects are important, they do not describe how a group functions. When only these facts are known, other important elements remain obscured. The following experience is a common occurrence in many schools:

> Eight of us, in addition to the principal and the superintendent, were in the group. Our job was to revise the general curriculum. This curriculum had become the "public dumping ground" for all of our poorer and problem students. . . . We were there for over an hour and, really, only one person beside the principal and the "super" said anything. The principal didn't say much either. The superintendent had a new curriculum all planned out prior to the time he had come to the meeting. It was our responsibility to "rubber stamp" what he had already decided to offer as a new curriculum. We voted for it and our group was then dismissed. Our Curriculum Committee functions like this most of the time. (Math teacher, high school)

"Group experiences" such as this committee meeting are but thinly disguised covers for authoritarianism and dictatorial policies of administrators. To be sure, there were ten members in the group (medium-size group); the purpose or function of the group was to revise the general curriculum (task-centered); the job was completed and the vote recorded, (movement or progress). The failure of such groups to be meaningful to any participant except the leader, as in the illustration cited, is not rooted in the kind of task the group undertakes. Curriculum revision is of usual concern to such a group. Teachers are well qualified to accomplish this assignment. The failure or the distortion of the functioning of the group arose from the "group process"—the manner in which the group functioned.

The terms content and process represent additional major dimensions of a group. These terms, as well as interaction, size, and purpose, help to define a group. Here are simple, beginning definitions of these two terms:

> 1. *Content:* the "what" of a group discussion. The subject matter of the group's deliberations or actions. Content may vary in infinite fashion: curricula, dancing, occupational study, self-appraisal, social graces, new football plays, and college choice are all possible as topics for a group discussion.

> 2. *Process:* the "how" of a group discussion, or the way in which the content is handled or discussed by the group. The methods of the leader; the degree and type of participation by members; the communication processes used; the rules, regulations, policies, or

procedures of form adopted by the group; the movement or progress of the discussion—these are among the many aspects which are considered to be "process" in groups.

CONTENT IN GROUPS

Each group exists for a particular purpose or to complete a specific task. Such a purpose or task will normally determine the content for the discussion or action of the group. The environment in which a group is established, or the need that is felt for the initiation of a group discussion, offers the gross content out of which specific group topics may be chosen. Industrial plants may discuss grievance procedures, demands for wage increases, or safety programs. Church groups may discuss a new budget for the Sunday school program, a building plan, or the early life of Christ. School groups take their content from the curriculum, special programs or projects, and new developments from within the school.

School guidance programs will normally offer a wide range of subject matter for adoption by groups. A typical high school guidance program might offer many major content units during the school year. Each gross environment would provide for many smaller group content adoptions. Orientation may be chosen as an example of one of these major program functions. Typical group content items are listed in the chart below:

SCHOOL ORIENTATION: MAJOR GUIDANCE UNIT

Specific Group Topics	*Probable Leaders*
1. Curricular programs	1. Faculty members
2. School services	2. Guidance personnel
3. Student activities	3. Upper-class students
4. Study habits	4. Reading specialists
5. Student-teacher relationships	5. Faculty members and upper-class students
6. Personal goals	6. School counselors
7. Rules and regulations	7. Student government leaders
8. Grading procedures	8. Faculty members
9. Psychological testing	9. Guidance personnel

The specific group topics listed would probably not all be included in any one program. Additional topics, and decisions concerning the inclusion of particular members of the student body and the choice of leaders, would depend upon local circumstance. Orientation is especially well suited to the use of group techniques. Hoffmann and Plutchik (1959) have devoted an entire book to the application of *small group discussion* techniques in orientation. However, they warn that small group techniques alone cannot "carry" an orientation program. This caution is also appropriate in other areas where group techniques are used. Small group procedures are only one method and must be supplemented at all times with individual approaches such as counseling and interviewing. Large group techniques such as the lecture or teaching are also used in orientation work.

Each major unit in a guidance program can be broken down in chart form, as was done for the orientation area. This breakdown of "content" areas in guidance illustrates the various topics which may be selected for use in group procedures. There are almost numberless opportunities for creative use of groups in guidance. Guidance directors, counselors, teachers, and students can all contribute to building an appropriate content approach that will best serve their particular school and program. Changing emphasis within the guidance program, changing emphasis of student needs, cyclical programming, philosophical biases—all these can influence the selection of content for groups in guidance. The group is a tool which may be employed in solving endless types of problems. A more detailed analysis of content in guidance groups will be the primary focus of the several chapters in Part Three.

PROCESS IN GROUPS

The word "process," when it is used to explain the dynamics of group operation, represents specific elements capable of influencing the success, failure, and over-all functioning of a group. "Group dynamics," a phrase defined earlier that has grown with the use of groups, may also refer to all of these factors. Anthropologists, sociologists, psychologists, psychiatrists, and educators, as well as specialists from other fields, have long been interested in groups and group functioning. Groups have been used in commonplace and unusual ways in all of these disciplines. A concept of group process, important in all uses of groups, has been developed from many sources.

General descriptions of the many specific group applications, theoretical concepts about group structures, as well as research reports on group concepts, can be found in many sources. Collections of theoretical and research findings can be found in Cartwright and Zander (1960), and Hare, Borgatta, and Bales (1955). Each of these editors has made major contributions in books and articles. The work of the "group dynamics" theorists, many of whom are organized in the National Training Laboratories, a division of the National Education Association, is basic to all applications of groups and current research. The early efforts of Lewin, Lippitt and White (1939), and the more recent publications of the National Training Laboratories (1958; 1959; 1960), well represent the group dynamics approach.

Special uses of groups in therapy situations can be found in Deveroux (1956), Moreno (1953), and Bach (1954). A major theoretical advance in group and human relations theory came through the industrial research programs which investigated workers in manufacturing and business areas. Roethlisberger and Dickson (1939), Whyte (1943; 1949), Dubin (1951; 1958), Tannenbaum, Weschler, and Massarik (1961), and Meier (1958) illustrate early and more recent progress in these areas. The many research reports as well as the applications of group methods to work in psychology and education are a major source of information and data for the delineation of group process and content in the sections and chapters to follow. Readers who wish to search further into any of the specifics of the ideas presented can refer to suggested readings and bibliography.

Investigations of the group as a social unit date back to efforts at the turn of the century, when observers and experimenters such as Triplett (1898), Simmel (1951), and Cooley (1909) were concerned with competition and co-operation within groups, group size and its influence, and similar topics. Beginning research in the area of leadership was carried out by Terman (1904); in social control, Thrasher (1927), F. H. Allport, (1920), and Furfey (1927); and in subgroup cultures and small group effects, by Puffer (1912), and Riddle (1925). Piaget's (1926) observations and knowledge, gathered by examination of children's games and other activities, were also important contributions for all persons in group research and theory building.

Research and concept building are still taking place in all areas represented by these pioneer efforts. Current studies of the dynamic structural factors within groups attempt to reveal and to measure the forces and effects which were observed in these early investigations. Educators and guidance workers constantly hope to apply many of these generalizations to school situations and to guidance and counseling approaches. Current research and theory make it possible to do this.

Analysis of the total process of a group in operation includes many elements. The following process factors are important when groups are used in guidance:

1. Organization and Purpose
2. Structure and Function
3. Communication and Perception
4. Motivation and Learning
5. Movement and Progress.

Organization and purpose

Groups may be formal or informal, approved or disapproved, official or unofficial, organized or disorganized, open or secret, task-centered or growth-centered. Each of these facts about a group can change its function, objective, and method of operation. Each group is a subculture and sub-unit of society with lesser or greater ability to cope with the demands of a total society when compared with the larger, organized complexes of society such as education, business, or the church.

The "gang" has long been a favorite social phenomenon for intensive study. Early efforts were cited in the historical survey of process sources. More recent studies have been made by Whyte (1943), Sherif and Sherif (1953), and Kvaraceous (1954). High school secret fraternities or sororities, sandlot athletic teams, the National Honor Society, Phi Beta Kappa, the varsity football team, the elementary school student government organization, groups used in a guidance program—all are generically related to the gang. These groups are collections of individuals organized for various purposes under different conditions; but all respond to similar forces and factors which influence their operations, successes, and failures. Some of these groups are approved, official, organized; others are spontaneously developed and dependent on circumstances for their ultimate outcome or continued life. Many forces operate within each group: group-developed objectives, leadership, membership roles and functions, communication networks, person perceptions, motivation, and learning. Comparable forces operating in different groups are similar. They are understandable and, to a degree, predictable to the trained observer and to the skilled group leader.

The factors of group function and purpose are often the most decisive forces operating within the structure of the group. Early researches highlighted these factors. Roethlisberger and Dickson (1939) summarized their findings in the *Hawthorne Studies*, and they stressed the beneficial effect of treating workers in groups as individual human beings. This "Hawthorne Effect" is a potential within many groups, and it is often overlooked or ignored by supervisors, teachers, parents, and group workers. Many groups exist to provide an opportunity for members to function as persons of dignity and worth. That this human need is basic is appropriately recognized in the counseling field by writers such as Rogers (1951), Arbuckle (1957), and Hahn and MacLean (1955). Workers in the guidance field have also stressed this factor, but harassed guidance persons in their administrative tasks sometimes neglect it. Lloyd-Jones and Smith (1938; 1954), Wrenn (1951; 1961), Glanz and Walston (1958), and many others stress personal worth, human dignity, and self-esteem. These particular concepts are well-known to group workers, counselors, and guidance personnel. They are representative of many factors that are basic to the purpose of an organized group.

Structure and function

> Four of the children were playing "boat" in our papier-mâché model of a boat that we had built during our unit on science and the sea. It was recess time and the other children were outside in the play area. I was about to send these four children outside also when I observed more closely what was taking place. There was a "Captain," a "First Mate," and a "Crew" of two. The Captain was getting "instructions" from the First Mate. The First Mate was also busy giving orders to the crew in the name of the Captain. The First Mate was obviously the leader of the play group. His job was to keep the Captain happy, the crew busy, and all interested in the game. He wanted most of all to play "boat." (Elementary school teacher)

This sort of group structure, with many variations, is common in many children's games and even in business. The "Captain" is the official leader; the "First Mate" is the actual leader. The members of the group obtain satisfactions through the success of the group and the efforts of the actual leader. The leader is aware of all the participants and of the "roles," or specific responsibilities, that are assumed by contributing members of the group. Children's games are revelations in group dynamics. The simple structure of the organization, the few, flexible rules, the high degree of member involvement, and the clear need for a leader help to reveal basic dynamics.

Every group has members and one or more leaders. Many roles must be filled by members in order to have a smoothly operating group. Sometimes these roles for group members are appointive or elective, such as those of secretary, master-at-arms, and vice-leader. Frequently these roles, and others in informal groups (task-prodder, social and emotional specialist), are not consciously recognized by the members or the leader. The clarity with which leaders and members understand and implement the roles that must be filled in a group will help to determine its patterns of operation and action.

Communication and perception

Groups are made up of persons. Each person within the group must react to, interact with, and reflect upon the actions of the other persons who are members, or are associated with the group. Asch (1952, p. 142) has put it thus:

> The paramount fact about human interactions is that they are happenings that are psychologically represented in each of the participants. In our relation to an object, perceiving, thinking, and feeling take place on one side, whereas in relations between persons these processes take place on both sides and in dependence upon one another. . . . We interact with others, not as the paramecium does by altering the surrounding medium chemically, nor as the ants do by smell, but via emotions and thought that are capable of taking into account the emotions and thoughts of others. Such interaction is to social interaction in general as consciousness is to biology in general.

Communication and person perception within groups is a complex and undependable element. The pressure for predictability and conformity within groups has led many writers to decry group pressures and demands upon individuals. Some writers see groups as moulding forces and even destroyers of individuality. Riesman *et al.* sum up this view in the final statement of *The Lonely Crowd*

> The idea that men are created free and equal is both true and mis-
> leading: men are created different; they lose their social freedom and
> their individual autonomy in seeking to become like each other.

The problem is to communicate, to perceive, to join with others in common tasks, and yet, retain one's identity and individual autonomy.

The area of person-perception is a field of increasing activity. In-vestigators have long been aware of the peculiarly involved actions and re-actions of those engaging in joint undertakings. The apparent simplicity of these processes, the seeming ease displayed by people in communicating with other people have made it difficult for research to be completed, or for principles to be extracted from the gross behaviors involved (Tagiuri and Petrullo, 1958). The facts and acts of human interactions, communica-tions and perceptions, or the psychology of human interactions has come to be known as "person-perception." Increasing theory-building efforts are being made; new research programs are being developed—these promise to isolate more and more of the needed data useful in understanding the processes involved in verbal interchanges and human interactions (David and Brengelmann, 1960; Heider, 1958).

Motivation and learning

People may behave in a bizarre fashion and do things for no apparent rea-sons. In spite of the seemingly inexplicable actions of persons both as in-dividuals and as members of groups, psychologists are able to point out that behavior is caused; it doesn't happen fortuitously. Human needs and physi-cal drives are similar in all persons in our culture. Learned human needs arise from the social environment in which we live. While behavior can often be anticipated, it is difficult to predict and control; hindsight and explanations of causes are more frequently possible. Social control has been a debatable issue for many generations. The need for social control and the problems inherent in social control are outlined in an article by Rogers and Skinner (1956). In the article the authors relate social goals to individual behavior, as well as to group behaviors.

Behavior is caused and orderly, in an individual and in a group; however, behavior changes. Individuals constantly change from birth to death. Learning is the key to changes in human behavior. Educational theory has always held that learning can take place in groups, and psy-chologists insist that learning is an individual process. The two points are not mutually exclusive. The group provides the environment which may enhance or inhibit learning. The object is to provide a stimulating and permissive climate for individual change and development in schoolroom classes and groups, and to encourage individual effort, autonomy, and independence.

All of the process factors previously presented bear upon learning and motivation. Many other factors affect the learning potential of persons within a group. Knowledge of personal motivations and behavior causes can help to establish and maintain climates favorable to learning. Students will learn as members of a student government group; students will learn as members of a street corner gang. What the individual learns within each group will depend upon his motivations and needs. At the same time, personal learnings will be affected by the objectives and purposes of the groups, the effectiveness of the leaders and other members, as well as the feelings, emotions, and thoughts that contribute to the interactions and human relations factors within the group.

Much research has been completed on motivation and learning in group life. Not all results are compatible. The group climates study by Lewin, Lippitt, and White (1939) was one of the early attempts to isolate some of these factors. More recent theory and research efforts will be examined more closely in later chapters. Such studies point directions, but do not answer many of the inherent questions concerning the motivations of persons in groups and the factors associated with learning. Certainly motivation and learning are factors that are vital within regular school classes, groups, groups within classes, and in groups in guidance programs.

Movement and progress

> Our "Occupations" course has been a failure. The students only take it because it is a required course. We are going to have to revise it or drop it from the curriculum. (Junior high school counselor)

> Student government in our school is a joke among the students and the faculty alike. (High school teacher)

> The "college planning" groups among our senior class have been an overwhelming success. It has been offered to all interested students, and faculty members have served as group leaders. (Senior class advisor)

> Our case study discussions in the freshman required psychology course have been stimulating and most productive. The groups have

functioned within the over-all framework of the classes, and it has added a new dimension to our class-room work. (College counselor and teacher)

Groups can fail miserably; groups can achieve success and provide meaningful satisfactions for all members. The proof of a group's functioning often is in its ability to do the job—to accomplish its objective. The degree of movement or progress in a group towards its stated task-centered or growth-centered goal can help to determine whether success or failure is in store for the persons associated in a common task.

Problem-solving in a history class, a student government committee, or a guidance group is a similar accomplishment. The problem-solving process is related to the steps in thinking as outlined by Dewey, the abstraction process in semantics, critical thinking, and the scientific method. In later chapters concerned with the treatment of process as a whole, the steps in the movement or progress of a group will be examined in detail.

Each of the major elements involved in an understanding of group process has been briefly presented in this introduction. Each concept will be examined specifically in Part Two.

PARTICIPANT LEARNINGS

Students and others as members in a group react differently to the group experience. Leaders, teachers, counselors, and guidance workers using group approaches evaluate their own participation and performance. In spite of the long history of human action in small and large groups, there is often an initial condition of unfamiliarity and disorientation for leaders and participants whenever groups are used in new or different ways, or in school programs wherever there has been a "former way" to do things. The usual result of the skillful application of group techniques is that participants and leaders lose their sense of hostility or feelings of discomfort, and come to prefer using group approaches for learning rather than holding exclusively to the better-known means of mass or individual treatment.

Counselors, teachers, and leaders

Group leaders, whether they are teachers, counselors, guidance workers, executives, or administrators of any type, are usually uneasy, insecure, and perhaps hostile as they begin to view systematically their own operation as leaders. Their attitude often is that they have been doing things "naturally," and they object to an organized study of methodology and techniques. Sometimes they feel threatened and under attack, believing that they must defend at all costs their present methods of operation. Successful leaders often fear that they may "upset a good thing," and unsuccessful leaders or group members are often more comfortable and secure when they are able to place the responsibility for failures on others, rather than on their own concepts or techniques.

Many years of experience in dealing with such attitudes on the part of new participants in group programs is summarized in the writings of those who specialize in training others in the techniques of group work. The training programs conducted at Bethel, Maine, by the National Training Laboratories (1958; 1959; 1960), as well as reports of successful training experiences in workshops and seminars in schools, industries, and community groups (Miles 1959; Miles and Corey, 1957), show that feelings of uncertainty and hostility can be overcome, and that participants can be helped to function and learn more effectively as members and leaders of groups.

Faculty members, through involvement in group procedures, have frequently become more active and positive in their attitudes about counseling, in helping students, and in the over-all guidance program. I. Gordon (1950; 1951; 1956) reports specifically on such procedures, and stresses the significance and utility of groups in the final results. Related activities with faculty members and teachers are widespread (Hoffman and Plutchik, 1959; Driver, 1958). Personnel at all levels of programming in education can profitably use group techniques.

There is great danger when well-trained specialists such as teachers, administrators, and even student leaders are "told" by group workers that they are ignorant of appropriate techniques which they need to fulfill their own responsibilities. Hostile reactions can preclude learning. Slow, careful involvement will help to reduce antagonism. Psychological knowledge of human motivation and basic needs is vital to the success of a groupwork program when training efforts are instituted in school systems or in other environments. Training techniques are available to help in establishing such a program. Experience gained in these techniques can sooth the tempers and fears of new participants, and help to make the group a useful device for more efficient and effective implementation of previously established programs in education, business, and community life. The writings of Miles (1959) are especially appropriate to this type of planning, as are earlier writings of Lippitt (1949), Lewin (1948), and M. Ross and Hendry (1957).

Students, adults, and group members

Group members often have no understanding of effectively planned and implemented group techniques when they work in groups. Groupwork, when expected, is "natural" and usual. This seeming contradiction to the attitudes of leaders is probably a result of planning and cultural experiences. Even in new situations where individual expectations have not been met, groups may be successfully accepted by participants without any particularly active awareness on their part. It seems easier to participate or be a group member in a new situation than a new leader. However, if new groups fail, the members are quick to attack and criticize the so-called progressive approaches. Such a reaction can be observed when a comparison is made of elementary and secondary school programs.

Elementary pupils, perhaps through general cultural learning, expect to be members of groups and to perform daily in small groups. High school pupils seem to have lost their familiarity and cultural expectations, in this respect, perhaps through constant experience with the "platoon system" employed in all classes after elementary school. Many high school students attack groups in educational activities as "unnatural." This attitude seems to be learned and can be reversed with effective and efficient use of groups (Wey, 1948).

Effective countermeasures to negative attitudes on the part of students and other group members depend upon efforts to change participants' expectations and to employ effective group techniques. Graduate school seminars and first grade reading groups are a part of the educational heritage that all students can anticipate. Between these two extremes there are many other areas, and types of programs, in which group procedures may be efficiently used. The caution that must be voiced concerns the quality and effectiveness of the group policies that are proposed.

Research has shown that group members can be involved in the process of learning and behavior change in groupwork. Early and recent experience with industrial workers revealed the dramatic behavior changes resulting when group members felt that they were valued as individual human beings (Fleishman, Harris, and Burtt, 1955; Roethlisberger and Dickson, 1939). These results have been observed in many studies since that time (Homans, 1950; Mackay, 1958; Brewer, 1958). The studies demonstrate learning through involvement of parents, students, workers, and community members in group activities and actions.

Group climate can not only dramatically change participants' attitudes, but also sometimes become such a strong influence on students' or members' behavior that dangers result. Mob action is well known as an extreme example of this principle. De-personalization or the lack of personal responsibility can sometimes occur on a much smaller and less dramatic scale. Festinger, Pepitone, and Newcomb (1952) report on this occurence. Other writers and research workers (Crutchfield in 1954 and Maxwell in 1954) report on related influences in the areas of group loyalties and feelings of cohesiveness which can block creative efforts on the part of individuals, and produce excessive attitudes of conformity. Groups are powerful medicines that can help or hurt personal development.

SUMMARY

Specific elements of a group have been presented. Process and content have been defined and analyzed briefly. Content is seen to be the subject matter of a group's discussion and can be drawn from an infinite variety of sources. Process is treated under five major headings: (1) Function and Purpose; (2) Leadership and Membership; (3) Communication and Perception; (4) Motivation and Learning; and (5) Movement or Progress.

Leaders and members of groups react to involvement in group activities with behavior of many types. Faculty members', counselors', students' and other group members' behaviors prior to, and following, group experiences are examined. Groups, as well as counseling, testing, and other multiple approaches to guidance of youth, are emphasized.

SUGGESTED READINGS

Bennett, Margaret E., "Functions and Procedures in Personnel Services," in National Association for the Study of Education, *Personnel Services in Education*, Fifty-Eighth Yearbook. Chicago: University of Chicago Press, 1959, 103–133.

Bonner, Hubert, *Group Dynamics*. New York: The Ronald Press Co., 1959.

Durham, L. E., and J. R. Gibb, *An Annotated Bibliography of Research National Training Laboratories, 1947–1960*. Washington, D. C.: National Training Laboratories, National Education Association, 1960.

Flanders, Ned A., *Teaching with Groups*. Minneapolis, Minn.: Burgess Pub. Co., 1954.

Gibb, J. R., and L. M. Gibb, *Applied Group Dynamics*. Washington, D.C.: National Training Laboratories, National Education Association, 1955.

Hare, Paul A., E. F. Borgatta, and R. F. Bales, eds., *Small Groups: Studies in Social Interaction*. New York: Alfred A. Knopf, Inc., 1955.

Herrold, Kenneth F., "Evaluation and Research in Group Dynamics," *Educational and Psychological Measurement*, 10, 1950, 492–504.

Knowles, M., and H. Knowles, *Introduction to Group Dynamics*. New York: Association Press, 1959.

Raven, B. H., "The Dynamics of Groups," *Review of Educational Research*, 29, 1959, 332–343.

Roseborough, Mary E., "Experimental Studies of Small Groups," *Psychological Bulletin*, 50, 1953, 275–303.

Sherif, Muzafer, and M. O. Wilson, eds., *Group Relations at the Cross Roads*. New York: Harper & Bros., 1953.

Siegel, S., and L. E. Fauraker, *Bargaining and Group Decision*. New York: McGraw-Hill Book Co., 1960.

Thelen, Herbert A., *Dynamics of Groups at Work*. Chicago: University of Chicago Press, 1954.

Thompson, G. G., "Children's Groups," in P. H. Mussen, ed., *Handbook of Research Methods in Child Development*. New York: John Wiley & Sons, Inc., 1960, 821–854.

PART TWO

Groups function in diverse ways. The major elements necessary for an understanding of the operation of groups can be presented in many patterns. Five basic approaches are represented in Part Two as the skeletal dimensions of groups in use:

1. Formation and Operation of Groups
2. Leaders, Members and Structure in Groups
3. Words and Meanings in Groups
4. Human Behavior in Groups
5. Problem Solving in Groups

Each of the listed topics is treated as a single chapter in the pages to follow.

3. THE FORMATION
AND OPERATION OF GROUPS:
organization and purpose

The spontaneously developed "gang" of Whyte's *Street Corner Society* (1943); the seven-member groups assigned by the teacher for the unit on the American Indian, in the Problems of American Democracy course in high school; the drug store gang; the home room group studying "Problems of Petting"; the "Panther Athletic Club" (a neighborhood sandlot team); the guidance class studying occupations—all are groups. The definitions offered in the opening chapter of this book were not precise enough to differentiate among such diverse collections of individuals gathered for varying purposes and functions. Groups are not easily classifiable. It is characteristic of groups to have many forms, many structures, and to fulfill many purposes and functions.

The variability of groups is a natural outcome of the basic fact of human existence. As humans we may do things alone, or we may do things together. Except for mobs, we organize ourselves or are normally organized into small or manageable units. Large groups or units, such as an army, a church, or a business, are organized into smaller units that are manageable and recognizable to those who are members. The family may be looked upon as a clan or a tribe during times of family reunions, but for practical purposes the family is made up of those who live together under one roof. Two people often seem to provide an exception to the rule of doing things alone or in groups. However, in some cases even a couple or two friends may be classified as a group.

Groups may begin in many ways. Time alone seems necessary for several high school youths in a corner drug store to unite into a loosely-knit group. Persons as unknown and unconcerned about one another as passengers on an airliner will draw together when they are forced down in a desolate location. Similarly, groups may become organized spontaneously as the local church faces a task of collecting enough money to support a capital improvement program, or they may *be* organized by ministers or social manipulators.

Regardless of the initiation process in a group, the first task which must be faced is the determination of the problem to be solved, the issue to be resolved, or the purpose to be achieved. A plan of action, or agenda, must be adopted—on a formal or informal level. The objectives of a group, the early action undertaken and completed, and the reactions of members to these specifics will determine whether or not the individual members will become a group.

Groups possess strange powers of control over their members. Loyalty to a group code is often placed above other standards and values which may be held by members on an individual basis. The source and strength of this power of the group is clearly related to the stability and continuity of a group, and its effect upon the subsociety which has fostered the group.

The process of group formation, organizational problems of groups, and the strength of groups will be the major topics considered in pages to follow in this chapter.

THE FORMATION OF GROUPS

Groups may develop spontaneously or through the active efforts of social organizers. Groups may also develop on a formal or informal basis, and they may be task-centered or growth-centered. The establishment and organization of a group is not fortuitous; it is the result of individual efforts of members or outside organizers. Groups are formed in order to meet the needs and motivations of these members or outsiders.

Spontaneous groups

Spontaneous groups are designed to meet the needs of individuals or groups whose needs are not presently being met. Individuals band together for protection, self-enhancement, or action. The tensions of everyday life for adults and for students are constant, and can serve as a motivating force.

Veterans' groups developed on college campuses after World War II and the Korean conflict because the men returning from the service felt that the existing student organizations did not meet their specific needs. The street corner gang develops in new or old neighborhoods out of similar frustration or community ignorance of the needs of the individuals involved. The needs may be as simple as that of "activity"—a significant need in the jungle-like maze of streets and buildings in large cities. Secret fraternities or sororities in high school are only one step removed from the street corner gangs of the large cities. The school with this secret society problem must examine the needs which are being met in the fraternities or sororities. The actions of students in these groups are need-satisfying; the social failure may be rooted in the school program where normal outlets do not exist for these particular students.

Groups which spontaneously develop may often offer public or published reasons for their existence. The actual reasons may be consciously or unconsciously below the surface of the group's actions. The "Pastime Athletic Club" in the neighborhood may be professedly an athletic group, and yet never play in any games or contests. The clubhouse, the socialization, the actions whatever they may be are not designed to assist in the stated goal of the group. Many school clubs are similar to this type of neighborhood group. The election of officers, the appearance of the group's picture in a yearbook, the collection of points for an award are not normal expected functions for a group, yet they seem to be the only activities which are supported by the group. The needs which are being met by the group's existence are not those of task accomplishment. In many ways, such groups are distortions of growth-centered groups; the individuals are seeking enhancement, protection, or action because of their own individual or group-centered psychological needs.

Three major types of psychological needs appear to be operating in the formation of any spontaneous group: (1) protection (2) enhancement, and (3) action. The learned social needs of acceptance, security, and affection are strong motivating forces in all human behavior. Individuals who are frustrated in their seekings for the satisfaction of these goals will turn to other outlets or other means of securing satisfactions. The splinter club group organized from among the "outs" in a senior class of a high school may seek recognition from the student council of the school or may organize as a non-school function. Acceptance, security among peers, the affection of others in the group—these needs all are powerful forces operating within the lives of the adolescent, the younger child, and the adult in the community. Enhancement of self through status, the esteem of others, prestige, and power are additional motivating forces operating in the lives of all persons. Action plans or activity patterns of spontaneous groups also point to lack of opportunity or frustration in a school or community.

ENVIRONMENTAL FACTORS. Spontaneous groups frequently form out of physical conditions or external arrangements which facilitate the development of a group. Housing development groups reported by Festinger (1951, 1953) indicated that contiguity, common facilities, and interaction opportunities were primary in the formation of subgroups within a university housing unit and other architecturally related groups. Common needs, whether they be those of sociability, as in this case, rather than protection or self-enhancement, as in previous examples, were also operative. Teachers, guidance workers, and special educational service officers, such as attendance officers or school social workers, have long noted the effect of environmental or physical factors in the formation of spontaneous groups in the school or neighborhood. The back corner of the classroom, a youth group at the church, adjoining backyards, common sectioning of classes, or other similar factors, are all influential and active in the spontaneous development of groups.

FORMAL AND INFORMAL STRUCTURE. The many lodge groups present in American society operate upon detailed and very specific rules of procedure, organizational patterns, and member relations. Officers are promoted through "chairs" and "offices"; ritualistic openings and closings are standard; tasks are rotated or shared on a particular plan. Within the same lodge or social group, an informal or unofficial organization often exists: "Oh no, we can't allow him to become———!" is typical of a conversation held between members of an unofficial and informal subgroup of the larger organization.

Other types of informal groups may operate entirely outside of any organized, recognized structure. The "professional" athletes on the varsity football or basketball team may form a minority group within the class and disturb the teacher greatly with their antics or their loud discussions of non-school and non-athletic activities. Industry has long been wary of the pressure exerted by the informal group in the plant or on the floor, the members of which constantly cry, "don't break the job." The control of production by informal groups, and the communication networks present in many plants has been studied and clarified: Roethlisberger and Dickson (1939); Jaques (1951); Homans (1950). Little or no evidence of a research nature exists that similar forces are operating within every classroom to a degree. However, teachers with experience can well describe the testing of the limits with a substitute, with a new teacher, and with a poor disciplinarian, as well as group controls on participation and performance. Gibb (1960) reveals such concerns as he discusses class "norms."

Most school organizations have their formal and informal aspects. The lines of communication, and reporting of actions, plans, and results through such lines of communication are of the joint formal and informal types. Some information is passed on in a formal sense, and then the editorial comment or the interpretation is offered to those who are members of the informal chain of command. Often, official or formal use is made of such informal or unofficial lines of communication, or of the actual informal groups, as in "official leaks" by political figures or by business executives. "Official rumors" are similar uses of the "grapevine," or other informal aspects in groups and organizations.

Unorganized groups are not the same as informal groups. Organization is on a separate continuum from formality. Informal and formal groups can be unorganized. Lack of organizational structure can be destructive to a group's progress and personal relationships. French (1941) showed the effects of organized versus unorganized groups in determining group operation.

Planned and organized groups

As patterns of operation within a group become stable an informal or spontaneous group can turn into an organized formal group. Other organized groups come into existence as a result of the efforts, planning, and foresight of individuals or groups who wish to accomplish a task, meet a need, or serve a function which has been established within the subsociety group.

Stogdill (1950) offers two major variables which define the operations of the formal or organized group: (1) *responsibility variables,* the work one is expected to do, and (2) *formal interaction variables,* the persons with whom one is expected to work. Essentially this implies that a planned organization will exist when a job must be done and when certain persons are expected to do it. The key word in this characterization of a formal or organized group is "expected." Stogdill defines the informal group by offering the same two variables, but substitutes the word *actually* for *expected.*

Groups are established because they provide an effective means to accomplish tasks and meet personal needs, and they can do so while they are attractive and socially desirable to the members who participate. Back (1951) is concerned with the various attractions and forces that bring groups together. He lists task attraction, personal attraction, and possible prestige gains as three sources, the strengths of which vary according to environmental conditions. All of these sources can contribute to the ability of the group to influence its members.

Many classifications of the types of planned or organized groups possible in our society could be offered. A simple and yet meaningful categorization includes four types:

1. Formal groups
2. Action groups
3. Study groups
4. Discussion groups

There are many subgroups in this classification, such as the "66" group, the "buzz" group, the "standing committee," and other titles which may be designated by the particular author of the classification or the parent organization that establishes the subgroup. So-called formal groups may become so informal that any line which is used to separate them becomes arbitrary.

FORMAL GROUPS. Formal groups are common throughout our society. Local or national government organizations, boards of education, teachers' associations, workingmen's unions, and similar formal organizations can be found in every community in America. These groups are characterized by the existence of officers, a constitution or by-laws, rules of procedure and action, written reports, and formal organized meetings. Such groups are usually permanent or semi-permanent, they are large, and they often have smaller subgroups of a similar formal nature, such as standing committees and executive councils.

Large formal organizations are designed to serve many people and to complete tasks that are difficult or impossible for one person or a few persons to accomplish. They are usually ponderous in their movement or progress and often have ritualized systems of communication within them. These units of society are well equipped to serve the continuing needs of the members and are purposely designed to be difficult to change. They are responsible to society and to the members in the conduct of business tasks and the maintenance of financial stability. The attractiveness of such groups is in their task orientation, their do-the-job nature, which especially validates such formal groups. Socialization, personal and emotional satisfactions, and status or prestige need-fulfillment are not intended to be the primary attractions of such groups, although they are often perquisites.

School groups, such as student government organizations, debate councils, athletic teams, class organizations and other "permanent" groups, are copied from the large, official groups of a formal nature existing in the outside community. Practice, experience, and attitude development are the usual reasons offered for the formation of such groups. Though copied from task groups, these school groups are, in reality, growth groups. Socialization, personal and emotional need fulfillment, and even status and prestige attractions are common in such so-called formal groups in a school.

Selected formal groups in the community and the school are designed to fulfill personal and emotional needs of the members rather than to accomplish tasks. The ladies' flower club and the varsity club in school are examples of this variation of the formal group. Actually, many supposed formal and task-centered groups lose their original function, or the needs of the groups change, and they become essentially status groups. Many so-called athletic clubs in the community, with permanent buildings, have no significant athletic function. The serving of meals and the need to be seen and to take guests (status and prestige needs) are the real reasons for the continued existence of the group. Often, in a school, class offices seem to serve only a prestige need. The functions may be carried on by a paternalistic principal or a directive class advisor. Student needs in class groups, or any groups except those of a highly ritualistic nature, such as the senior prom, may be denied any existence.

ACTION GROUPS. There are many organized groups which are not formal and do not reflect the status quo of the community. Action groups are developed in order to change the status quo, or to bring about desired improvements within a society or subcultural unit. Thelen (1954) describes the nature and activity of such groups in his analysis of groups at work. The fields of human relations, civil rights, community action, and related areas offer primary examples of planned action groups.

Action groups are persons brought together for the primary task of *doing* something. These groups most frequently stress the job to be done. Individuals are chosen for membership because of their ability to do the job and forward the objectives of the group. Growth, at best, may be a secondary goal; or there may be an attempt to include individual members so that they may be helped to become better task workers through experience.

Social action groups in the community are often models for school groups within a more controlled environment. Fund raising committees of a student council, big brother programs, and similar efforts are attempts to do a job. The social action group, with its stress upon accomplishment, is not frequently found in a school situation. School officials, teachers, and even guidance workers are often afraid of such groups because of their radical or liberal stripe derived from the community. Also, a school is supposed to be devoted to learning and the excuse is often offered, when such groups are contemplated, that it would be permissible to make a study of the problem, but that action would have to be left to forces outside the school. "Sit-in" and "Freedom Rider" demonstrations planned by student groups in the South are clear examples of the informal action group.

The skills developed by leaders in the field of action group effort represent some of the most outstanding benefits of group work. Specific methods of resolving racial, religious, and other intergroup conflicts have been developed by social psychologists, groupwork specialists, and social workers. Although on the perimeter of efforts of school guidance workers, the work of Watson (1946), Dean and Rosen (1955), G. W. Allport (1951), and Lippitt (1949) provides practical approaches which can be adapted for use in action groups in a school or community.

STUDY GROUPS. Action groups are primarily concerned with the task at hand; study groups, conversely, are designed to help members to learn and to understand or, in short, to gain knowledge. The assumption is often clear in study groups that action is to be eschewed, even if it seems appropriate. Educational environments are particularly suitable for the use of study groups. A class is a formal study group; the subdivisions of classes as they are organized into small groups are growth groups as well as study groups.

Study groups are frequently informal. The organizational rules of the group are kept to a minimum. The trappings and rules of procedure found in formal groups would defeat the purposes of the study group. Confusion in this area is revealed when a teacher or a group leader attempts to use "Robert's Rules" within a small study group. Formal rules of procedure are needed in large groups; however, their employment in an inappropriate situation is similar to the situation of the golfer who insists that he wishes to use his driver in order to putt.

An outstanding use of the study group concept, with all of its advantages, is described in the volume, *With Focus on Human Relations*, by Taba and Elkins (1950). This is the story of an eighth grade class which, in the process of studying social science, puts into practice the principles of human relations and interpersonal emotional learnings. The teacher in this situation used a wide variety of groupwork techniques in order to accomplish the goals of the project. This publication is one of a series devoted to the concept that group techniques in education can enrich the curriculum and aid students in learning the important elements of citizenship and maturity while also completing the usual educational projects and activities in various class situations. The 1960 National Society for the Study of Education yearbook is titled, *The Dynamics of Instructional Groups*. Groups, classes and education do belong together.

DISCUSSION GROUPS. Discussion groups, by design, are essentially growth and socio-emotional groups. Action is assumed *not* to be a concern of the members of the group. Discussion groups may be used in class structures, as preludes to study and action groups in community organizations or in guidance programs. Discussion groups are frequently used to explore a given area of concern. If conclusions resulting from discussion are satisfactory, then the group may organize a study or an action group.

A technical variation of the discussion group is the therapeutic group. A therapy-oriented group is a growth group of an extreme form, and is a type of discussion group. No action is necessary or planned in a therapy group. The expected result is within the person—the added maturity or personal insight obtained through discussion and skilled leadership on the part of the group therapist. Many authors have aided guidance workers in adapting the discussion group as a therapeutic group within a school program. Driver's *Multiple Counseling* (1958), and Bach's *Intensive Group Psychotherapy* (1954) are examples of efforts in this direction. This special application of the discussion group in the guidance program will be presented in detail in Part Three.

Groups can be formed spontaneously or as a result of a planned pattern of action initiated by persons inside or outside the group. Extremely technically-minded persons could claim, with some justification, that all groups are spontaneously formed, since the idea has to develop in someone. The idea that an outside manipulator establishes a group by decree has not been intended when planned groups have been discussed. Groups begin to gel or to hang together, according to many principles. Regardless of the factors underlying the formation of a group, the first practical problem which must be faced by a group is, "What do we do?"

An objective or purpose within a group is a vital concern to the members, the organizers, or anyone who plans to evaluate the results of the group's efforts. The purpose of the group may vary from that of an exchange of ideas and concepts, as in a discussion group, to a specific plan of action, as in a community action group. Normal group development will flow smoothly from an organizing state to the development of an objective or purpose for the group. Whenever a group is confused, uncertain, or in conflict about its purpose, the root of the difficulty may often be traced back to the formation process and confusion in the minds of those who organized it. Such confusion serves as a divisive force. The group cannot begin to function effectively without a clear understanding of the problem or the objective. The process may not be obvious or even conscious (a group therapy unit presupposes common purpose), but purpose exists in a successful group.

Objectives

Objectives, like good theories, are very practical items. A concrete situation such as an auto trip can illustrate the usefulness of an objective. Whenever a person undertakes an auto trip he has in mind an objective which may or may not be shared. The objective may be a specific destination, or the objective may be to enjoy the scenery and the pleasures of an unplanned excursion. A purpose has been established in either case.

All members can profit from an early examination of the objective which is appropriate for the group. In fact, following an introduction of the members to each other, virtually nothing is more appropriate than a statement of objective, or purpose for existence. Many groups will bog down at this point and never progress any further. Certainly, if the group cannot agree upon any need for its existence, or any problem for its attention, it may be desirable for it to disband. It is surprising to alert observers how frequently persons are very willing to "get down to business," without the least concern about the objective or basic reason for the existence of the group.

Objectives or purposes are not necessarily lofty. A problem, a specific concern, a confusion in human interaction—all are legitimate concerns for those who are affected. Many group leaders crystallize purpose by asking the group: "Well, what's the problem we have to face?" or, "Let's decide exactly what we are to do now." These statements are simple, but reveal a concern for one of the first problems to be solved by any group if it is to avoid frustrating confusion and disagreement.

Levels of aspiration

Many groups are sincere and responsible in their determination of a purpose or objective; in fact, they are so bent upon doing the job that they attempt to do too much. Group activities by their very nature are not speedy means of solving problems. Speed is an advantage of the authoritarian or dictatorial method. Groups are effective in involving persons in decision making and often become effective in the long run, but are deliberate and even painfully slow getting under way. Attainable goals and objectives are important to new groups in order to avoid early failure and frustration; older and more experienced groups are capable of revising and expanding their plans after they have succeeded in solving a portion of the total problem. Therefore, for an inexperienced group, a series of objectives or purposes is more desirable than a broad goal which can be only dimly seen. However, goals need to be increasingly difficult and rewarding for the group members if the group is to be constantly challenged.

The level of a goal or objective needs to be established, reviewed, and revised as a group progresses. The leader, general group members, and special members, such as the secretary or recorder, all need to share the responsibility in this matter. Constant or even periodic revision of objectives, and revision of the level of aspiration for the group may distress some members of the group. Rigid, authoritarian persons object to the flexibility which is needed in group operation. Our Constitution was formulated by a group of persons who had joined together in order to revise the Articles of Confederation. These Americans were flexible!

The identification of the problem is the first step in the structuring or formation of a group. The determination of purpose aids the members to understand their own roles and their own attitudes toward the problems to be solved. Individual action, thought, and participation need to be focused on the mutually understood purpose of the group. Thelen (1954, p. 253) is unequivocal in his characterization of the need for purpose or an objective in a group:

> Without it [an objective problem] there would be no basis for differentiating roles, for settling leadership competition, for organizing effort. There would be no criteria for testing ideas, and the group would end in nothing but a series of divisive moves for individual power.

The agenda

A spontaneously formed or preplanned group must establish its objectives and purposes and then lay out the steps which will be followed in order to achieve the stated goal. Simple examination of the process involved in this task would demand that the objectives be broken down into manageable units and examined in an order which would provide for effective and meaningful problem-solving. As the group has isolated short-term problems, long-term goals, and ultimate purposes, agenda are a natural outgrowth of the discussion. The leader, the secretary, or the recorder can organize and present for group approval formal or informal agenda.

An understanding of the psycho-social nature of any group is necessary prior to establishment of agenda. The construction and formulation of any group and the adoption of specific objectives and goals within a group are both processes which involve conflict and compromise among members. Each member has needs and forces motivating and driving him towards group involvement. A term with many meanings has been developed which can help to clarify this problem: the hidden agenda. The hidden agenda concept can refer to at least three major variables: (1) a manipulative desire on the part of the leader or the power members to "take" the group to a preplanned conclusion; (2) the personal, private goals and objectives of the individuals comprising the group; and (3) the group's unconscious or private agenda.

The leader or the power members of a group can secretly caucus or arrive at an understanding for the planned operation of the group. This action is contrary to effective group techniques and is, at best, slick dictatorship. At times such control is practiced by leaders and responsible persons in many groups. The business meeting where the group adopts a plan of action which has previously been typed and is brought out by the leader or chairman at the end of the meeting (having been in the briefcase all during the meeting) is, at times, a facetious result of this practice.

Manipulation of a group by a leader or by powerful members is an attempt to cover authoritarian action with "democratic packaging." Such action is often far more repulsive than direct decision-making on the part of a leader or responsible administrator. Our world is one in which decisions must be made and assignments determined, and not always through group action. Hidden agenda tactics of this type reveal an insecure leader or power group; approval is sought and power feared. Such actions are, perhaps, the greatest insult which can be offered to group members.

Hidden agenda of the individual members are far more frequent and common in group actions and discussions. Such hidden agenda exist both consciously and unconsciously. Leaders and groups need to deal with this type of action in varying fashions. Conscious adoption of private agenda by an individual indicates a personal need for action. A group member who is constantly defeating the purposes of the group through long and detailed personal recitals and descriptions of personal experiences is really saying psychologically, "I must have an audience . . . I need to have the attention and concern of others. . . . My needs in these areas are greater than the needs of the group."

The personal, private, preconscious needs of a group can also form hidden agenda. The neighborhood athletic association referred to earlier is typical of a group with hidden agenda. The group does not exist for athletic activity in spite of its name; the group never plays any games or fields a team. The group is organized for purposes of sociability, prestige, and status. The name on the jacket is an indication that the member *is somebody*. An adolescent may vehemently deny the existence of the needs of the group in such areas whenever a public examination is conducted; a private, personal report from the members will clearly establish such needs (Kvaraceus, 1954, 1959). A psychiatrist was quoted in the daily press: "Don't be too quick in taking away the 'duckcuts' from the boys in the high schools; it may be all they own!" Hidden, private meanings are vital to persons and groups. Similarly, an exclusive athletic club for the scions of society also exists for "hidden" or at best non-admitted reasons.

More deeply hidden or unconscious needs operating within the group may be present in small or large groups. Sociability, fun, relaxation and fellowship are openly accepted as some of the objectives of the men's club in the local church, the American Medical Association, and the American Personnel and Guidance Association. Such values or hidden agenda are seldom mentioned when members are urged to join in meetings and to attend local or national conventions. Hidden needs in some groups are destructive to the group and can sometimes wreak havoc upon society. A roaming gang in a teeming city drifts into a dimly lit park; hostile feelings against society and the established order may be translated into action in the sadistic and vicious mauling or murder of an innocent member of society.

The variations of the individual or group hidden agenda are numberless. The form which the digression will take is related to the needs, the pressures and personal goals operative within the personality of each member, and the total "group field." Many persons fear power and feel threatened when they find themselves in disagreement with the ideas of the leader or a powerful, but small subgroup. The perceptions, statements, actions, and feelings of the persons involved in this type of situation are affected. Experimental evidence concerning the effects of high status and power upon individuals with low status and power have demonstrated this phenomenon in groups (Hurwitz, Zander, and Hymovitch, 1953). Similar results have been observed in individual psychological development in all areas of adjustment psychology. The motivations, needs and experiences of persons as a part of their personality structures are constant influences in life, and the individual's own needs can dominate a group's activities if the conditions are right and the pressures strong.

Leaders, members, observers, and evaluators need to keep in mind the issue of hidden agenda which affect all groups. The obvious manipulation of a group by a leader or by group members occurs less often, and is, therefore, less of a problem than the interference which is constantly present as an individual attempts to cope with the problems of living while he is also a member of a group. Thelen (1954, p. 253), while pointing out the overriding need for an objective problem for the group to solve, states that without a well-defined objective, problem, or purpose the hidden agenda of each person can destroy the functioning of the group.

STRENGTH AND VITALITY IN GROUPS

Young children's behavior is often inexplicable except as peer pressures are understood. The elementary school pupil who refuses to wear rubbers and a raincoat, to the distress of his parents, seems to be "unbalanced," willful, rebellious, even self-destructive. The pleas of parents, teachers, relatives, is useless. Only when it is understood that the neighborhood "gang" credo includes, "only sissies wear rubbers and raincoats," can the behavior be made meaningful. The child is struggling for acceptance and membership within an informal, but potent peer group. The standards of the group may not, and often do not, conform to the standards which adults might wish the group to adopt. Regardless of adult feelings, the group's power is effective. The individual is enmeshed in a conflict situation—his parents versus his gang or group. This conflict is common in individuals at all age levels. Society can be substituted for the parents, and the individual must resolve the issue as best he can.

The strength of the pressure which can be exerted by a group is the result of its organizational strength and the attractiveness of the group to its members. The pressure for conformity to group standards is increased as membership benefits and values grow. The style of leadership within a group is another variable which can determine the degree of pressure exerted upon persons to conform to the standards of the group (Bonner, 1959, p. 83; Bovard, 1951b). The degree of in-group feeling present can not only affect standards and pressures for members, but can also affect communication within the group. Furthermore, such in-group feelings are a strong factor in determining the effectiveness of the group's working power, and in revealing its hostile attitudes towards society, or its effect for the good of society.

Group attractiveness

Individual groups possess different degrees of attractiveness to potential members. The Varsity Club in a high school is a high status group open only to members of athletic teams. The private club of the upper-uppers in old Yankeetown is open only to a select few, and consequently it represents a similarly high status goal for community members. Money, power, even friends in high places will not bring membership to those who are not qualified. The pressures within such groups are often as great upon members as upon outsiders who wish to join. Formal and informal mores govern the actions of the members. The expulsion of a member of the "four hundred" because of a misdemeanor or a divorce is an example of the pressure exerted upon members to conform to the standards of the group. Stealing, on the part of a new member of a street corner gang, as an initiation device, or the strict payment of high dues in the new golf club: both are examples of forces acting upon members of groups.

When the standards of a group are in opposition to the standards of society, both the group and society exert pressure on the individual to conform. The society may be the whole of which we are all a part, or a student society in a school. Conflict often arises within the individual who wants to remain in good standing with the group and finds that in order to do this he must oppose the standards of society. With regard to society, the purpose which the group fulfills may or may not be desirable, and society will benefit or suffer accordingly.

The pressures upon the individual member arising from the group are called "norms" by Gibb (1960, p. 117). He describes their effect upon members of classroom groups and of out-of-class groups. He characterizes norms as shared expectations of group members. The purposes, the functions, the shared expectations of the group—these are the raw materials of the power behind the pressure and standards which are established in a group.

Group stability

Groups which develop attractiveness for members can become stable groups; members will tend to remain within the group and carry out its purposes and functions. Measures of group attractiveness (Libo, 1953) can be related to the continued success or stability of the group. Groups in which there was attractiveness between and among members, and for the group, tended to be stable; where opposite conditions existed, the group very frequently disintegrated and members tended to withdraw from activities.

As a group can become attractive and stable for its members, so it may develop strong norms or standards to which members may adhere. Standards and pressures may be symptomatic of the degree of strength of purpose and stability of a group. Observers can determine the group's stability, attractiveness and power on the basis of the behavior of the group.

The concepts of group stability, attractiveness, pressures, and standards are, of course, relative and varying terms. These ideas are on continuum and can not be recognized in any single instant of time. A developmental observational schedule of the operation of any group, in a school or community, can provide an observer with an estimate of the conditions which exist within the group, and the motivating forces operating within the individual members as they face and solve problems outside of the group.

Cohesiveness

Many writers in the field of group dynamics are prone to equate group purpose, organization, morale, teamwork, and even productivity with the over-all term *cohesiveness*. This term is something of an omnibus concept encompassing some, but not all, of the interrelated concepts listed above. Two major concepts of cohesiveness have begun to emerge out of all of the theoretical speculation concerning groups. Cohesiveness may be defined in two ways: (1) the morale, the "togetherness" of a group; (2) the shared understandings of the purpose and function of a group (Bonner, 1959, 67 ff.). Considerable research about the effects of morale and cohesiveness within groups was conducted shortly after World War II (Katz and Hyman, 1947). Cohesive groups, groups with high morale, were able to withstand greater deprivation and to bear up under trying conditions better than groups with low morale. The relationship between cohesiveness (morale) and productivity is not clear. Groups with high morale or a high degree of cohesiveness have not always been the most effective groups in accomplishing a task. Experiments by French (1941), and others quoted by Schachter, Ellertson, McBride, and Gregory (1951), show cause for questioning the validity of the idea that cohesiveness and productivity are related directly.

The second concept of cohesiveness is that of attractiveness to a group as earlier discussed. Bonner (1959, 76 ff.) discusses this concept as have many other authors quoted by Cartwright and Zander (1960). Experiments attempting to relate cohesiveness to group productivity show conflicting results (Schachter, Ellertson, and McBride, 1951; Kahn and Katz, 1953). It would seem that the basic notion of cohesiveness is descriptive and illustrative of a dimension of group climate or attitudes, but not predictive of the output or results achieved by a group.

The problem of relating cohesiveness and productivity is partially clarified as the concept of cohesiveness is also seen to be a measure of the success of the organizational structure of a group. The group that has achieved a purpose and is organized to do a job, and has high morale, will be attractive to the members and to outsiders. However, an army may have high morale and may appear effective in its colorful dress uniform, and yet it may not be a fighting army when called upon to fight.

Recent research indicates that the answer to group productivity may lie in areas other than cohesiveness or group morale or attractiveness. Specific progress has been made in predicting the productivity of a group through knowledge of the relationships which exist between and among the members and the leaders, the communication or interaction process, and the decision-making procedures (Fiedler, 1960b). A detailed analysis of group productivity and these factors will follow in later chapters as these other aspects of group functioning are examined.

Cohesiveness is, however, basic to the organization and structure of the group. Once organized or spontaneously developed, the group must establish objectives, adopt agenda of an informal or formal nature, and begin to work. At this point one may assess the morale, attractiveness, or perhaps the cohesiveness which exists within the group. Prior to the completion of the task of the group, or the accomplishment of the growth objectives established for the members, the state of cohesiveness can affect many other factors vital to the ultimate success of the group. Primary among these factors are the interpersonal relationships of the members, the communication processes used, and the continued development of the group in the direction of problem solving and the accomplishment of its objective.

INTERACTION AND COHESIVENESS.   The degree to which a group can work together with mutual satisfaction and high morale, as a definition of cohesiveness, leaves many questions unanswered. While cohesiveness has been seen to be the attractiveness present in the group for the members, it has been more clearly seen as a definitive variable within the structure and functioning of groups.

The early stages of a group will provide opportunities for the clarification of goals and objectives. As members work together they begin to develop affective reactions to one another. These member relations and goal-directed activities can be controlled. Sherif and Sherif (1953) illustrated this with group manipulation by sponsors and leaders. It was shown that friendliness and concern for one another build feelings of security within the members of the group and help to fulfill the needs of members participating in the activities and problem-solving stages of group functioning. Cohesiveness is here a positive factor and one of the concepts which can help to explain the success of some groups and the failure of others. Benne and Muntyan (1951, p. 71) call this stage of group develop-ment the "building of a feeling of permissiveness." The accepting attitudes of members, one to another, is the foundation of this mutual respect and understanding. Many writers have stressed this aspect of group work to the virtual exclusion of all other aspects of functioning. Critics (Whyte, W. H., 1956; Bonner, 1959;) have frequently pointed out that this is not the end goal of group work, but the atmosphere or conditions which should predispose a group to do the job or to complete the task. The climate or the cohesiveness is not an end in itself; it is a precursor and concomitant of action or problem solving. Cohesiveness, of course, can continue to grow and to develop as the group continues to solve problems and functions throughout its various cycles of existence.

Cohesiveness, like certain medicines, is desirable and catalytic within a group, but can be overdone and can be destructive. Cliques, sub-group alignments, or even majority-minority splits are outcomes of strong feelings of a positive nature toward other members of the group. Such sub-groups are divisive in their essential nature (Huszar, 1945). Research has also shown that such cohesiveness carried to an extreme can develop at-titudes within a group which lead to the rejection of fringe or deviate mem-bers of the group. Schachter (1951) found clear evidence that this phe-nomenon occurred more readily as the groups developed a high degree of attractiveness.

The research findings in this area can be validated in the experience of many teachers, guidance workers, or group leaders. As groups begin, they are sincerely interested in the involvement of all members in the task at hand. As the groups begin to function effectively, and as the members become attracted to one another through mutual interactions and problem solving experiences, they tend to become intolerant of the members of the group who are nonproductive, or deviant in other ways. Such a happening can also be related to the overzealous attitudes of the group or its mem-bers toward the task at hand. The socio-emotional aspects of the group experiences are cast aside as being too demanding upon the members or not worth the effort if the job is to be done.

Cohesiveness in groups can be looked upon as a type of glue which can hold the members together. However, as in many cases where too much glue is used, the articles will not stick together. Group members need to be aware of the positive and the negative aspects of cohesiveness and be alert to the symptoms and actual presence of destructive forces within a group which can be covered by the guise of task orientation or group loyalty.

OUT-GROUP RELATIONS.   A corollary of the interactive nature of cohesiveness is the attitudes and feelings expressed by group members to nonmembers or "non-belongers." Just as peripheral members of a group may be rejected by the group as a whole, so persons outside of the group are rejected because they are non-members. This condition is seemingly related to the development of strong feelings of in-group loyalty, and yet it would also seem to be a warning sign. When group members must actively deny and reject others, when they must attempt to build themselves up through the process of tearing others down, it would seem to raise questions of security and independence. Group research has not clarified this problem as cohesiveness has been delineated and studied. Experience from other areas can perhaps serve to partially explain such happenings.

Psychologists have long recognized, in taking case histories and testing protocols, that extrapunitive aggression is related to frustration and insecurity. The external reactions are covers and reactions to internal feelings. Political scientists have noted such reactions on the part of insecure, frustrated nations. Hitler and other dictators have covered insecurity and frustration by making scapegoats of groups of persons (races) or even nations. The process here seems to be similar to the aggressive feelings expressed by members in groups with so-called high cohesiveness. Perhaps the high cohesiveness is a cover for fundamental insecurity. Such speculation may be useful to the group leader or worker in selected situations; however, research is still needed in order to relate and clarify such interdisciplinary concepts of human behavior.

SUMMARY

Groups can be formed spontaneously or may be organized by social planners. The formation of spontaneous groups depends upon such variables as the persons involved, the environment, and the needs or desires of the participants. Personal needs leading to the formation of groups are (1) protection, (2) enhancement, and (3) action. Organized groups usually follow one of four major patterns: (1) formal, (2) action, (3) study, or (4) discussion. The establishment of a group goal or objective is the first task facing a newly-formed group. Varying levels of aspiration may characterize groups. Appropriate and accomplishable objectives can mean much to the early success of any group; later group action can lead to the development of more complex and conceptually mature goals. The agenda represent the specific action plan of the group. "Hidden agenda" of individual and group natures affect all group functioning. The strength and vitality of a group are determined by the attractiveness of the group to the members, the stability of the group, and the degree of cohesiveness developed among the members. Organizational strength and group power are concepts which define the nature of the group and point a group toward its goals. The nature of the goals and objectives characterizes the group as desirable or undesirable to society.

SUGGESTED READINGS

Bass, Bernard M., *Leadership, Psychology, and Organization.* New York: Harper & Bros., 1960.

Dubin, Robert, *Human Relations in Administration.* Englewood Cliffs, N.J.: Prentice-Hall, Inc., 1951.

———, *The World of Work: Industrial Sociology and Human Relations.* Englewood Cliffs, N.J.: Prentice-Hall, Inc., 1958.

———, "Human Relations in Formal Organizations," *Review of Educational Research,* 29, 1959, 357–366.

Keedy, T. C. Jr., "Factors in the Cohesiveness of Small Groups," *Sociology and Social Research,* 40, 1956, 329–332.

March, J. G., and H. A. Simon, *Organizations.* New York: John Wiley & Sons, Inc., 1958.

Roethlisberger, F. J., *Management and Morale.* Cambridge, Mass.: Harvard University Press, 1941.

Roethlisberger, F. J., and W. J. Dickson, *Management and the Worker.* Cambridge, Mass.: Harvard University Press, 1939.

Tannenbaum, R., I. R. Weschler, and F. Massarik, *Leadership and Organization.* New York: McGraw-Hill Book Co., 1961.

Thelen, Herbert A., "Work-Emotionality Theory of the Group as Organism," in Sigmund Koch, ed., *Psychology: A Study of a Science,* Vol. 3, Study I. New York: McGraw-Hill Book Co., 1959, 544–611.

Watson, Goodwin B., *Action for Unity.* New York: Harper & Bros., 1947.

4. THE LEADER,
THE MEMBERS, THE GROUP:
structure and function

"Who's going to be the leader?" "Who's going to take the notes and keep the records for the group?" "Aren't we going to be able to get anyone who can help us with this job?" "Who said we have to . . .?" "It seems as though we are going about this job in the wrong way; don't you think that we need to stop and take a look at how we are working together?"

These issues and many other questions are constantly asked by participants and leaders at all age levels as groups function. Such questions reflect concerns with some of the most serious issues in all of the functioning and operation of groups. These issues relate to the nature and function of leadership, the operation and responsibility of members, the types and sizes of groups, and the nature of power, authority, and interaction relationships of groups, their leaders, and their members.

Research in the field of dynamics of group operation has been productive in identifying areas and issues. However, not all conclusions are accepted by persons concerned with the development of theory in group dynamics. Controversy and conflict abound in the growing literature of the functioning of a group. The concerns of identification, selection, and operation of leaders and members in a group are confusing to all who delve into research and attempt to obtain guidance for their own perform-ance as group members and leaders. Perspective is desirable, but any per-son who says, "this is the pattern, this is the truth. . . ." is likely to be a fool or a charlatan. However, practitioners need to be given some direction, some information which can make a task easier and the results more meaningful. The analysis of issues which follows is intended to give per-spective to the observer outside of the research milieu of group dynamics. Controversy and conflict are inevitable, and all sides are not equally justi-fied in their claims to practical implications. The positions to be outlined have been selected because they appear to be of functional application in guidance and counseling activities in educational environment.

LEADERSHIP

Theories of leadership date back to early historical writings and problems of politics and culture. The "Great Man" theory has been offered in op-position to the "Situational Leader." Authoritarian, democratic, and laissez-faire patterns of leadership have been analyzed to determine their effects upon the members in groups and the productivity of groups. Socio-metric or interaction types of measures of leadership have been designed, and they have been partially challenged by a concept of "syntality" or functioning, problem-solving influence of leaders and members.

There is no single method of selecting, appointing, or devising a leader for a group which will avoid all problems and guarantee the effective functioning of a group. Most frequently, theory and research have con-cluded that the environment and the purpose of a group are determining factors in the functioning of a leader. This conclusion is reasonable and useful to group workers. Prior to an analysis of conclusions, it is necessary to examine the major concepts of leadership and the research findings developed in accord with theoretical speculation.

Classical leadership concepts

The concept of leadership types in the field of group dynamics is deeply rooted in the experimental work of Kurt Lewin and investigators that worked with him. The widely-known and debatable classification of leaders into the classical types of "authoritarian," "democratic," and "laissez-faire" is based on concepts and experiences obtained from experimental work with youth groups in recreational settings. The early "Lewin, Lippitt, and White" (1939) experiments, and later reports by Lippitt (1940) studied the effects of various types of leadership upon the activities and feelings of the group members.

AUTHORITARIAN LEADERSHIP. The authoritarian leader is characterized as a person who uses personal power to determine group goals, objectives, and actions. He is the center of the group's functioning. His methods of control are domination, threat, and punishment. The authoritarian leader does not act with the consent or approval of the members of the group, but is responsible only to himself. Fear and anxiety are not only climatic conditions of the group, but also tools for the leader to use in manipulating the members.

Group members in authoritarian groups are constantly in conflict with one another seeking approval, favors, and privileges from the leader. Scapegoating, aggressive, hostile acts towards other group members, and non-productive actions have been attributed to members in groups with authoritarian leaders.

Political dictatorships and autocratic governments have frequently been cited as examples of authoritarian leadership. The unlimited powers of Stalin, Hitler, and other leaders of this and other centuries have been models for group theorists for illustrations of leader power, leadership methods, and effects upon followers or members. The concept of the authoritarian leader has been used in the analysis of autocratic administrators and principals in schools in directive and counselor-centered approaches to individual therapy and counseling. Teachers have also been characterized as authoritarian and dictatorial when they tend to use techniques which smack of the dictator or the autocrat.

DEMOCRATIC LEADERSHIP. The idea of democratic leadership is imbedded in our culture. Positive attitudes of democratic leadership include the acceptance of the ethic of group participation in planning, decision-making and implementation of plans and decisions (T. Gordon, 1955).

A democratic leader is a facilitating, co-ordinating, and group-centered person. He is capable of promoting participation and psychological involvement on the part of members and is willing to place personal interests, ideas and plans in a position subordinate to those of the group. He is interested and skilled in the development of leadership qualities in group members, and is capable of sharing the responsibilities of leadership with other capable persons.

A democratic leader's power is derived from the group, and the group has the authority to withdraw the right to power from the leader. The power relationship of the leader and the group members, as well as the characteristics of the operation of democratic leadership, lead to involvement and participation of members. Responsibility and authority is shared; aggressive and hostile reactions towards the leader and other members are kept at a minimum. The leader and the group attempt to adopt flexible, realistic methods of solving problems while respecting each other as persons with feelings, needs, and individual motivations.

Examples of democratic leaders and groups are frequently drawn from political contexts such as the government of the United States, the United Nations, and the legislatively oriented British form of government. Counselors and guidance persons are often presented "democratic" methods of treatment and counseling. Client-centered or patient-centered types of techniques are similar to democratically oriented approaches, although the comparison is implied more often than stated. Teachers and administration officials are urged by writers and specialists in education to adopt "group dynamics" approaches in order to make their operations more "democratic."

Few writers have attempted to define in a few words the meaning of democracy as it applies to the leader in the group situation. Bonner (1953, p. 400) sums up the qualities of democratic leadership in this excerpt:

> The democratic leader is fundamentally motivated . . . by persuasion, conciliation, and a tolerance for human weakness. He is conspicuously less concerned with discipline, and his relation with his followers is friendly rather than distant and authoritarian. He tends to trust people's good sense and to believe that, with adequate guidance, they can attain their own ends. His effect on his followers is seldom dramatic, for they sense in him only a common man like themselves. He need not use propaganda in the opprobrious sense, for having faith in his people's intelligence, he relies mostly upon facts and logical argument.

Bonner's very general definition will displease many political scientists and many theorists in group dynamics. However, he has stated simply most of the essential characteristics and beliefs appropriate for democratic leaders in small group situations. Variations are, of course, legion; the essentials appear to be similar.

"LAISSEZ-FAIRE" LEADERSHIP.   The "laissez-faire" leader as characterized by Lewin, Lippitt, and White (1939) is more accurately described as a passive or "anarchy-type" leader. C. G. Browne (1958), and Bonner (1959), among others, have supported this position.

The type of leader referred to by these authors is easily recognized by school personnel and guidance workers. The do-nothing leader allows the group to develop as chance or individual members desire. Little or no direction is available from the leader.

Members working with a "do-nothing" leader are bored and disinterested; sometimes they may be characterized as aggressive, hostile, and non-cooperative. However, virtually any type of structure or climate may be imposed by the members of the group since they have the total responsibility for the development of the group. Many such groups resemble authoritarian groups in terms of reactions to one another; other groups, through personal value structures of the members, may develop more democratic actions and climates.

The non-leader assumes no power or authority for the decision-making process or other activities faced by the group. Power and authority are "lying around loose" and individual members (emergent leaders) may assume such responsibility.

CLASSICAL THEORY: A CRITIQUE.   The distinct separation of leadership into three categories has been modified by most research persons since the original formulation by Lewin, Lippitt, and White. The types of leadership they identify seldom exist separately. More frequently, there is overlapping, and operational procedures contain elements of each category. Seldom will pure "leadership types" be observed.

Many skilled leaders use the trappings of democratic leadership as a cover for skilled autocratic manipulations. Apparent autocrats are often much more democratic in their actual functioning than superficial observation would initially indicate. The types and the "poles" of leadership are guides for group leaders; actual practice seems to stretch the concept of democratic leadership into autocratic-democratic and laissez-faire—democratic, as well as pure democratic. Skilled group leaders need to analyze leadership in different conceptualizations in order to understand more fully the actual meaning of democratic leadership. Only when the diverse types of democratic leadership are understood can an observer say that a person is operating as a "democratic leader."

Functional leadership types

Production, output, or even group accomplishment was not a primary concern of those who were first concerned with the classical leadership types. Lewin, Lippitt, and White (1939) paid little attention to such items. They indicated only briefly that group performance was higher in the authoritarian group. They also stated that although this was true, the quality of the performance of the democratic groups was higher. Other investigators have found that efficiency seems to be best served by autocratic methods (Shaw, 1955; Guetskow, Kelly, and McKeachie, 1954). This last experiment was organized on the campus of the University of Michigan and the experimenters modeled the procedure on the original experiment of Lewin, Lippitt, and White (1939).

The research specialists who have found autocratic methods to be more efficient have usually stated that not only quality of performance, but also personal values and socio-emotional satisfactions are higher in student-centered or democratic groups. Classical democratic-type leadership did not produce the productivity results expected or hoped for by experimenters.

The idea of functional or useful problem-solving leadership has been isolated as a concept which could lead to more effective performance on the part of groups. Participatory, supervisory, and consultative became terms which were descriptive of the roles which were fulfilled by leaders. It is important to note that these terms were not to be coupled with the classical leadership types earlier illustrated, but, rather, were meant to indicate variations within the scheme of democratic leadership.

PARTICIPATORY LEADERSHIP. A functional or participatory leader is not an isolated, "out in front" leader. He is one *of* the group and has a part in the problems, decisions, actions, and even the failures and successes of the group. Leadership in this view is a collection of functions, tasks, and responsibilities which are shared and implemented by both a leader and a group. The leader is more *active* than other members in initiating ideas and concerns for group problem solving, but is different from the group members only in *degree* of activity, not in the *kind* of activity accomplished.

This concept of leadership agrees with the democratic concepts of leadership delineated by theorists in the more "classical" views of leadership.

The kind of leadership which provides for each member of the group to share leadership functions, or to be a leader "a little," has been explored and catalogued by Cattell and co-workers (Cattell, 1951; Cattell and Stice, 1953, 1954). Cattell has related his concepts of the measurement of personality and group leadership to a multi-factor view of personality. He sees personality as consisting of behaviorially centered characteristics which can be measured and catalogued. The group leader who participates and affects the group with which he is working can be described in terms of these measurable characteristics (Cattell and Stice, 1954).

Cattell's concept of participatory leadership is referred to as "group syntality." Cattell hypothesizes that "syntality" refers to the properties of the group which result from the efforts (participation) by the group and the leader. Participation and sharing are expressions which are related to his theoretical constructs, though certainly not equal or identical to them.

A willingness to "get in and work with" a group provides opportunities to be a working leader. Teachers and group leaders who have been willing to participate and work with groups will recognize this approach. The functions originally carried on singly by the leader can be shared as the group members become capable of taking on responsibilities. Participatory-type leadership in the democratic tradition and spirit attempts to develop leadership in others, and the leader seeks to work himself out of a job as leader.

Participatory leaders are not passive or restricted in their activity with a group. Research has shown that this type of leader rates significantly higher than other members of the group in such activities as analyzing problems, initiating action, and proposing solutions (Carter, Haythorn, Schriver, and Lanzetta, 1951). More recent research has shown that not only were leaders more active in the process of decision-making, but when leaders were group-centered rather than leader-centered, and when members and the leader participated in the process of reaching conclusions, the groups were willing to undertake more difficult tasks and were more satisfied with group functioning (Ziller, 1957).

Studies of group production and outcome have shown that participatory leadership has surpassed other methods (Coch and French, 1948; Preston and Heinz, 1949; Bovard, 1951a). The groups studied not only were able to do the job, they were also more friendly in their interactions, and possessed a high level of cohesiveness. Other studies have confirmed most of these conclusions, and have refined certain aspects. Berkowitz (1953) found that when leadership functions were shared by designated or institutionalized leaders, cohesiveness tended to be lower. Group members seemed to expect strong leadership when leaders were officially designated. Members objected when leadership was shared with them in urgent situations. They expected the leaders to *be* "leaders" while, as members, they were to be free to participate and take the initiative when they wished to do so.

SUPERVISORY LEADERSHIP. Teachers, counselors, educators of all types, and industrial foremen have needed, not only to participate in the activity of groups, but also, through adequate techniques, to aid groups to grow in skill and to do the job alone. Effective supervision has as its goal the eventual independent functioning of those who are supervised. Effective supervisory leadership is a further development of participatory-type leadership.

Some investigators tend to consider the concept of supervisory leadership as opposed to participatory leadership (Preston and Heintz, 1949). Their definition of the concept of supervisory leadership places a supervisor in an aloof, non-participating role. Such a view is not in accord with effective theories of teaching, counseling, and learning. These appointed supervisors or designated leaders are only leaders or "heads" in a bureaucratic or name only sense. More accurately, such research would seem to be placing "good" supervision against "poor" supervision; the good supervisor (participating) comes out ahead. The teacher or group leader who can begin with groups in an active, co-operative role, and then withdraw gradually as skills are developed by the members, can move along to supervise other groups.

The supervisory leader needs to make group members aware of time in the process of group functioning and leader roles. The goal, for leader and group, needs to be the independent functioning of the group. Emergent leaders need to be trained to assume roles previously filled by supervisory leaders. The work of the National Training Laboratory at Bethel, Maine, and the writings of those who are concerned with the development of leaders and group efficiency are fully in accord with this view of supervisory leaders (Miles, 1959; M. Ross and Hendry, 1957).

CONSULTATIVE LEADERSHIP. A third, related type of participatory leadership is involved when a group seeks the aid of a qualified specialist. A school group is drawn to the librarian when occupational information is needed; a church planning group may sit down with a consulting architect in order to plan changes in the church building; a women's political discussion group may invite a political science professor from the neighboring university—a specialist is sought in each of these cases.

The specialist knows more about a particular situation than the group with whom he is consulting; however, without the group, the consultant cannot solve the problems at hand. The concept of working together is frequently forgotten when the specialist arrives. The specialist will begin slowly, but continue to talk more and more. Sometimes he ends by giving a speech, even to a small group. If the specialist then goes home, the group members may have more knowledge than they did prior to his coming, but the business of combining their problem with his knowledge still remains.

The outside expert needs to prepare his participation on the basis of knowledge of the group's problems or concerns. The group members need to realize that their knowledge of their own needs is as important as any outside information. The dual responsibilities of the specialist and the group must be clearly defined if the specialist's participation is not to take the form of a lecture (Bradford, 1949).

At the start, the consultant possesses no power in the group other than an inherent power resulting from particular knowledge. He is an assistant to the group members. The role of leadership which emerges as the consultant works with the group must be one of a participating, co-operating nature. The lack of involvement with any of the members provides the consultant with a strength or at least an advantage of objectivity. The nature of the consultant places him in the position of a "stranger," as Simmel (1951) characterizes the outside specialist who aids a group in solving a problem.

Skillful interpretation of the role of a consultative leader demands understanding of the equality of the roles to be played by the specialist and the group. Only as each respects the talent of the other in the problem-solving situation can the outcome be worthy of the efforts of both parties.

Other leader types

Many types of leaders have been identified by the theorists and observers of our history. The *charismatic* leader is the person who leads because he possesses the "gift of leadership." This gift is a part of the personality, body, and spirit of the leader. Such leaders have been known in our civilization, but seldom within the scope of school, community, or industry. Often, local leaders are discussed by teachers, business officers, or admirers as if they *did* possess such a gift. However, it is clear upon closer examination that such skill in leadership is related to specific abilities.

The bureaucratic leader is common in our society. Persons known as bureaucratic leaders are leaders because of the "office" they hold. Military officers, business executives, and many appointed leaders are of this type. The "office" gives power, responsibility, and opportunity to be a leader. The degree of leadership actually present in the person is as varied as the types of situations in which bureaucratic leaders are found. Bureaucratic leadership is not inherently inefficient or lacking in importance. When the person *is* a leader, and is also in the "office" of responsibility, then the tasks or the responsibilities of leadership may be fulfilled in a completely effective manner. Where an ineffective leader is charged with an official leadership role (or office), an "emergent leader," who must work with the ineffective leader, will often arise from within the group.

Dubin (1951) and other industrial sociologists describe the attributes of the "office" as it is structured in an organizational pattern. Much of the success of modern industrial organization and management depends upon the concept of office. The military has long held to a similar concept of leadership. Soldiers or other servicemen have regularly been instructed to salute the automobile of an officer, whether or not he is in the car. The "office" is being honored. Extreme examples of this practice can also be found in the privileges and perquisites accorded many business executives.

School situations are surprisingly similar to the military and the business worlds in their use of bureaucratic "office." The class president, the treasurer with no funds, the secretary who keeps no records, and other student positions in clubs, class organizations, and student government illustrate such situations. Faculty and administrators also utilize bureaucratic leadership. The system or the structure of the school is maintained through a series of "fictions" (Dubin, 1951, pp. 336–345)—"believing to be true, that which is not. . . ."

Leadership functions

Various types of leadership have been examined in connection with selected concepts of what the leader is and what the leader does in group situations. Inherent in all discussions of leadership types is the notion that there are responsibilities and functions which must be carried on by all leaders.

BASIC FUNCTIONS.   Cartwright and Zander (1960, p. 496) cite two major functions which are the responsibility of all groups: *goal achievement* and *group maintenance*. These terms are related to the concepts of task-centered and growth-centered groups. Leaders and groups must assume that there is a job to do or a growth goal to reach. As the leader and the group assume responsibility for the task, they are tending toward goal achievement. The initiation of action, the development of plans, the evaluation of plans, the implementation of plans—these are task-centered responsibilities. Group maintenance responsibilities are those of "maintaining" the group as an entity to solve problems or to complete a task. The socio-emotional needs of persons—human relations concerns, the need to participate, respect for the minority faction in the group—these are group maintenance concerns of both the leader and the group.

TASKS OF LEADERS.   A more general view of the functions of the leader in the group concerns actions that help the group to achieve its purpose. Group goals have to be established as the group evolves. Agenda must be developed and must reflect the group's concerns. The group must progress to its goal, and the meanings of the interactions of the group must be clarified, while respect must be maintained for individual members. These tasks and concerns are functions of the leader. They are also issues for each member.

More specific functions of the leader, as he works with a group, depend upon the type of leadership role to be filled. The democratic leader will balance the needs of task or goal orientation with respect for the person or the individual members of the group. Hayes (Glanz, and Walston, 1958, p. 34) lists four major functions that the democratic leader must perform as a group progresses: (1) focus discussion, (2) regulate discussion, (3) guide discussion, and (4) interpret and draw together group conclusions. The democratic leader will attempt to aid the group through many different approaches. The leader needs to take his cue from the problem-solving steps which must be completed by the group. The progress of the group, discussed in a later chapter, can provide the leader with an outline of specific functions which must be fulfilled as the group achieves its objective.

Leadership and personality

The goal of relating successful leadership function to specific personality traits has been one of the most sought after in all of the literature of groups and leaders. Success has been elusive, and no investigator has been able to draw a meaningful picture of a leader by describing the traits which he must possess. Attempting to order the massive research data that had accumulated since 1900, Mann (1959) sought to integrate the findings regarding the behavior of persons in groups with their personality traits. Most relationships were of low or barely significant order. Leadership and intelligence appeared to be most closely related; leadership was also positively but slightly related to adjustment, extroversion, dominance, masculinity, and empathy. Other behavior traits in groups were even less clearly related to personality characteristics.

Mann (1959) found that intelligence related most significantly to leadership behavior and yet other findings have shown that even this variable will be rejected by groups if the leader is too far above the group in intelligence (Hollingsworth, 1942). Clearly there is no simple road to selecting or predicting leadership according to the personality traits demonstrated by persons. The complexity of the leadership role in any group and the variable tasks to which groups may address themselves have convinced researchers that there is no discrete "leader type." Tannenbaum and Massarik (1957) stress the complex interrelationships of the group, the leader, and the situation at hand.

Progress in understanding the personality of the leader has come not in seeking isolated variables such as height, weight, or intelligence, or in such gross terms as adjustment, but in understanding the "behavioristic" elements of personality, and studying the performance of the group (Cattell, 1951; Cattell and Stice, 1953; and Cattell and Stice, 1954). Cattell and his co-workers are well known for the *16 P.F. Questionnaire* (Cattell, *et al.* 1956), which is an attempt to measure specific behaviorally-based elements of personality. These traits are such familiar ones as dominance and emotional maturity, but other, more unfamiliar concepts are derived from statistical analysis of the behavior items on the questionnaire. Cattell and Stice (1954) have begun to report meaningful results on the research task of identifying behavior traits which separate leaders from non-leaders.

"Syntality" in group behavior, with measurement of participatory leadership, is a concept of "productive, do-the-job leadership," which complements sociometric or "perceived" methods previously used (Moreno, 1953; Jennings, 1959) to measure and identify leaders in group situations. Cattell's works are complex and often difficult for the practitioner to apply. As more data become available they may aid in the problem of identifying potentials in particular leaders for particular types of tasks with particular groups of persons. This approach to the measurement of the personality of the leader assumes that the nature of the participatory leader will vary as specific situational groups and tasks vary.

Leadership: A critique

Leadership is an old and yet a new concern for persons in a democracy. Leadership was present in all of the activities which led to the founding of the United States of America. However, Krech and Cruchfield (1959) point out that it was not until 1896 that a book on leadership was catalogued in the Library of Congress. The tremendous surge of books on leadership, the how-to-do-it manuals for teachers, business men, and industrial executives attest to the attempt to understand the techniques of leadership.

The National Training Laboratory has been dedicated to the proposition that leadership and group skills can be learned and used in varying degrees by all persons. Leadership is not an inherited characteristic or "gift"; the democratic way of life assumes the principle that power to govern is delegated by the people. Research is beginning to uncover methods of understanding leadership and the functioning of leaders in a group situation. It is rewarding to note that the newer and perhaps more promising approaches to leadership stress that in a group, everyone leads "a little." The leader is like the members of the group and is not on a white horse out in front, charging ahead. Leaders in one group may be followers in another. Potential for leadership appears to be related to personality characteristics of a complex rather than simple nature. Training and experience can aid persons in leadership and followership functions as their talents are usable from situation to situation.

MEMBERSHIP ROLES IN GROUPS

The leader is often looked upon as the most important factor in the operation of a group. This is like saying the engine is the most important factor in the operation of an automobile. Group members, however, perform a function in the group similar to that of the wheels on the car; a car can go nowhere without wheels, and a group can go nowhere without the support of its members. In another sense, the group members are like the "line" on the football team, while the leader is similar to the quarterback. Success in groups, as in any co-operative endeavor, depends upon members' skill.

Leaders can be selected in many fashions. The members of the group, by their actions and co-operation, can determine the success of the leader and the group. The role of members in a group intensifies the stress of the factors operating upon a group because group members have definite needs and personalities of their own which are brought into the group meeting (hidden agenda). Group members seem to seek leaders who reflect their own basic needs. Sanford (1952) found that group members with authoritarian needs and rigid personalities prefer leaders of the same type; members who place much value upon discussion and human values tend to seek "equalitarian" leaders.

The members of a group are the other face of the coin of leadership. The success of the group depends upon the joint efforts of members and leaders. The group members, as well as the leader, must be responsible for the two major functions in a group—goal achievement, and group maintenance. Specific roles in these two categories will be identified and illustrated as responsibilities of the group members.

"Key" roles

Groups and group members develop the concept of "key" members of the group. These members may have official or unofficial status within the group. They may be senior (influence) members to whom the leader and the group look for advice and counsel. Conversely, influential members of a group who are not in sympathy with the objectives of a group can destroy the group unit in early sessions. It is impossible to cite the many titles which can be used to identify certain members of groups. A lodge may honor a revered member with the title of "Most Worshipful High and Holy Western Advisor." On the other hand, "Assistant Presidents" have worked effectively in the administrations of many presidents of the United States, and they have never had an official title.

Groups generally recognize selected roles and identify individual members to fill them. A *vice-chairman* (vice-leader, vice-coordinator, etc.) and a *secretary* (recorder, scribe, amanuensis) are the most common. The *process-observer* and *resource specialist* are specific key roles which are somewhat new to the small-group concept.

PROCESS-OBSERVER. The process-observer in a small or medium-sized group is somewhat similar to the parliamentarian in a large formal group. However, the process-observer can be a member of the group (though sometimes he is external to the group) and is not as restricted to points of order or enforcement of rules of procedure. The process-observer is charged with conducting a continuing analysis of how the group is functioning. In short, a process-observer is the analyst of group functioning in terms of process or non-content behavior. Earlier distinctions of content and process need to be recalled in order to structure clearly the responsibilities of the process observer. The person charged with this task watches, listens, and in many cases, interprets the "how" of the discussion of the group. He is not concerned with the content discussion of the group. He is concerned with such things as clarification of goal, focus of discussion, participation on the part of the members, interaction patterns between leader and members, interaction patterns between and among members, individual "out of group" behavior, hostility and aggression exhibited between and among members, movement or progress of the group towards its stated goals, and functioning of the leader.

The task of the process-observer is monumental. He is the specialist in the area of "group dynamics"; his is the responsibility to be the conscience, the evaluator, the diagnostician, and the physician to the group. Unquestionably, the process-observer needs to be well-informed about the dynamics and operations of groups. His role is also one which is threatening to the leader and to the members of the group. Tact, skill, understanding, and patience are needed for group members who aspire to the adequate fulfillment of the responsibilities of this key position. Dickerman, in Benne and Muntyan (1951, pp. 173–185), reflects the concern with which members of the National Training Laboratory view the important tasks that are assigned to the process-observer. Exceedingly flexible and varied approaches to this task are needed. Training in the use of an observer as a member or an outsider of the group is vital if the attempt is not to disintegrate into bickering and defensive reactions on the part of members of the group.

RESOURCE SPECIALISTS. Many groups will bring in an outside consultant for aid with problems they have isolated. The outside specialist may be viewed as a participator-leader, as earlier described, or a "key" member. It makes no difference which title is used. The significant element in the use of the consultant or the resource specialist is a realization that his function is not comparable to, and not a substitute for, a continued co-operative problem-solving attitude on the part of the members and the leader. The outside person adds a third quality to the group; often such a third force can add significantly to the success of the group. Perspective, an interrupted sense of time and continuity, and knowledge are the strengths which the outsider brings. Simmel's short essay on the "stranger" referred to above (Dubin, 1951), should be read by all specialists who plan to work with groups and *also* by group members before they attempt to work with outsiders.

Other group member roles

Every group will have other roles to be filled by members. School groups, particularly younger school groups, have a variety of roles which occur with an almost mystical or compulsive regularity. The clown, the fall-guy, the mascot, the daredevil, and the baby are roles which are familiar to the elementary school teacher. Redl and Wattenberg (1959) illustrate these roles and explain them in terms of personal needs and motivations on the part of the individuals assuming the roles and the members of the group who need, use, and defend such roles. In group behavior, as in individual behavior, actions are caused; they do not occur spontaneously.

Shared leadership

Leadership and group membership overlap in every phase of group activities. A concept of shared leadership involves the action of a participatory leader and leader-oriented members. The "little" leadership which is assumed by all members of the group is important. The members need to be aware of their own roles and functions as "assistant leaders" in all the operations of the group.

POWER IN GROUPS

You children are now "group one" and "group two." You are to study and to collect flowers. Each group will select certain flowers to collect and to mount in a scrapbook that the group, as a whole, will maintain. I will hold conferences with each of the groups and help you to plan your projects and begin your scrapbooks. (Sixth grade science teacher)

The success of the project described above by the teacher will depend upon her conferences with the groups, and the type of leadership, organization, task orientation, and other variables that enter into such a plan. A destructive element can be introduced if the teacher dominates. Many school youngsters can characterize such a group with one or two simple comments: "Yeah! We'll hold a conference and she'll tell us what we gotta do, whether we want to do it or not." Or, "Gee I bet this will be fun. . . . We organized groups before in our social studies class and we really had a ball."

Power is a latent, but constantly present element within the functioning of a class, a group, or an industrial work group. Bierstedt (1950), a sociologist viewing the human structure of society, sees power as the element underlying all organized interactions of groups and individuals. He sees it as a sustaining and supporting force. Groups and leaders must recognize power as a factor to be evaluated and utilized. Authority is a manifestation of power. Bierstedt categorizes authority as "institutionalized power." Authority becomes the outward symbol of power. Authority can be observed; its force rests on the power underlying its exercise.

The authority of the teacher rests upon her power to punish, reward or take action upon the students in the group studying flowers for science. Her power to give grades is institutionalized through the principal, the school board, the state legislature. The grades she gives to students are representative of the judgment she renders, based upon student performance. Children quickly understand the nature of power and authority in their early experiences in school and in the family. Later sophistication and the "fuzzing" of power and authority with tact, suggestion, and other socially acceptable means frequently confuse the issue.

Students, adults, workers, and particularly young children become suspicious very quickly whenever the power structure becomes uncertain. "Does he really mean it?" This is frequently the reaction when a group is given the power and authority to determine its objectives. One of the vital tasks of the leader and the group is to clarify and structure the power and authority concepts within the group. The concept of democratic participating leadership is based upon a rationale of "shared power." The authoritarian or dictatorial leader rests upon a base of power reserved for the leader. The classical laissez-faire leader and group is a wandering, uncertain organization because of an abdication by the group and leader from the exercise of authority. "Anarchy" was a term various authors preferred for this type of group. An anarchy exists where there is no order, no institutionalized authority—in short, no organized power.

Psychologists have identified power and authority as important variables to which persons react. Some individuals fear and distrust power and authority of all types and degrees; other persons develop a strong need for the clearly ordered structures which authority can create. Extreme reactions of these types can strongly influence behavior. Facetiously, but with insight, the remark can sometimes be made: "No, I never understood him until I found out that he disliked ALL policemen."

Democratic groups with concepts of shared participation, authority, and power demand that members as well as leaders be able to understand, accept, and utilize power relations in a group situation. Perceptions of group members, judgments and conclusions of group members, and the effects of leadership as related to power can be demonstrated in simple experiments (Gnagney, 1960; Lippitt, Polansky, and Rosen, 1952).

Democratic participation in group problem-solving situations is dependent upon the most mature concept of power identifiable; democratic participants and leaders must "carry around" internal power controls. Self-directed, self-governed individuals are needed in order to have a democratic society as well as a democratic group (Redl and Wineman, 1952). Visitors or refugees from authoritarian societies often marvel at the carelessness with which goods and foods are delivered early in the morning in cities and towns, before any storekeeper can receive or "guard" them. Internal controls and "internalized authority" are important elements in such simple customs in a democracy. The availability of goods and foodstuffs is, of course, related in such an illustration. The peaceful exchange of power from Winston Churchill to Clement Attlee in 1946, MacArthur's release by Truman—these are acts within a society dedicated to peaceful and orderly acceptance of power. Power and authority may be right or wrong; procedures exist for orderly challenge and question. Groups within a democracy wishing to reflect the refined elements of a self-ordered society must recognize the need for order, authority, and power.

GROUP SIZE

The issue of size for a group is a problem and nagging concern for group leaders, members, and organizers. There is no definitive research which has concluded that, for a particular purpose, the size of a group must be ————! Various purposes require various size groups. Such a conclusion is distressing to any person seeking aid in an educational, industrial, or community setting. However, there are generalizations which can be applied with discretion.

A principle

Thelen (1949) offers a principle which can aid in the analysis of the appropriate size of a group. He uses the term "least group size" in which "achievement" and "socialization" skills are present to do the job. His meaning for achievement is similar to that of task or goal needs discussed earlier. Building skills are needed if the group is a construction gang; writing skills, if the group is attempting to produce a play. "Socialization" is the concern for the socio-emotional needs or service needs of a group. When the least possible number of members are present to take care of these two needs, for the group task at hand, the group is of optimum size.

The reasonable application of a principle such as Thelen offers can help any group leader, member, or organizer to decide the optimum size for the groups under consideration. The nature of the task and the personalities of persons involved can become the stumbling blocks to such an analysis. The organization, purpose, and structure of a group are factors which must be considered when optimum size is judged. Skill in all areas of group operation and an understanding of group dynamics must precede determination of size.

Size variables

Specific factors influence the determination of the optimum size of a group. Purpose is a simple and yet decisive consideration to be analyzed prior to the determination of group size. A class of thirty students cannot effectively observe the functioning of a watch repair man on a field trip. The same group of thirty students could profitably observe the production line assembly of watches in a large factory or assembly plant. Physical facilities impose obvious limitations upon size. Other easily understood variables need not be identified.

An armchair speculator could not determine the dimensions of friendship groups, groups desiring maximum interaction, groups attempting to achieve consensus, therapy groups, and others. Research has supplied partial answers.

FRIENDSHIP GROUPS. Natural friendship groups of small children are small and restrictive. Sociometric research (Redl and Wattenberg, 1959) has revealed that such groups tend to have five or six members. This data has been collected in classroom situations, and may or may not apply outside of classrooms; the probability would seem to be high that it would.

Groups of more than five or six members seem to develop "fringers," "hangers-on," or "rejects." The implications of such findings can be useful in planning group activities. If organizers expect friendship patterns and friendly out-of-group relationships to be concomitants of in-group activity, it would seem desirable to establish groups of five or six members or multiples thereof. Groups of nine to ten or fourteen to sixteen would tend to shut out small numbers of persons from outside activities and produce fringe relationships or rejection patterns. That this does happen would seem to be supported by school and industrial observation, but certainly not rigorous research.

Interaction variables

The opportunity for interaction on a verbal level often is inversely proportional to the number of members present in a group. The modifying term, often, must be used to qualify such a generalization relating to interaction and size. Below certain levels of size, groups cannot form an organized pattern; communication breaks down and stimulation ceases. "What else is there to say?" Such a comment is often heard in a small group. There is of course, most often, a great deal more that needs to be and can be said; inter-stimulation is needed in order to bring out the best in members. Experiments with animals and observations of one's friends can illustrate this principle. Fully fed chickens, when joined at the feedbox by hungry chickens, start to eat again. How frequently have unexpected guests arrived and satiated hosts joined, even with gusto, the refreshment ritual?

More ordered research into the factor of size and interaction was completed by Hare (1952) when he investigated the achievement of consensus by groups of various sizes. Hare found that as group size increased from five to twelve, consensus, or percentage of agreement, among members decreased. Interaction decreased as group size increased; personal satisfaction was related to the opportunity to express ideas and opinions, even if they were not adopted by the group. Hare also noted trends toward factionalism as groups became larger.

Support for the concept of a direct relationship of increase in size to decrease in participation was noted by Bales and Borgatta (1955, p. 401). These authors also attempted to test the hypothesis of inherent conflict in even-numbered groups but without clearcut results.

No pattern of greater efficiency in smaller groups as compared with larger groups exists in the research literature of learning. Contrary results seem to appear with startling regularity. Large-scale instructional techniques involving closed circuit television; large class groups of over thirty-five students; and small class groups of twenty-five to thirty-five students were compared, in terms of the retention of the subject matter of the instruction, after a period of one or two years. Retention of subject matter did not relate to the size of the instructional group. The students preferred the small groups but appeared to function as effectively in terms of retention in all situations (Siegel, Adams, and Macomber, 1960).

McKeachie (1961), in analyzing the work of the teacher, investigates learning efficiency and related values in small and large groups. The volume of research is considerable, but conclusions are different in competing experiments. The degree of learning appeared to be similar in groups of comparable size, regardless of whether student-centered or teacher-centered techniques were applied.

Small classes were found to be more efficient by Cheydleur (1945), in comprehensive projects extending over twenty-four years at the University of Winsconsin. McKeachie (1961) refers to the "Pyramid Group" plan of Pennsylvania State University where six freshmen, six sophomores, two juniors, and a senior as group leader, were compared with larger control groups of persons who had equal time in learning experience in psychology. Achieved results (Carpenter, 1959 a and b; Davage, 1958, 1959; Davage and Carpenter, 1958) were called "fantastic" by McKeachie—the small groups clearly surpassed the large groups.

The evidence is coming in slowly but clearly that non-subject matter learnings (socio-emotional, adjustive, self-confidence, and maturity) are achieved through small group instruction with more efficiency than in large groups. The achievement results or traditional learnings were equal in large and small groups, and tended to be better in teacher-centered groups, regardless of size.

A FINAL WORD

Group structure and function have been clarified as research has progressed into more and more of the thorny issues which seem to stand in the way of a meaningful theory of groups and group activity. Early problems have been surmounted. Democratic leadership has been defined more carefully, and it has been demonstrably superior to other types of leadership. Early concerns about the inefficiency of democratic leadership have been allayed, and participatory-democratic leadership has enabled groups to reach achievement goals as well as socio-emotional goals.

Members have begun to assume an importance commensurate with that of the leaders. This is a natural outcome of democratic-participatory leadership. Group members have been developed into "little leaders" and "sharers" in power and authority. At the same time, evidence is becoming available that the democratic leader can be a strong, initiating, participating leader, and still achieve all of the goals which have been established for groups within a democratic framework. Bonner (1959, p. 193) particularly takes a stand for effective, strong leadership as a natural concomitant of participatory-democratic leadership. This author would agree with Bonner (1959), Berkowitz (1953), and other research specialists quoted in this chapter, that the leader and the group members both have dual roles in forming democratically organized and efficient groups; the leader's dual role demands that he lead, initiate, and participate while being concerned about personal values. This approach has always accompanied the growth of democratic leadership and followership. The democratic problem-solving method is concrete, specific, and useful. The "Alphonse-Gaston" type of democratic leadership can destroy groups, leaders, members, and ultimately, a faith in the democratic method of problem-solving.

Small groups recognizing the nature and function of power and authority, made up of responsible members and initiating, participating, and psychologically mature democratic leaders, can produce efficiently, and will always be testimony to the concept of human dignity. This precept of faith in a democratic, group problem-solving method has not as yet been fully vindicated by all research results; however, this writer believes that the tide is running stronger, and that theory, with productive changes, will continue to be supported by research.

SUMMARY

Leadership is the first major element within the structure of the group. Early research and theory categorized leadership into three classical types: autocratic, democratic, and laissez-faire. More recent investigation into the functions of leaders has revealed three variations of the "democratic" leader. (1) Participatory, (2) supervisory, and (3) consultative leaders are functional leaders. Charismatic and bureaucratic type leaders are also briefly examined.

Two basic functions of all leaders are (1) goal achievement concerns and (2) group maintenance issues. Personality and leadership are related factors; the exact relationship is not discernible.

Group members are "partial leaders" as well as supportive elements within a group. Goal achievement and group maintenance are concerns of members as well as leaders. Key member roles are those of vice-leader, recorder or secretary, process-observer, and resource specialist.

Power and size are two major factors in group structure. Power provides the force for order and regularity in interpersonal relationships in and out of groups. Authority is defined as institutionalized power. A principle of "least group size" is outlined. Size variables are related to interaction and learning in groups.

SUGGESTED READINGS

Bass, Bernard M., *Leadership, Psychology, and Organizational Behavior*. New York: Harper & Bros., 1960.

Browne, C. G., and T. S. Cohn, eds., *The Study of Leadership*. Danville, Ill.: The Interstate Printers and Publishers, Inc., 1958.

Cattell, Raymond B., "Personality Theory Growing from Multivariate Quantitative Research," in Sigmund Koch, ed., *Psychology: A Study of a Science*, Vol. 3, Study I. New York: McGraw-Hill Book Co., 1959, 257–327.

Gordon, Thomas, *Group-Centered Leadership*, Boston: Houghton Mifflin Co., 1955.

Guetskow, Harold, ed., *Groups, Leadership and Men*. Pittsburgh, Pa.: Carnegie Press, Carnegie Institute of Technology, 1951.

Haiman, Franklyn S., *Group Leadership in Democratic Action*. Boston: Houghton Mifflin Co., 1951.

Hanna, L. A., *et al.*, *Group Processes in Supervision*. Washington, D.C.: Association for Supervision and Curriculum Development, National Education Association, 1948.

Ross, M. G., and C. E. Hendry, *New Understandings of Leadership*. New York: Association Press, 1957.

Tannenbaum, R., I. R. Weschler, and F. Massarik, *Leadership and Organization*. New York: McGraw-Hill Book Co., 1961.

Wagner, J. A., *Successful Leadership in Groups and Organizations*. San Francisco: Howard Chandler, 1959.

5. WORDS AND MEANINGS IN GROUPS: perception, communication

> I do not love thee, Doctor Fell.
> The reason why I cannot tell;
> But this alone I know full well,
> I do not love thee, Doctor Fell.

Tom Brown's words, written while a student at Christ Church, Oxford, are typical of students of all ages, and illustrate the problem of understanding the process of perception and communication in groups. Some persons are able to relate to one another instantly; others appear to be hostile for no apparent reason. Group development and productivity are dependent upon the individual relationships of the members of the group. The total group atmosphere for problem solving is an aggregate of individual reactions plus the greater element of "group field."

Heider (1958) is concerned with human interaction and its seeming simplicity:

These intuitively understood and "obvious" human relations can . . . be just as challenging and psychologically significant as the deeper and stranger phenomena. (p. 1)

The problems of "common-sense psychology" are deceptive in seeming simple. Combs and Snygg (1959) remind us that "believing is seeing," not "seeing is believing."

Psychology has examined with care the problems of perception and knowing—the issue of "what is 'out there' and how do we know what is out there." Not only is this a concern for things but also for people. Asch (1952) points out that while things cannot act back, people not only *can*, but can also affect our own "seeing," feeling, and actions towards them (see earlier quotation, Chapter 2).

Words, connotations, the nuances and juxtaposition of words make up much of the environment in which a group operates. Even in a group, each person is the center of his own psychological world; words, perceptions, and relationships with other members of his group are designed to maintain, protect and enhance the self. Still, a collection of individuals forming a group must communicate through words and actions their common needs and their willingness to work together and to solve problems through common effort. Groups, like individuals, can succeed and fail in communication and in tasks.

Many factors complicate the understanding of the meanings of words used by individuals within a group. Atmospheres of co-operation and competition introduce elements of set or predisposition which can affect members' interrelationships. Authority, power, or physical arrangements which result in restricted patterns of communication can also severely hamper group effectiveness.

Specific techniques, such as role-playing, or assumption of others' roles, can often provide a means for overcoming barriers of communication. The adaptive behavior of the members of the group, and their ability to relate to one another and understand each other are important to the development of a creative, problem-solving unit.

PERCEPTION AND MEANING

The psychology of perception has been concerned with the process by which objects and persons become "known." Sense organs receive stimuli and transmit them to the central nervous system for interpretation. The issue of perception "versus" cognition has been a concern of many writers. Some psychologists (Taft, 1960) seem to wish to separate the processes; others (F. H. Allport, 1955; Heider, 1958) believe the distinction between these processes is blurred, and there is a growing interest in a gross theory which can encompass the total "knowing" process.

Objects have size constancy, yet our eyes see them as smaller or larger as they vary in distance. We learn to make interpretative judgments about the size of objects in relation to their distance from us. Similarly, we have personality perceptions which vary as circumstances vary. The most important variable in person perception (cognition or knowing) is the person doing the perceiving or knowing.

Counselors and guidance persons have faced the issue of perception in training and in practice. Counseling involves listening and the observation of another person in an attempt to understand, interpret, and even empathize. To empathize assumes that the counselor is able to know and to understand the feelings which are being "felt" by another person. The guidance person in a group situation is called upon to "read" many persons, and each person within a group is similarly called upon to "read" others. As counselors and guidance persons are able to utilize such skills in group situations, and as they are able to help others to develop these skills in leading and working with groups, so guidance workers and counselors can bring an advantage to the functioning of groups.

Individual behavior

Snygg and Combs, in *Individual Behavior* (1949), offered a new frame of reference for psychology. They theorized that each person views the world around him in a personal, private fashion. Psychologists had long looked at the person and his traits *from the outside*. Snygg and Combs offered principles with which the psychologist could look *with the person, out onto the world*.

The concept of individual "hidden agenda" (Chapter 3) is an example of the private outlook of a person within a group. We all have personal agenda; our world is a private, self-centered existence. This does not mean that selfishness, in the commonly understood sense, is the dominating force in all persons; rather, each person's world is created from the inside out. The self creates a phenomenological world in which all things are judged from a self-central position.

THE SELF-CONCEPT.   The self as seen by the self is a constantly growing and developing concept for the person from the time of birth until death: "I am a person who is . . .," "I am a person that is capable of . . .," "I am a person who believes . . .," "No, I could not do that; I am not that kind of person. . . ." The unique psychological totality of a person, and his personality and character develop as he learns and grows.

The primary psychological task of the person or the "self" is the "defense and enhancement of the self" (Combs and Snygg, 1959). The ordering, regulating force for a person is his concept of himself. When he is attacked, defense is necessary; when freedom of operation is present, the self seeks enhancement. The self concept is therefore vital in all personal interactions. Guidance workers and counselors are concerned with aiding students to understand themselves, to assess their strengths and weaknesses, to develop educational and vocational plans (Glanz and Walston, 1958; Katz, 1960; Mahoney and Engle, 1961). Working with persons in groups, counselors and guidance workers can utilize previous learnings about the concept of self.

THE PERCEPTUAL FIELD.   The world of perception is not a world of reality, nor is it made up of physically present and constant objects and persons. The perceptual world is a place perceived and "known" by the person. We see what we want to see; we hear what we want to hear; each person's world is a self-oriented world (Combs and Snygg, 1959). The person orders and regulates his world in an individualistic, personal fashion. Strengths, weaknesses, educational plans, vocational aspirations, and even the day-to-day functioning of the person, are characterized by an interpretation of "self in a world."

The implications of these concepts for groups and the operation of individuals within groups is startling. A group is a collection of individuals, each with a private view of the group, the group's meaning, and what *he* wants the group to do. That a group can ever succeed, or that group structure can weld together separate, self-oriented persons is a tribute to human engineering.

The "other person"

The other person is the person outside of the self. The other person is a part of the world and the phenomenal field which is the background and foreground within which the self must "defend and enhance" itself.

A dual perceptual problem exists as the individual perceives another person. The observer must fill in "blanks" in another person's words and actions. All that is observable and known is only a part of the total conclusions which are to be drawn. At the same time, a person perceives another person in accordance with his own needs and concept of self. The first problem—that of drawing conclusions from partial information—has been the subject of considerable research and investigation in recent years (Tagiuri, 1960; Heider, 1958; Tagiuri and Petrullo, 1958). Tagiuri (1960) has examined the conclusions that are drawn from movement; Heider (1958) has attempted to analyze the "common sense" basis for human interaction; Tagiuri and Petrullo (1958) have edited a series of research and theoretical papers concerning the dynamic new area of person perception. Psychological theory and group dynamics research in the area of perceptual distortion of "other persons" resulting from self needs have been related to "person perception."

A science of "person perception" is still in the future. Experiments have uncovered tendencies and proclivities of persons, but there is no clear cut theory which can guide the group workers. Psychological theory in the area of self-determined perceptions is a better known area of theory and research. "Projection," the imputation of one's own weaknesses, strengths, traits, or characteristics to another person, has long been known and studied. Group experiments have shown that persons are inclined to judge others in light of their own reactions to other persons. Tagiuri, Blake, and Bruner (1953) illustrate this principle by having judges evaluate others as they believe others relate to themselves. Individual stereotypes and prejudices also interfere with objective perception. Haire and Grunes (1950) highlighted this phenomenon when they asked persons to describe a factory worker by choosing from a series of adjectives which were offered as possibly characteristic of the worker. The subjects had no difficulty when the adjectives fitted their own preconceived notions about factory workers; but when the adjective "intelligent" was added to the list, confusion arose.

Perception of others is an outgrowth of perception of one's self. The psychologist who first stated, "as ye judge yourself, so shall ye judge others," meant it as a contrast to commonly accepted views of interaction and perception.

A final word about interpersonal perception and interactions within groups: Fiedler (1958, 1960a, b) has proposed that group success relates to perceptions and interactions of leaders and group members. This concept makes sense when viewed as an outgrowth of the concepts of participatory leadership and group performance. Group success, as seen by Fiedler, is the complex outcome of similar perceptions by the leader and the members and of the interpersonal relations of the leader and the members. This view of groups is well documented with research and will be examined in a later chapter as an element in the productivity of groups.

Language and meaning

The use of words in conversations and in group discussions is one of the problems in the interrelated areas of object perception and person perception. Krech and Crutchfield (1959, pp. 469–472) present problems inherent in the physical perception of sound and words. They point out that individual perceptions of intensity, frequency, and distortion are different. They do not deal with the semantic issue of interpretation of meaning, although this is perhaps the most significant factor in hearing. Personal needs can distort sound patterns (we hear what we want to hear) and can also impart meanings not intended by the speaker. The need to distort meaning can subvert the most precise use of words by the other person.

Roethlisberger (1941) analyzes the essential nature of the environment in which a business executive works and characterizes it as *verbal*. Three functions of language are selected as appropriate for examination within the verbal environment of the business official: (Roethlisberger, 1941, pp. 88–92) (1) logico-experimental, (2) emotive, and (3) self-expressive. The language of events, facts, and things is called logico-experimental. When attempts are made to influence others, words can be used in an emotive sense. Self-expressive language is used to satisfy desires. In daydreaming, reverie and status situations, self-expressive language would be used. For example, when a man says to a friend, "I had lunch with the president of the company," his intention may be to enhance his own status. Stephen Potter has called such techniques "one-upmanship" in his incisive and satirical books on the social scene. Not only in industry, but also in education do lines of communication become confused when persons use the same words with different meanings. Such is the problem of semantics. Communication becomes, in addition, an exercise in interpretation of personal characteristics and emotional states, as the several levels of word meaning are understood.

Counselors and guidance workers have long been aware of the need to deal with both intellectual and emotional content of words. A youngster may attempt to obtain aid from a teacher in a guidance course, without revealing the personal nature of his problem, by prefacing his question with the words: "I have a friend who . . .," or "I know someone who. . . ." The distressed student who is seeking information concerning which college to attend may simply be sizing up the counselor in order to determine whether or not he is the sort of person to be trusted. If the student decides the counselor can be trusted, then and only then, will the more personal problem be revealed for discussion. Skilled counselors strive constantly to understand and to reflect the emotional content of the ideas expressed by a student or a client.

Arbuckle (1957) clearly points out this responsibility of the counselor:

> The counselor's listening is not just a blind, polite sort of thing, but it is a careful *understanding* listening, the sort of listening that may be quite fatiguing, and it requires skill and understanding on the part of the counselor. As the counselor listens, he in a way internalizes with the client, but does not identify, and as the client talks the counselor moves closer to the feelings that the client is expressing. [Arbuckle, 1957, p. 144].

A skilled group leader and a responsible group member need to listen, to understand, and to accept, as a counselor does in counseling. The group is a collection of persons all expressing facts, sentiments, and needs. Observation, listening, and understanding are related aspects of person perception. As understanding occurs in members and leader, as meaning becomes clear in the process of perception, cognition, and interaction, the group begins to establish systematized communication which can allow it to function effectively.

INTERACTION AND COMMUNICATION

Communication within a group is dependent upon variables arising out of the personalities of the persons involved and the nature of the communication pattern. The "self" and the "other person" are but two of the major variables. Other important variables are the organizational structure of the group; the emotional climate of the group, such as feelings of co-operation or competition; the complex factors of interpersonal feelings and attitudes

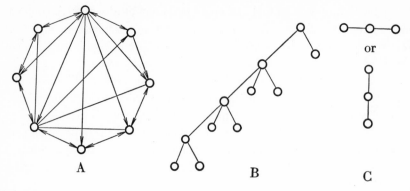

FIG. 5.1

towards members by members; and even problems of perspective of group members, arising out of prestige or position. Each of these factors is influential, as members of a group attempt to talk, work, and plan together.

Communication patterns

Groups may be patterned in many ways in order to facilitate the exchange of ideas and the sharing of words and meanings. Three essential communication patterns are illustrated in Figure 5.1 which is shown above. Pattern (A) represents an interchanging pattern of a small group. Each member is able to communicate with the person on either side, and with members across the group in any direction or pattern. Pattern (B) represents a typical line and staff chart found in many business organizations, community groups, and educational institutions. Pattern (C) represents a one to one linkage of persons. Such a pattern can exist within a small group if cross communications are impossible, and within a line and staff chart on either a horizontal or a vertical basis. Pattern (C) is more of an experimental structure which is only occasionally found in real life groups.

The small group pattern of interchanging lines of communication is limited by the size of the group. In groups of over twelve persons, frustration and inability to participate adequately were observed in experimental situations (Hare, 1952). As the number of persons in a group increases, the problem of communication increases. Public schools are generally unable to establish classes of twelve or under. Usually classes are too large to use the small group type of communication and discussion. Variations of

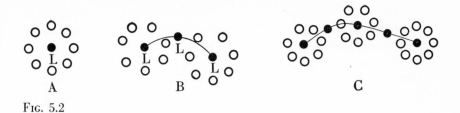

Fig. 5.2

the small-group pattern often can be obtained through the mediating efforts of the leader, or the use of assistant leaders with sections of larger groups. Figure 5.2 illustrates variations of the small group *interchanging* pattern of communication.

(A) illustrates the leader assuming a middle position and able to mediate and control the discussion. (B) represents a development of two separate groups. The leader may alternate between the groups or may observe while an assistant or student leaders serve the group. (C) extends pattern (B): the leader supervises three individual groups which can be served with assistant leaders.

The line and staff chart is often referred to as the "dangling puppet" type of communication pattern. It is usually efficient in passing information *down* and inefficient in passing information *up*. Such characteristics are well suited to authoritarian types of business, service, or community groups; however, small group communication and understanding are difficult if such a pattern is not modified (H. H. Kelley, 1960). Below, Figure 5.3 schematically demonstrates a method of modifying the more rigid line chart.

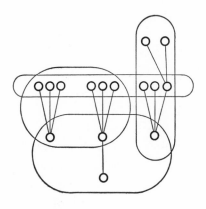

Fig. 5.3

Other variations are possible; certainly a flexible approach to communication patterns within a group of any size pays dividends in greater understanding on the part of the participants.

Research into the problems of communication in groups has taken various forms. Many efforts are related to a design of experimentation originated by Bavelas (1960). His early efforts in 1950 spurred other researchers to follow his lead. Cartwright and Zander (1960) have reprinted his article in the second edition of their review of research designs which they cite as models for further research. The work of Bavelas, as well as related experiments, has determined that centralized communication patterns, with one person in a controlling position, are evolved quickly by experimental groups with specific tasks to perform. Such centralized patterns are stable and efficient, but they develop lower levels of satisfaction and morale on the part of members than do decentralized patterns. Dispersed or decentralized communication patterns have appeared less efficient, but have engendered more satisfaction on the part of the participating members. Similar results were obtained by Shaw (1954, 1955) in studying patterns of communication which he characterized as "authoritarian" and "non-authoritarian." His conclusions were generally in agreement with the other studies quoted, though not in the same specific terms. Restricted channels of communication that shut out members, also breed low morale (Gilchrist, Shaw, and Walker, 1954).

The research results are in accord with other theoretical positions advanced earlier about groups, leadership, followership, and productivity. These experiments were all completed with laboratory type groups having specific tasks. Generalization to other types of groups is of course dangerous, but possibly appropriate.

Co-operation and competition

Individuals within a group may work together in a co-operative fashion, or may attempt to work for self-enhancing goals exclusive of the group. (The goals of the group in a co-operative situation are self-enhancing as the group succeeds). Certainly much has been written about the competitive spirit which can produce high levels of productivity. At the same time co-operation has been extolled as a value in a democratic society. It is obvious that within a single group there is of necessity only one method which can be used at any instant of time. The concepts of co-operation and competition are mutually exclusive within a small group. However, variation can provide for co-operative groups to compete with other groups.

Clichés in our language reveal a faith in both of these patterns of co-operation and competition: "Stand together or fall separately!"; "the competition brings out the best in him!" Group theory has stressed the co-operative approach. Laboratory research has supported this position. Deutch (1949) established tasks for groups that were accomplishable through co-operative effort, and tasks that were accomplishable only through individual effort. Controlled experimentation favored the co-operative groups. The results showed that (1) members in the co-operative groups were more effective in terms of production, (2) affective or human relationship factors were positive in the co-operative groups and negative in the competitive groups, (3) co-operative members were able to work together more effectively towards accomplishment in that they were able to "substitute" for one another as the need arose, (4) the competitive groups were less able to communicate with one another, and (5) the competitive groups were more poorly oriented to the task and less orderly in solving problems. Exceptions to productivity superiority by co-operative groups were noted in tasks which were primarily individualistic in nature. In general, Deutch concluded that there was greater organizational productivity in co-operative groups.

Other studies have demonstrated these principles and have also shown that a co-operative group does less well in a task which is individualistic in nature, or which demands complex reasoning. Essentially, these results support the position that co-operation in groups is more efficient than competition whenever it is possible to solve problems jointly rather than individually.

A unique contribution to the understanding of the co-operative relationship, which is necessary to the efficient functioning of a group, was offered by Ghiselli and Lodahl (1958). A miniature railroad track layout was used to test groups of three persons. The task was to work co-operatively a pattern of track switches in order to allow the trains to travel. The subjects had previously been tested to determine whether they were quick or slow in decision making. Groups of quick persons did no better than groups of slow decision makers. When one rapid decision maker was combined with two slow decision makers, productivity jumped. The conclusions drawn were similar to the age-old saying that "Too many cooks spoil the broth," or "Some have to be braves and some chiefs; everyone cannot be a

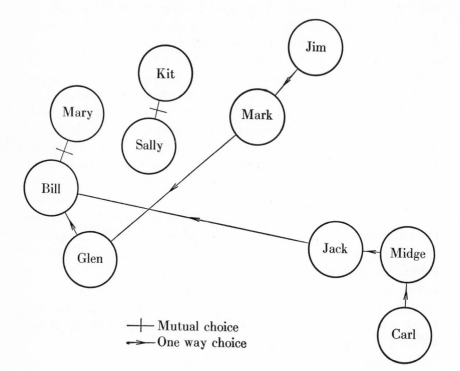

+—— Mutual choice
•—>—One way choice

FIG. 5.4 *Ten students, partial chart of choices (first choices only)—after Jennings.*

chief!" Co-operation, productivity, patterns of communication and division of responsibilities are necessities for efficient group functioning.

Sociometric interactions

> Our next unit in the guidance course will be to investigate and to discuss the four curricula that will be available for you when you enter the ninth grade next year. Will you please list for me on the small three- by five-inch cards I have given you, the names of the three persons with whom you would prefer to work and study. We will form groups of six to eight persons on the basis of your choices. We will discuss specific case studies in the group meetings, and you will need to apply the material on self-analysis that you have been collect-

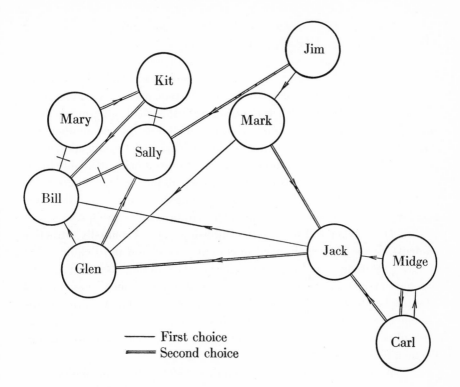

FIG. 5.5 *Ten students, two choices—after Jennings.*

ing in the unit of the course we have just completed. (Eighth grade "group guidance" teacher)

The teacher in the preceding illustration will have a major clerical task if she attempts to structure the groups according to student choices. However, if she takes advantage of her information, she will be able to establish groups with a "built-in" communication system and will learn much about the nature of the social relations of the group. As the teacher charts the choices and studies the interrelationships between them, she will have contructed a sociogram and will be analyzing sociometric data on group members. The sociogram was first offered by Moreno (1934), and Jennings (1934, 1959). Variations have been developed by Gardner and Thompson (1959), and Gronlund (1959).

Figure 5.4 shows the beginnings of a sociogram; Figure 5.5 shows some of the complexities of charting all the choices of students in response to the teacher's request (after Jennings' methods).

Sociometric choices and the buildings of sociograms help the group planner to understand the affective relationships in a large group of persons. The partial sociogram showing only first choices of students identifies two couples in which the paired students chose each other, and other one-way choices. (Figure 5.4). The analysis of two student choices confirms the observation made on the structure of Figure 5.4; a small sub-group is made up of four persons, all of whom have mutual choices for one another. Isolates (students for whom there are no choices) appear. An indication of the social atmosphere and the climate of interaction is quickly available to the teacher. Popular leaders are quickly apparent, cliques appear, and rejected students assume fringe roles. The sociogram holds a mirror up to the class. Similar analyses are of course possible within smaller groups.

The teacher will be able to establish groups of mutually attractive students. Some groups will need to contain second and third choices, but student preferences are known and effects can be anticipated. Such groupings have much to recommend them over arbitrary or "hunch" assignments. The teacher has collected considerable diagnostic data. As units of the guidance course are completed and as new choices are made for new groups, she will be able to chart a continuing pattern of the social relationships of the members of the class.

Moreno (1934, 1953) and Jennings (1947, 1959) have pioneered the research into the techniques and specific applications of "sociometry." The American Council on Education published *Sociometry in Group Relations* by Helen Hall Jennings in 1948, and published a revised edition in 1959. This ninety-nine page manual examines the philosophy, techniques, advantages, disadvantages and applications of sociometric measurement in group work.

Sociometry provides a means for a teacher or a group planner to provide learning situations for students and group members. Matters of group structure, such as who is in charge, who is the leader, what positions are occupied by whom, how is the power structure established, what are the status roles of members, can be changed as each new group is formed to undertake new tasks. Non-experienced leaders can be placed in groups and given an opportunity to develop, free from the dominating effect of more status-laden experienced leaders. The teacher, or the group planner, is free to place members with respect to structures or roles, power (social influence), responsibility capabilities, and other factors which need to be developed by students of all levels of experience. The sociogram can provide the group leader with a chart of the existing patterns of social interaction.

What the group planner accomplishes depends upon the skill with which he handles the available data. Advanced approaches to "sociometry" are available to group leaders via the newer applications of the "Syracuse Individual Choice Patterns" (Gardner and Thompson, 1959).

Role playing: A communication aid

Children often "play act" the role of father, mother, teacher, Davy Crockett, or Daniel Boone. Adolescents and adults are less interested in "play acting," except on a stage. However, the fun and learning opportunities of such experiences *are* available to adults and students in group settings.

A typical example of role playing in a high school follows:

FATHER: (*played by Jim, a sixteen-year-old senior*) No. . . . No. . . . I have told you a hundred times, that you are not going to be able to drive until you are eighteen years old!

MOTHER: (*played by Sally, a sixteen-year-old senior*) Maybe you are being a little hard on him; maybe you ought to reconsider your decision. . . .

SON JACK: (*played by a seventeen-year-old senior*) All of the fellows in the neighborhood have already gotten their drivers' licenses. A guy can't do anything in this house. . . .

FATHER: Now wait a minute . . . you have no right to talk that way to your mother and me. You know the statistics about teen-age drivers, and the problems of accidents and the rates the insurance company charges.

SON JACK: Yes, I know, I know . . . you have told me about it, but all you have to do is look around the neighborhood; no fellow around here has ever had an accident.

The scene continues in front of a guidance class concerned with "parent-child" relations. The father attempts to convince the son of the dangers, the costs, and his concern for his son's physical well-being. Following the role-playing scene, the "actors" hold a discussion with the group leader and attempt to evaluate their own feelings and attitudes about the problem. Usual statements about the experience are as follows:

JIM: (*playing the role of Father*) You know it was easy to play that part. My father has said those same things to me so many times that it was as if I was in the same situation that I am in so often at home.

GROUP LEADER: Tell us about your feelings and attitudes toward your "son."

JIM: You know I was getting real mad at him. Even though it was a make-believe situation I was getting all riled up at my "son" because of the silly things he was saying.

Make-believe situations which are real to the participants evoke feelings and provide an opportunity of "seeing" into another person's feelings. Briefly, the emotional self of the other person is revealed and understood; the inner world, the private world of feeling and emotion of the "other person" is partially available to an outsider. Role playing provides a technique by which it is transiently possible to succeed at what is implicit in saying, "Now if I were you. . . ." Successful role playing, however, dictates that the feelings and attitudes of the other person be expressed effectively. As feelings and emotions are experienced, the person begins to understand better the position and the outlook of the other person.

Role playing as a technique in group situations is appropriate in many different circumstances. Foremen's training sessions often include the switching of the roles of worker and foreman. The foreman needs to see the problem from the perspective of the worker. Role switches can be adopted as a communication device in any situation in which one person is familiar enough with another's role to assume it on a temporary basis. There are no scripts, no lines to learn; role playing is dependent upon a thorough understanding of the role undertaken. The words, actions, positions and ideas must come out of the actual (temporary) attempt of the role player to "play the part." Situations must be clear cut. Family conflicts, grievance procedures, embarrassing moments, job interviews, and common social experiences are only a few of the scenes which may be played.

The group, the actors, and the group leader need to discuss the plan of action in general terms and need to secure the vicarious involvement of all persons as well as the major "actors." Follow-up discussion is needed to extract the total value from such a program. Insights may be simple (Dad does get mad . . .), but they are felt on a first-hand basis.

Role playing is based on a sound fact of human behavior and personality structure. In life, we must all assume roles. The pychologist points out that the person learns to act in accordance with the roles which are assigned in the environment (Hilgard, 1957). The self-concept is developed out of the role experiences which the child completes (Glanz and Walston, 1958). Confusion and disintegration of personality is often revealed through "role confusion" (or "role diffusion")—an inability to integrate the many roles expected by society or the self. (Hilgard, 1957, pp. 475–76; Erikson, 1956).

The concept of role has been a part of psychological and sociological theory for many years. Mead (1934), and Linton (1936) wrote about the concept and its significance in personality and in communication. Later theorists have made much of the expectations of group members as leaders or as persons in various group positions, and of the "role system" with its relation to responsibility and authority in groups (Stogdill, 1959). Bates (1956), and Bates and Cloyd (1956) have analyzed the complex interrelationships of roles, personality, and group functioning. Krech and Crutchfield (1959) even speak of a "loose concept of social homeostasis" in which society requires that important roles in its organizations and groups be filled when vacated. L. Thompson (1956) supports a similar view.

The importance of the concept of role in personality and the social order underlies the discussion of leadership and membership functions in Chapter 4. Role playing is not an easy accomplishment; it demands an understanding of the "stuff" of personality, groups, and the social order.

Role playing provides a means not only of clarifying problems of communication and meaning in groups, but also of providing an incisive learning experience for the participants (Klein, 1956). Role playing adds a further dimension to the use of groups in many different types of guidance and counseling situations. Part Three will include many additional applications of role playing.

GROUP CLIMATES

Acceptance, understanding, and permissiveness are key words that have been used to characterize counseling relationships. The climate which exists as a counselor and a student, or client, work together to solve a problem has been singled out as one of the most significant aspects of counseling (Rogers, 1942, 1951). The importance of the emotional climate of the counseling relationship has not always been understood as well as it is now. Rogers, along with others of his tradition (Arbuckle, 1957, 1961; Snyder, 1947), first emphasized the importance of the climate of counseling as it related to client progress. A person is not free to explore new learnings and behaviors in a threatening atmosphere. When threatened, he will defend the self; as security and acceptance are experienced, the person becomes free to examine the organization of the self and the patterns of adjustment which characterize the personality (Combs and Snygg, 1959).

The problem of group climate is closely related to the climate issue in counseling (Rogers and Roethlisberger, 1952). Group or multiple counseling procedures have acknowledged the need for establishment of a permissive, accepting and understanding climate or atmosphere. Task-oriented groups are not always as concerned about this factor as growth groups. However, any group which attempts to obtain the co-operation and involvement of group members needs to be concerned about the climate problem. Group members who are threatened and feel the need to defend themselves are more engrossed with that problem than with the stated objective of the group (Exline, 1957). Climate is therefore a determiner of the communication level which exists among members. Creative contributions and effective problem solving depend upon the best talents available to the group; attention to psychological climate can provide for the necessary freedom for the individuals who comprise the group.

Differing climates exist in task-centered and growth-centered groups. The characteristics of authoritarian, democratic, and laissez-faire groups were discussed in Chapter 4, as leadership and attitudes of members were examined. Many other classifications of groups can also be offered in which climate plays a major role in the determination of the success of the groups, as well as in the potency and efficiency of the communication process. Educational environments have promoted a concern with a division of groups into teacher-centered and student-centered. Group theorists and experimenters have been vitally involved in the determination of the characteristics of two other types of groups: the leaderless group and the problem-centered group. Each of these different types of groups need to be reviewed to reveal the factors of climate as they affect communication, productivity, and member and leader behavior.

Teacher-centered and student-centered groups

The teacher in an educational class is the leader, the supervisor, the resource specialist, the power figure who wields authority. Additional circumstances often provide for the teacher to be the decision maker, task assigning chief, recorder, process-observer, and social arbiter. The teacher in this circumstance is the captain, the first mate, the crew, all rolled into one; the students in the class, or in a small subgroup of eight to ten, are the passengers in the boat. The students in such a situation have about as much effect on guiding group activity as a steerage passenger has on piloting an ocean liner. The atmosphere in such a group is often one of threat and attack. The student is constantly on trial to prove himself in knowledge and skill. The teacher is always in the background with a "little black book" in which she can enter marks of her authority.

The success of students in such a situation is quite remarkable. That there has been success and learning is unquestioned; but could there have been more success with other group procedures? Evidence is contradictory, and in many senses the "outlying precincts" have still to be heard from. Methods of assessing outcomes follow a traditional system. New methods of measurement are needed to document fully the learnings which are possible in such group situations.

Teacher-centered groups or classes at best are learning programs under the direction of a specialist who is a talented leader. If the leader is effective and able to stimulate and involve students in learning, the results are outstanding. When teachers are unskilled or ineffectual, the results may be catastrophic; positive learning is suspended and damaging learnings assume control. Nathaniel Cantor (1950, 1953) was dedicated to an exposition of the problem of learning and the conditions necessary for meaningful learning. When arbitrary use of authority is resorted to by a teacher in groups and classroom situations, the teacher is a supporter of the authoritarian tradition. Huszar (1945) points out the tradition of authoritarian control in the American educational system. Cantor and Huszar see the teacher as the primary factor in determining the learning atmosphere in the classroom.

The exposed, almost defenseless position of small groups makes them more sensitive to the power, authority and traditional effects of teachers. Teachers who serve as group leaders are frequently forced to compensate for the expectations of the students; the semi-authoritarian role of the teacher is well known and widely accepted in our culture. A participatory supervising concept of leadership has to be established, often in the face of student resistance.

Student-centered groups are characterized by an involvement of students in responsibilities which have traditionally been the prerogative of the teacher; group goals, methods of learning, and even pupil evaluation are determined by students alone, or in concert with the teacher. Student-centered groups are open in climate and structure. There is an atmosphere of discussion and shared responsibility. Whenever patterns of problem solving fail, or activities do not lead to progress towards the goal, the group must bear responsibility along with the teacher; there is no single scapegoat or focus for hostility. Affective elements within a group receive attention equal to that given to intellectual goals. Stress is given to learning skills of human relations and co-operation, as well as learning a specific subject or accomplishing a task. There is an opportunity for student-to-student reactions as well as student-teacher interchanges. The concept of equality of responsibility and equality of persons engaged in a joint process replaces the "white horse" type of leader and followers.

COMPARATIVE CHARACTERISTICS.   McKeachie (1961) has summarized the characteristics of student-centered groups. The following chart shows the differences between the two approaches (adapted from McKeachie, 1961):

STUDENT-CENTERED APPROACHES	TEACHER-CENTERED APPROACHES
Goals	
1. Determined by group	1. Determined by instructor
2. Emphasis upon affective and attitudinal changes	2. Emphasis upon intellectual changes
3. Stress upon group cohesiveness	3. No attempt to develop group cohesiveness
Classroom Activities	
1. Much student participation	1. Much instructor participation
2. Student-student interaction	2. Instructor-student interaction
3. Acceptance of errors and irrelevant contributions	3. Correction, criticism, or rejection of errors and irrelevancies
4. Group-determined activities	4. Instructor-determined activities
5. Wide range of discussion topics	5. Course material discussion
6. De-emphasis of tests and grades	6. Traditional tests and grading
7. Student-instructor evaluation	7. Instructor-determined evaluation

McKeachie's chart illustrates the extreme forms of both teacher-centered and student-centered groups. Many learning situations are combinations of both techniques.

RESEARCH FINDINGS.   Many studies have been conducted in attempts to assess the outcomes of teaching and learning experiences characteristic of each of the positions outlined in the foregoing chart. No clear-cut advantage in subject matter achievement has been established on either side. Student-centered groups do, however, show more growth in the socio-emotional and self-growth areas. Faw (1949) found superiority in both achievement and socio-emotional growth for student-centered groups. Asch (1951) carried out a similar experiment and found that in achievement and intellectual growth the edge was on the side of teacher-centered techniques. Krumboltz and Farquar (1957), and Maloney (1956) found results favoring achievement patterns in teacher-centered groups, but also found student-centered techniques superior in the socio-emotional measures. McKeachie (1961; Birney and McKeachie, 1955) believes that there is a slight superiority in student-centered approaches, but that the edge is *slight*. He also states that the superiority in the areas of student learnings of a nonsubject-matter or intellectual achievement type is markedly in favor of the student-centered devices and approaches.

Student-centered groups have assumed a double task and have attempted to meet the traditional standards on the evaluation scales of the past. Even if there is a slight increase in terms of intellectual achievement with teacher-centered groups, there is much support for the position that the task of education is broader than that of imparting facts. Understanding, attitudes, utilization of potential within students, respect for persons, and democratic problem-solving techniques are also a part of education in a democracy.

Leaderless groups

Leaderless groups are similar to the laissez-faire groups described by Lewin, Lippitt and White (1939). Instead of submitting to vacillating leadership, a leaderlesss group frankly accepts the fact that there is no appointed or expected pattern of leadership. The climate of such a group is one of insecurity and confusion. The condition is useful in providing an opportunity for the "emergent leader." It has been shown in research that when a leaderless group is established the talkative, outgoing person will begin to assume leadership (Bass, 1951). In addition the leaderless group, as a work-sample test, can be used to predict the future success of persons in training within a leadership course (Bass and Coates, 1952).

Guidance persons can use the leaderless group structure to induct students into an understanding of power, leadership, and group performance. Supervisory operation, with stress upon the need to develop leadership talents in others, has not yet taken full advantage of the possibilities of this technique. Critics of groupwork often cite leaderless groups as proof of the "nonsense" of the group approach (W. H. Whyte, 1956, p. 55).

The technique is effective and usable in a total approach to groups. However, any technique can be misapplied. Leaderless groups, in and of themselves, are usually of little use in reaching an objective in an efficient manner and are to be used, rather, for diagnostic and predictive purposes.

Problem-centered groups

Problem-centered groups would seem to offer a perfect middle ground for leaders and members. A climate of acceptance, understanding, and permissiveness, with focus on the task, would seem to offer the pot of gold at the end of the groupworker's rainbow. However, such a description of the perfect group is still nothing more than a description. All of the desirable characteristics of a democratic group with effective leaders and members, as cited in the preceding material, would apply in a problem-centered group.

Many writers have suggested problem-centered groups as a procedure; success would be guaranteed if the process were as simple to use, as it is to describe. Whenever the leader and the members can accept the position that the problem is the overwhelmingly vital issue, and still care for group "maintenance" roles, the problem-centered group can exist. Perhaps a more realistic view of the concept is to assume that it is a combination of all the desirable techniques of groupwork. The problem-centered group is an ideal for which any group can strive.

SUMMARY

The words and meanings used by members of any group are related to the effectiveness of the communication process within the group. Interpretations of meanings from word use depend upon the process of perception. Perception involves an understanding of the ideas of "self-concept" and "other person." Words can have different meanings and interpretations to different persons. Communication processes can only be understood as all of these variables are understood.

Communication among members of a group is affected by the patterns of interaction which are established within a social organization. Standard patterns of communication are offered along with variations that can provide for increased degrees of communication. Co-operation and competition can affect a group's functioning and the communication process within a group. Sociometric devices and role-playing patterns aid in the understanding process among group members.

Four types of group climates are variables affecting the communication process. Groups may be centered around a teacher, around the students, around no one, or around the problem.

SUGGESTED READINGS

Allport, F. H., *Theories of Perception and the Concept of Structure*. New York: John Wiley & Sons, Inc., 1955.

Brunswick, E., *Perception and the Representative Design of Psychological Experiments*. Berkeley, Calif.: University of California, 1956.

Festinger, Leon A., *A Theory of Cognitive Dissonance*. Evanston, Ill.: Row, Peterson & Co., 1957.

Gronlund, N. E., *Sociometry in the Classroom*. New York: Harper & Bros., 1959.

Kelly, George A., *The Psychology of Personal Constructs*, Vols. 1, 2. New York: W. W. Norton & Co., 1955.

Piaget, Jean, *The Language and Thought of the Child*. New York: Harcourt, Brace & Co., 1926.

Raven, Bertram H., "Social Influence on Opinions and the Communication of Related Content," *Journal of Abnormal and Social Psychology*, 58, 1959, 119–128.

Ruesch, J., and W. Kees, *Nonverbal Communication*. Berkeley, Calif.: University of California Press, 1956.

Taft, Ronald, "The Ability to Judge People," *Psychological Bulletin*, 52, 1955, 1–23.

Tagiuri, R., and L. Petrullo, eds., *Person Perception and Interpersonal Behavior*. Stanford: Stanford University Press, 1958.

Thibaut, John W., and H. H. Kelley, *The Social Psychology of Groups*. New York: John Wiley & Sons, 1959.

Thorpe, L. P., *et al.*, *Studying Social Relationships in the Classroom: Sociometric Methods for the Teacher*. Chicago: Science Research Associates, 1959.

6. HUMAN BEHAVIOR IN GROUPS: motivation and learning

Human behavior has long held a fascination for all persons. An interest in the underlying causes of human actions helps to account for the ubiquitous "street corner psychologist." Group leaders, and ideally the members of a group as well, should be beginning psychologists, with some formal background, in order to understand and to interpret the behavior of members in a group. This task is difficult because human behavior is complex. As a member of a group a person becomes responsive to fellow members. His personal actions, emotions, and beliefs become mingled with group behaviors, emotions, and beliefs.

Psychology offers principles which are useful in understanding human behavior. In psychology there are few, if any, immutable laws, such as there are in the physical sciences. Yet, psychology attempts to be more precise than the broader social sciences. Psychology stands somewhere between the physical and social sciences and has some of the weaknesses and strengths of both. Predictability is a major problem in any approach to the study of human behavior. Psychologists are frequently more effective in explaining why a person behaved in a certain fashion than they are in explaining how or why a person *will* behave. The variables in the causation of human behavior are many and complex.

Predictability, if ever achieved, can lead to control and possibly manipulation. The control of human behavior can be inimical to the concept of group development and the use of small groups in education. Skinner (1956) raises the question, "Are we to be controlled by accident, by tyrants, or by ourselves in effective cultural design?" The dignity and uniqueness of man are considerations which Skinner treats, and he emphasizes the need for knowledge and skill in the control of human behavior within the traditional value system of western civilization and democracy. Carl Rogers and B. F. Skinner, in a symposium (1956), both supported control as a goal of psychology. They do not agree upon methods but each seeks to establish, through control, an open, free democratic society (cf. Rogers, 1961).

Predictability and control for creativity are complex ultimate goals which must be preceded by an understanding and acceptance of human behavior, the causes of human behavior, the adjustment process, and the development of personal goals and objectives. Persons complete even simple acts because of many different reasons. Complex behavior may arise out of infinitely more complex causes. Conflict, anxiety and tension additionally can accompany and complicate the process of meeting and solving life's problems.

Man establishes many complex goals for himself and for groups. Goals demand progress in the achievement and adjustment processes; learning becomes the concept which can explain man's behavioral change. The topics which need to be exposed for group workers and leaders, so that they may begin to understand why people behave as they do as individuals and in groups, are outlined in the pages which follow. Selected principles of human behavior, an analysis of individual and group needs, and the effect of learning upon human behavior are the subjects of this chapter.

HUMAN BEHAVIOR

Man's behavior was explained as a result of "humors" in ancient times, "devils and little gods" in unenlightened periods, and "instincts" in the recent past. Teachers, parents, and counselors are often inclined to mention all of these causes when they attempt to explain a particularly puzzling or distressing bit of human behavior. A major breakthrough in psychology resulted from the efforts of Sigmund Freud when he demonstrated that all behavior is caused. Human actions were shown to be results of forces, factors, and feelings which could be isolated and studied. Freud's early efforts, and the theories of those of his followers who have received acceptance as psychologists, have attempted to spell out the factors which underlie human behavior. Many theories have been offered to explain the rationale of man's behavior. The adjustment process is a term which can encompass the major theories of modern dynamic psychological theory and classical psychological concepts.

The adjustment process

Astronomers need to use a telescope; biologists are dependent upon a microscope. A major tool for use in the understanding of human behavior is the "adjustment process." Although a concept is different from a tool such as a microscope or a telescope, the uses to which the concept of the adjustment process may be put allow the comparison to be developed. The adjustment process (cf. original in Shaffer and Shoben, 1956) may be diagrammed as in Figure 6.1 (Glanz and Walston, pp .49–50, 1958).

> "D" represents the drives, needs, or stimuli acting upon man. Man seeks water, food, air or other goals which can fulfill his basic needs. "T" stands for the thwarting, blocking, and frustrations which man

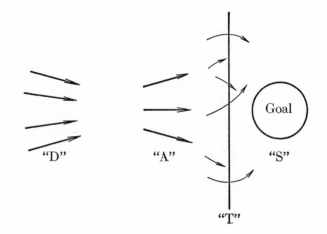

Fig. 6.1

encounters in obtaining his desired goal or satisfactions, "S." "A" represents the means by which man solves his problems (mechanisms of adjustment).

An example will serve to illustrate and further explain the adjustment process. A man is thirsty. "D," his chemical balance and tissue moisture level, is beginning to be upset. The man begins to seek means of obtaining satisfaction, "S." The drive leads to activity. If water is at hand (a glass by his chair), he has no problem in order to solve his problem (achieving satisfaction). If water is not nearby (thwarting and resulting frustration), "T" occurs. He must go to the kitchen or to the well; he must solve the problem. "A" (adjustment mechanism) represents the means he selects.

The physiological drives and social needs underlying man's behavior can reveal much of the direction and the types of adjustments which he will make. Comparably, the goals and objectives which he chooses illuminate the object of his seeking and striving (Shaffer and Shoben, 1956; Dashiell, 1949).

The adjustment process involves the entire organism. Emotional reactions accompany thwarting, and frustration can lead to anger, depression, hostility, aggression, and other reactions. Anxiety, or a generalized fear of the future, in varyng degrees, is an expected result whenever important goals are blocked. Tension and bodily stress can also build in the process. Many adjustments of the organism can reduce tension and anxiety, but a positive, integrated solution to the problem is the most successful means for resolving stress.

Homeostasis

Individuals are constantly seeking a state of balance in the physical and social interactions which make up the problem-solving nature of life. Cannon (1939) first used the term homeostasis to describe the wisdom which the body possessed; the term has been applied in a more general sense to a balance which is social and cultural (Stagner, 1951; Dempsey, 1951).

Social needs or physiological drives upset the balance or homeostasis of the individual. Objectives of food, water, status, acceptance, are sought by the organism as goals which can restore the balance. Blocking or frustration may intervene and the person must adopt a problem-solving technique which can reduce the frustration. Homeostasis and the adjustment process relate to the process of problem solving and the concept of balance in personal and social behavior.

Homeostasis, as a constant goal or objective for humans, and the adjustment process which leads to homeostasis, are observable concepts; however, both are gross and delicate as they operate. A person may seek status or prestige. This goal may be established in many specific patterns throughout the life of the person. Perfect balance or homeostasis is never achieved; the person is constantly seeking prestige or status in new situations or new environments—the adjustment process is continuous. A disturbance in the physiological balance of the body creates a specific need. For example, lack of water within the body creates a physiological need which is experienced as thirst. Beer, water, coffee, goats' milk and many other drinks can restore physiological balance. The process is completed, balance is restored and new needs arise; the process of making adjustments which tend toward homeostasis is constant.

Selected principles

The behavior of a thirsty rat in a maze leading to water can demonstrate the adjustment process, homeostasis, and trial and error learning through positive reinforcement or conditioning. Hitler's actions in Germany prior to World War II illustrate the principles of "status needs" and "prestige principles." The German people, sick of a post World War I recovery period, were seeking opportunities for achieving status as a nation and as persons in the eyes of the world. The methods, actions, even the patterns of adjustment used to attempt to establish the "balance" of the German nation and its peoples, have been analyzed by many social psychologists. Similarities exist between the example of a laboratory experiment and the example of a nation's problem; principles of psychology can be offered which apply to both situations.

(1) *All behavior is caused.* The rat seeks water because of chemical imbalance. A thirsty and hungry rat can be placed in a conflict situation in which both needs cannot be satisfied at the same time. Conflict, anxiety, tension, and even neurotic behavior can be induced in an animal in a laboratory situation. The actions, the behaviors of the rat can be traced to specific factors which can be controlled. Behavior can be understood and even predicted as the principle is delineated that all behavior has causes. The warped behavior of a Hitler, a Himmler, or an Eichmann can be traced to specific causes, learned social needs and the effect of a society on human

personality. The levels of complexity of causes of behavior in these two cases are quite different, yet the principle of causation of behavior is common to both.

Human behavior is lawful and ordered. The present ability of the psychologist to discover and isolate principles of action, to test and validate theory, and to formulate laws of behavior could be likened to the frustrated state of the Greek physician, or the colonial surgeon in America, who accepted the principle of causation but refused to operate upon the assumption that "bad blood" caused the diseases he was called upon to cure. Psychologists know that much work and study lies ahead prior to a scientific formulation of the "why" and "how" of all human behavior. People do not behave in a certain fashion because of the movements of the stars, the location of bumps on the head, or because of "little demons" running around inside of the body.

Physiological drives; learned social needs; blockings, thwartings, and frustrations; goals and objectives; emotions, tensions, and anxieties— such are the variables which cause human behavior.

(2) *Each person is different.* Different rats respond in different fashions to a deprivation of water. Not every German approved of the tactics and operations of the government of Adolph Hitler. Children in a schoolroom may appear to be alike as the teacher faces a new class; however, only a short time is needed for the teacher to learn that each member of the group operates in highly individualistic fashion.

Identical twins, developed from the splitting of one ovum, are as alike as nature can make two individuals. Studies of identical twins reveal that enviromental experiences, varying maturational rates, and learned personality patterns produce two distinct individuals. Such individuals, although alike, are without question two separate, unique persons. That no two persons are alike is a fact which is ignored in every classroom and throughout life outside of the classroom. The similarities of persons are classified, and patterns of operation are established in order to simplify production, studying, and even living. The classification of persons into groups always assumes that there are similarities. The principle of individual differences dictates that the organizer, the teacher, the group leader, always recognize that each person is unique.

(3) *The child is the father of the man.* The importance of the early experiences of man in forming and determining the quality and direction of later experiences has not long been recognized in psychological theory. Freud is largely responsible for highlighting its meaningfulness.

The child was frequently seen in earlier days as a small adult. Nineteenth century paintings depicted children with adultlike heads and childlike bodies.

Personality is formed out of learning experiences which take place from the moment of, and perhaps before, birth. The trial and error nature of early adjustments, the attitudes and value scales of parents or close adults, the early rewards and reinforcements for particular behavior actions and patterns—these forces and experiences are the raw materials of personality and the style of life which crystalizes out of learning experiences.

(4) *Personality is learned.* Personality, as a learned pattern of behavior, is a natural consequence of childhood experiences. The physical giant may be a cowardly, frightened, anxious adult. Physical and structural elements within the person do not wholly determine the patterns of behavior he adopts as persistent methods of solving personality problems. Blind persons may be aggressive, hostile, angry at society; or they may be gentle, positive in their dealings with others, and warmly attracted to society and other persons. The lack of sight is a physical factor. The important element within personality is the *learned* reaction towards the loss of sight.

The complex processes of personality formation are rooted in the adjustment processes which take place in the first few years of life. As a life style is adopted, as appropriate roles are selected from many possible roles and patterns of adjustment, personality becomes a persistent method of problem solving. Personality is exhibited to the public view; the internal view of the exterior patterns of personality is the idea of the self, the self-concept.

(5) *The basic psychological need of the person is the maintenance and enhancement of self.* Combs and Snygg (1959) delineate this principle in a singularly simple and meaningful fashion. Determined trait-theory psychologists have resisted the idea that the "internal view" of the person is a workable, logical and lawful approach to explaining human behavior. Without reference to the internal view of behavior, there is frequently precious little which one may use as a guide for understanding human behavior. "Now, why in the world did Jim ever do that?" Many are the teachers, counselors, group leaders or members who have uttered this phrase. There is little doubt that Jim has needs of many sorts that have directed his behavior. The search for psychological adequacy is constant within all persons. Even the behavior of a psychotic in a mental hospital

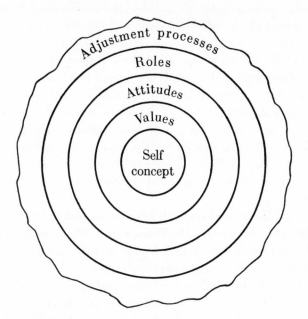

FIG. 6.2 *Physical, mental, and emotional demands on the individual.*

becomes logical and consistent, if the premises upon which the person operates are understood.

The self-concept serves as a directing and controlling force in the functioning of personality. Values, attitudes, and roles are developed as surrounding elements which provide for the operation and extension of the self within an environment. The adjustment patterns and problem-solving methods which are selected by the person provide for his contact with the perceptual field. The personality, with the self as the central directing force, is shown in Figure 6.2 (after Glanz and Walston, p. 77, 1958).

Groups in action

Persons remain individuals within a group, and yet as members of a group people often behave differently from the way they do as individuals. Chapter 3 related behavior to group strength, attractiveness, cohesiveness, and stability. Groups act and react in patterns which reveal that a group can respond to environmental forces and solve problems as a unit. Such group functioning is related to the methods used by the individual.

Some groups adopt goals and objectives which are determined from the additive total of the individual goals and objectives of members. Other groups seem to develop goals and objectives which are the property of the group as a whole, from a group entity which is greater than the sum of the objectives of members. This second concept, not yet clearly defined through research, has been discussed by many writers in the field of group work. Cartwright and Zander (1960, pp. 349–50) believe that the group can *develop* a goal or an objective and can work towards such a selected goal. This ability is postulated as a factor that separates successful groups from failure groups. Their volume of collected research devotes an entire section to studies related to this problem (Cartwright and Zander, 1960, pp. 345–486).

Related theory and research have shown that the homeostasis concept can be applied to groups (L. Thompson, 1956), and that elements of the adjustment process also seem to be a part of the functioning of groups. Horwitz (1960) reveals that individually perceived tension aroused by group goals can be reduced as the group goals are achieved. Raven and Rietsema (1957) have stated that an individual's behavior in a group is related to the degree of understanding possessed about the goals and objectives of the group. Adjustment to the group, involvement with group tasks, and identification with members, as well as feelings of negativism about the group, are all related to the individual's perception of the group goal and path.

Individuals respond to the pressures exerted upon them by the persons around them. Adjustment, and action of a problem-solving nature are not wholly individually determined procedures. The group can determine member actions. This principle is highlighted by Fleishman, Harris, and Burtt (1955), and by Gagne and Fleishman (1959), in analyzing the responses of foremen trained in leadership and group dynamics skills. The foremen often "reverted" to previously learned patterns of behavior as they found themselves in a work environment in which supervisors' expectations were at variance with what had been learned. Sensitivity, flexibility, and human relations attitudes could not prosper in an environment where rewards and positive reinforcements were offered for behavior of a different type (Fleishman, Harris, and Burtt, 1955). Gagne and Fleishman (1959, p. 402) report the spurious success judged by trainees in a human relations training program. Supervisors evaluated their performance as being less effective than the level reported by the trainees. Often one wants to succeed and believes that one has succeeded in spite of minimal success.

Lippitt had noticed the occurrence of regression in training individuals, and attempted to train "teams" of workers. He found (Lippitt, 1949) that teams were more successful in carrying out training goals than were individuals. Groups provided the strength and stability which were not present within any single person. Groups can therefore impart adjustment and coping skills which individuals lack.

Individuals and groups go through similar processes in problem solving, but groups may not be equated with individuals as operating organisms within an over-all process of adjustment. The group is affected by and is related to the effectiveness of individual adjustments, yet the group operates as an entity with processes and problem-solving techniques of its own. Conflict and confusion arise when the group, made up of individuals and also existing as a total force, is analyzed. Research is needed and is being performed; as results become available, group workers as well as psychologists will be able to avoid the "blood-letting" treatment for problems and for analysis of data. The principles exist; the process of theory validation is more mundane and time consuming. As research progresses, so group effectiveness can progress.

DRIVES AND NEEDS IN OPERATION

Human and animal behavior need to be understood inside and outside of the laboratory. Experiments with motivation and the causes of human behavior have led to theories, and to applications of theories to day-to-day activities. Short of giving a course in general psychology, and a course in the principles of adjustment, it is impossible to trace all of the experimental and research work which has led to current beliefs in the area of human motivation. Major contributions in this area of study have come from yearly symposia at the University of Nebraska, and the annual publications, since 1953, of the Nebraska Series on Motivation. J. S. Brown (1961) offers a research view of the role of motivation in personality.

One of the most comprehensive theories of motivation has been offered by Abraham Maslow (1954). Maslow's theories, certainly not all fully validated, are concerned with human motivation in action. Even as partial answers, Maslow's ideas offer concepts which must be examined as causative factors in human behavior; they must also be related to the operation of individuals in groups, and to the operation of groups.

A theory of motivation

Maslow (1954, pp. 80–106) has summarized his long-standing concern for the causation of human behavior in a book which attempts an organized presentation of the total spectrum of motivational factors operating within human beings. He presents seven groups of "basic needs":

1. Physiological Needs
2. Safety Needs
3. Belongingness and Love Needs
4. Esteem Needs
5. Self-Actualization Needs
6. Desires to Know and to Understand
7. Aesthetic Needs

A HIERARCHICAL PATTERN OF NEEDS? Maslow, as well as other writers, believes that for most persons there exists a pattern of need satisfaction which reveals some needs as more basic than others. The physiological needs, such as those for food, water, oxygen, elimination, are seen to be prepotent. Maslow states this directly (1954, p. 82):

> A person who is lacking food, safety, love, and esteem would most probably hunger for food more strongly than for anything else.

As physiological needs are satisfied, the person moves forward and attempts to satisfy needs of a higher or "upper" level of human behavior. Similarly, additional needs are revealed as previously prepotent needs are satisfied. There is no clear-cut consecutive pattern, and there is much overlapping of motivational forces within each person. Individual differences and the complexity of the learning process dictate that variations must exist from person to person. A theory which attempts to bring order to the mass of theoretical and research data available to the "motivational" psychologist should provide for these variations.

MOTIVATIONAL COMPLEXITY. Maslow (1954) warns against the assumption of a single cause. Human behavior is so complicated and overlaid with individual learnings that it is impossible to ascribe any single act to any one cause. The patterns of personality which are developed as the individual lives and learns create a unique individual in each case (Murphy, 1947; Hall and Lindzay, 1957). The basic physiological drives and the socially-determined needs of the person face thwarting, blocking and frustration throughout life. As adjustment patterns are formed, as personality patterns are developed, as life styles are created, a person becomes capable of solving problems in a characteristically unique pattern which reflects his individual approach to human interaction.

Maslow's theory of motivation has been attacked by more "scientific" psychologists who complain that it is too vague, too general, too "unscientific." The terms which he has used are terms which have been offered by psychologists prior to his time, and they will be used by speculative and research specialists after his time. His major contribution is a basic orderliness which he presents for the outsider. Each group of "basic needs" which he offers can be attacked by persons who wish to show that there are exceptions to his formulation. Exceptions exist, and Maslow is willing to state these exceptions. However, a theory needs to exist in order to advance experimentation and research. As more basic postulates are proven, and shown to be lawful, they can be substituted or used with his offerings. The guidance worker, the counselor, and the group worker need a basic framework to which existing knowledge can be related. Maslow provides this framework.

Motivation specifics in groups

The speculative theories of Combs and Snygg (1959) concerning perceptual phenomena and the development of the self concept are not inimical to the writings of Maslow (1954). Moreover, there are further sources which tend to relate and to substantiate the theoretical positions of all of these writers. Specific issues can bring home motivational theory to a group worker. The analysis of the operation of the following forces of human behavior in groups is drawn from the theoretical positions of Maslow (1954), Combs and Snygg (1959), and Shaffer and Shoben (1956).

ACCEPTANCE. The feeling of belonging (belongingness according to Maslow) is a strong and significant element in group activity. The rejection of members can create problems in group stability and the cohesiveness of the group. When respect for individual members of the group exists, the members report that involvement is high and that it helps them to learn. Thistlethwaite (1960) collected these data in a study of National Merit scholars who reported upon teachers whose help they valued. Any person who has ever been a member of a group will recognize acceptance as a stimulating force.

Graduate class instructors who train students in the use of group dynamics in guidance and other environments have often used the concept of acceptance to "bring home" the meaning of rejection by group members. The instructors established groups and told all members save one to ignore and reject one member. This rejected member later reported his feelings to the class. Many a "rejected" member reported the "real" feelings of rejection which he experienced (cf. Festinger, 1954).

ESTEEM.   Self-esteem needs are basic to personality. How many groups exist within a school system or within a neighborhood simply to have a president, a vice president and other officers. Often it seems that except for the election of these officers, and the resulting esteem which is obtained by the elected officials, there is no other activity necessary to the group's continued existence. The class president and the student council chairman are prestige offices in schools where student activities are purposely kept on an "esteem only" level. Administrators and teachers are often protecting their own feelings of security when they limit the scope of student offices.

STATUS.   Social psychologists have shown that status is a motivating force in all areas of life. Status is an advanced, formal type of esteem. Status refers to the rights, privileges, immunities, and duties reserved for persons within organizations, groups, or businesses. The military, the academic, and church worlds are prime examples of the use of status as a motivating and controlling device. Robes, marks of rank, perquisites of office are all important symbols for which individuals seek and work. Status is not meant as a dangerous or as an evil element within such organizations. Status formalizes esteem and security needs.

The function of status in group life is carefully outlined by Chester I. Barnard (1951). Barnard sees status as an outward symbol which differentiates organizational patterns and clarifies responsibility. His concept is that status has a use, in and of itself, as a reward for the ego, and as a tool to enable an organization to get work done, such as charity drives and service tasks. The payment for unselfish charitable work is often in the currency of status or prestige.

Status is a powerful tool for the teacher or the group worker. The bestowal of a leadership function upon a member of the group, even in a training session, or the appointment of a "blackboard monitor" in the first grade are examples of bestowal of status for motivational reasons. The climate of the group, the techniques of leadership, and the level of sophistication of group members are all variables which can affect the use of status or the award of esteem (Redl and Wattenberg, p. 287, 1959).

MISCELLANY. The concepts which are related to the motivation of persons both inside and outside of groups are almost numberless. Variations upon Maslow's theories could be offered as composers offer variations on a theme. Power, prestige and authority are often sought as ends in themselves by persons who need to reinforce their own frightened selves. Related behavior is often recognizable in the person who shuns any responsibility, fears any specific assignment. To test the self is to open the self to failure; the self that is not tested cannot fail. Psychological security is a demanding taskmaster and ranks next after physiological needs in Maslow's theory of basic needs (Maslow, 1954).

Each person will satisfy the needs of the self and of his own personality in a particular fashion. We may be certain that such behavior is caused, that such behavior is learned, that such behavior serves a meaningful end for the individual, and that human behavior is complex. The street corner psychologist and the research psychologist are still seeking final answers.

LEARNING AND GROUPS

Teachers, educators, and even psychologists should be concerned most with the learning process. Educators organize and offer curricula for learning; teachers interact with students in order to produce learning. Psychologists view the learning process as the keystone of psychology and human behavior (Morgan, 1956, p. 108). Learning, however, remains one of the most confused areas in all of the theoretical and research data that have been presented to the prospective educator or applied psychologist.

Morgan (1956, p. 107) defines learning as "any relatively permanent change in behavior that is the result of past experience." Hilgard (1957, p. 232) prefers "... the process by which an activity originates or is changed through responding to a situation." A further clarification is offered by Hilgard: "Not all changes in behavior are classifiable as learning. . . ." Learning is defined by Combs and Snygg (1959, p. 190), as the "... process by which an individual is able to change his behavior, usually in some more constructive fashion." Such definitions are *somewhat* different and *something* less than scientific in their use of "relatively," or "usually."

The task of precisely defining or isolating *the* scientific learning process (if it could exist) has not yet taken place. Many theories and approaches to learning exist; individuals learn in various ways, as individuals as well as in groups. Learning may also be enhanced or made more efficient by certain actions and conditions. Practical-minded teachers, counselors, and group workers need to adapt the successful principles and approaches which have thus far been clarified by theorists and research workers in spite of the relative confusion.

Learning theories

Morgan offers a three-pronged approach to learning theory. He lists "classical conditioning," "instrumental learning," and "perceptual learning" (Morgan, 1956, p. 108). Hilgard (1957) prefers to list the major approaches without giving a pattern which can organize and order them. Classical and operant conditioning both stress the effect of reinforcement or reward which aids the learner to behave in a certain fashion. The achievement of understanding or insight is variously classified as a learning experience and as a thinking process. Perceptual learning is explained as the process of narrowing responses, by discrimination and differentiation, to specific stimuli. Such perceptions are related to needs and motives and can be obtained through reinforcements and conditioning as well as by "seeing through," as insight is often named.

Research with animals has been prolific of learning theory; research with humans has often been discouraging. The human organism is so much more complex, and the process of learning is so involved, that experimenters have not been able to isolate the significant variables and construct laws of learning. Hilgard (1957, p. 244) states that ". . . the Law of Effect (E. Thorndike, 1911) . . . is virtually a statement of operant conditioning." Thorndike's Law of Effect stressed the importance of reward in strengthening a particular response. A modern psychologist states that a most recent work in learning is a restatement of a theory posed over fifty years ago.

Progress, though erratic, has been continually made in the application of learning theory to individual and group behavior. A recent experiment showed the effectiveness of operant conditioning (rewarding desirable behavior) as persons were taught discussion skills in small groups. Loree and Koch (1960) used a tape recorder to permit groups to listen to their performance. Experimental groups heard the leader stop the tape and complement or support (reinforce or reward) selected behaviors. Control groups simply listened to their performances. The experimental group improved more than the control group.

Knowledge of the results of performance is also a type of reward serving to reinforce behavior. R. L. Thorndike (1938) reported that a group was able to solve a problem in a more effective fashion than an individual, when many alternatives were presented. Such research would seem to support the concepts of "mental trial and error" as well as insightful or understanding types of learning. However, as the level of complexity of the problem became higher, the individuals performed more effectively than the groups. McCurdy and Lambert (1952) contradict Thorndike's results. since they found that individuals were more effective in problem solving than groups. Clear-cut answers do not emerge as learning theory research and studies concerning the efficiency of groups in problem solving (or learning) are analyzed. The efficiency of groups is perhaps even an independent variable in the issue and will be treated in detail in Chapter 7.

Teachers, counselors, and group workers have long operated on the belief that rewards and "positive reinforcements" are more effective than punishment in the development of particular behavior, or in the promotion of learning. "Seeing through," "insight," or "learning through understanding" are also staple operational guides in modern school systems. Nathaniel Cantor (1950, 1953), in *The Teaching-Learning Process,* and *The Learning Process,* stresses such principles on a theoretical basis, and presents a position demanding a total understanding of all approaches to learning and the importance of the climate or atmosphere within which learning takes place. Progress in approaches to learning has been greater in recent decades than progress in isolating and formulating precise laws of learning. Some of the psychologists and theorists in this area have also been closely related to the field of counseling and guidance. An examination of their work can help in understanding the role of learning and its relationship to group operation.

Approaches to learning

Specificity in learning theory has been almost impossible to obtain. Generalized approaches to learning and the creation of conditions favorable to learning have been more fruitful avenues of investigation. Carl Rogers

(1942, 1951) revolutionized the entire counseling and therapy worlds when he promoted a "non-directive or client-centered" approach to helping others. He postulated that growth, learning, and new behaviors could be developed by persons as a *"climate* or *atmosphere* was produced which could free the internally motivated client. Combs and Snygg (1959, 1949) developed a theory of individual psychology which theorized that the person in a threatening atmosphere could only defend himself psychologically. An accepting, understanding, and free atmosphere was necessary for enhancement or self-directed learning. These writers (Rogers; Combs and Snygg) operating from different premises (counseling and psychological theory) were saying similar things. They were not learning theorists, but were offering gross and "human" approaches to learning. Their relationship to John Dewey, to the theory of Lewin, Lippitt, and White (1939), and to classical Freudian theory is not a distant one.

The view of the "climate" or "atmosphere" for learning did not depend upon any specific "law of learning." Recognition was given to the complexities of learning, and an assumption was made that however learning took place, it could take place more effectively within an environment of acceptance, understanding, and freedom for individual creativity.

Persons need to perceive in order to learn. As perceptions are developed, the process of differentiation or the narrowing of appropriate responses to the appropriate stimulus can proceed. Each of the processes of perception and differentiation is dependent upon the ability of the organism to explore, seek, extend the self, and in all ways become more open and conscious of other persons, things, and combinations. The defensive, fearful, distrustful person is occupied with the self; defense has priority over enhancement.

Perceptual learning is a cumulative, building type of learning. Simpler learnings, experience, growth, and maturation must precede later, more complex learnings. The child in the first grade can draw wagons on top of wheels . . . axles are not needed. Maturation of thought processes and the accumulation of experiences are needed prior to an understanding (learning) of the importance of axles (Combs and Snygg, pp. 197–98).

The complexity of learning and its relationship to personal perceptual factors is pointed up in a charming illustration by Combs and Snygg (1959). The child is more effective in learning the route to school than in predicting and understanding what the first grade teacher expects. Sidewalks are consistent and predictable; people are non-consistent and non-predictable.

Climate and perceptual approaches to learning stress that learning is a personal, highly individualistic procedure. Here perhaps lies the nub in the problem of developing a comprehensive theory of learning. People are so complex and the processes of learning are so intricate that the goal of specific prediction is still in the future.

Research and "proof" are as erratic in approaches to learning as in learning theories. However, approaches to learning attempt to explain more phenomena. Even with similar results of research it would seem that "approaches" are as valuable as specific learning theories. Rogers and Diamond (1954) present a volume of research to support their positions. Combs and Snygg (1959) present an extended bibliography on research related to their theories.

Significant research in industry has supported the "climate" and "atmosphere" concepts of learning. Fleishmann (1953) showed the influence of learned behavior in climates dominated by status-laden supervisors; behavior was as the climate dictated. A study by Fleishman, Harris, and Burt (1955), referred to earlier, also demonstrated the influence of an industrial plant climate. Trainees lost their newly acquired human relations skills when they performed in an atmosphere in which different expectations were experienced. Behavior was adjusted to agree with the climate of expectation. Dubin (1951) stresses that learned behavior on the part of labor union leaders will reflect the leadership qualities and the performances (climate and atmosphere) of management. McKeachie (1956; 1958; 1961) has collected tremendous amounts of research and has attempted to isolate the variables of group effectiveness and productivity as they relate to atmospheres and climates. His teaching-methods research studies are all related to the concept of learning-efficiency. His conclusions (1961) show a small but meaningful edge for student-centered climates over teacher-centered and non-accepting attitudes in measured productivity. Learnings in the areas of emotional growth, maturity, attitudes and related variables are clearly in favor of the open, accepting atmospheres.

Learning in groups

Groups in which a democratic atmosphere exists, and in which participatory type leadership techniques are used, are designed to provide a meaningful climate for learning (cf. Della-Piana, 1956). Writers and research workers referred to in earlier sections were not concerned with group functioning and yet were describing dimensions of effective groups. The accepting, understanding, creative climate of a democratic group with a democratic leader provides an almost theoretically perfect situation for learning.

Response to the climate or the character of the group situation cannot, however, produce learning in and of itself. (Client-centered counselors, group workers and leaders would here disagree.) When the proper climate exists, additional techniques, at least in non-therapy type groups, seem to be needed; there must be an effective next step. Inquiry, gentle prodding, verbal reinforcement, idea manipulation, and success can breed personality change and productive achievement.

Group leaders, counselors, and planners of group activities need to be aware of motivational factors and the esoteric expression of motivational needs of each person. Group experiences are related to individual counseling, individual thought and growth, and privacy. Multiple approaches are designed to aid students and persons out of school to proceed at their own pace and to develop their learnings in their own manner. (Driver, 1958; Glanz, Hayes, and Penney, 1959).

All members of the so-called helping professions need to realize that the principle of individual differences dictates that until a validated and comprehensive Law(s) of Learning is developed, possibly out of recent work by Mowrer (1960a; 1960b), all types of learning experiences will have various effects upon different persons. The variables introduced by personality factors in the individual create such problems. Passive learners may profit, like Pavlov's dog, from classical conditioning experiences. Active, participating persons will respond to rewards, reinforcements, and support.

All persons need to think problems through to learn by understanding relationships and by manipulating relationships so that the "aha!" type of experience can occur. As a group member, each person can profit from the interactions of others in a learning process; alone, the person can further his learnings only through individual efforts. Research workers place group experiences in opposition to individual effort in order to control variables in the experiment. Practice shows that individual and group approaches supplement each other. Counselors, guidance workers, group workers, and teachers need to recognize the great overlapping of their functions. Learning is the tie that binds each approach to the other. The classroom, the counseling office, and the group workroom are environments in which identical principles of behavior change or behavior originations apply.

SUMMARY

Human behavior in groups is complex. The basic processes of adjustment and homeostasis can help to bring order to individual as well as group behavior. Additional principles that can aid in understanding human behavior in groups are: (1) behavior causation; (2) individual differences; (3) the importance of childhood; (4) personality as a learned process; and (5) the maintenance and enhancement of the self.

The theory that the complexity of human motivation can be simplified as a concept of hierarchical needs (Maslow) is analyzed. Acceptance, esteem, status and power are examined as motivational forces in groups.

Learning theories and approaches to learning are presented as they apply to human behavior in groups. Research data are presented that show the importance of climate and atmosphere in group operation.

SUGGESTED READINGS

Brown, Judson S., *The Motivation of Behavior*. New York: McGraw-Hill Book Co., 1961.

Dollard, John, and Neal E. Miller, *Personality and Psychotherapy: An Analysis in Terms of Learning, Thinking, and Culture*. New York: McGraw-Hill Book Co., 1950.

Hall, C. S., and G. Lindzay, *Theories of Personality*. New York: John Wiley & Sons, Inc., 1957.

Klein, D. B., *Mental Hygiene*, (rev. ed.). New York: Holt, Rinehart and Winston, Inc., 1956.

Lane, H., and M. Beauchamp, *Understanding Human Development*. Englewood Cliffs, N.J.: Prentice-Hall Inc., 1959.

Leeper, R. W., and P. Madison, *Toward Understanding Human Personalities*. New York: Appleton-Century-Crofts, Inc., 1959.

Lindgren, Henry C., *Mental Health in Education*. New York: Holt, Rinehart and Winston, Inc., 1954.

Maloney, R. M., "Group Learning Through Discussion," *Journal of Social Psychology*, 43, 1956, 3–9.

Patty, William L., and Louise S. Johnson, *Personality and Adjustment*. New York: McGraw-Hill Book Co., 1953.

Redl, Fritz, *Understanding Children's Behavior*. New York: Bureau of Publications, Teachers College, Columbia University, 1949.

Stock, Dorothy, and Herbert A. Thelen, *Emotional Dynamics and Group Culture*. New York: New York University Press, 1958.

Weaver, Anthony, *They Steal For Love*. New York: International Universities Press, 1959.

Zaleznik, A., C. R. Christensen, and F. J. Roethlisberger, *The Motivation, Productivity, and Satisfaction of Workers: A Prediction Study*. Boston: Harvard University Division of Research, Graduate School of Business Administration, 1958.

7. PROBLEM SOLVING
IN GROUPS: movement and progress

Erich, Gary, David, Paul, Larry, Sue, and Jack make up a group of children living in a typical suburban community. Within one week, their summer activities, as a group, include giving a puppet show; opening a museum filled with turtles, snakes, ducks, clam shells, and birds' nests; printing a newspaper; and building an airplane. Each task is discussed and assignments are made for the members of the group. Hours of wild activity precede each event. The group seldom completes one task before another appears more interesting and desirable; the old task is put aside (all equipment and gear must be saved for the *next* time), and the group moves on to the new problem. The inability of the group to follow through, to assess the total nature of the adopted task, or to succeed completely as a group may brand the youngsters failures as group specialists; but, as growing, learning persons, they seem to be most successful.

Many school or community groups seem similar to a neighborhood group of children. It is always fun to plan, to organize, to think of all the things that may be accomplished; but so frequently the steps necessary for ultimate success are viewed as interfering elements. The group cannot progress from the planning and organizing stage to the *doing* or *activity* stage.

Selected growth groups sometimes feel that they need not concern themselves about action or the completion of the task. However, even a student council constitution committee can learn more about the processes of democracy if they actually prepare a revised constitution rather than simply talk about the need for a committee report. A discussion group needs content for its discussion. The children's museum referred to actually opened for a few hours. Two or three pennies were collected from dozens of children who were "shanghied" into visiting the museum. The money was discovered by one of the parents several weeks after the museum had closed. It had never been divided among the entrepreneurs. Even as success is achieved, the group proves its interest in growth and experiences rather than the financial return, a task concern.

There are separate stages of group functioning; specific steps are necessary in order to have a group succeed in its given task. Earlier sections have described the group processes of organizing, adopting agenda, selecting leaders and members, and communicating ideas and feelings; the group is ready to do a job. Phases of problem solving are present in group action as they are in individual problem solving. The failure of a group to progress through steps or phases holds it dead center, like a baseball team, equipped, on the field, with umpires and spectators, but without opponents.

The steps of group progress in problem solving are not precise, nor are they specifically consecutive; however, phases can be isolated and described. As a group progresses and succeeds in its tasks and subtasks, decisions must be made. A vote can be taken in order to decide each issue. Yet, is voting the only method of arriving at decisions within a democratic group? What are its other methods of resolving problems, of making decisions? Many methods of decision making are appropriate for selected situations. These methods include decision by the leader, majority vote of the group, division of the group into smaller subunits in favor of specific proposals, achievement of consensus, and a block-and-gap method of achieving consensus. The sections to follow will outline the phases of a group's problem-solving behavior, the methods of decision making, the effectiveness of group action, and an approach for diagnosing and correcting group failures.

PROBLEM-SOLVING PHASES

The process of changing behavior or learning is complex, and it is related
to the variables of motivation and experience, as has been indicated in
previous sections on group behaviors. The problem-solving behavior of
individuals is similar to that of groups. Some group tasks are simpler than
individual tasks because many persons are present (R. L. Thorndike,
1938). Conversely, sometimes group procedures are more complex and
difficult than individual problem-solving (H. H. Kelley and Thibaut, 1954;
Thibaut and H. H. Kelley, 1959). When groups are able to face and solve
problems in a more effective fashion than is possible by an individual, it is
usually because of the advantage of the presence of many persons who can
offer ideas and suggestions, and can evaluate trial solutions. Certain problems of a complex nature hamper groups because of the same factors which
are advantageous under other circumstances.

Problem solving in groups or in individuals is akin to the process
of thinking as outlined by Dewey (1933). The stages of action are also
closely related to the scientific method. The similarity of these processes
was recognized early in the history of group analysis (Elliot, 1928). Many
efforts have been recorded as theorists and experimenters have sought to
identify and classify the steps common to all groups. No clear-cut patterns
or definite research results are yet available. Several promising approaches
will be presented. The common elements will be stressed to determine
what conclusions can be offered for the guidance of group workers concerned with understanding group progress.

A process description

Problem solving on either an individual or a group basis is variable and
situational. Generalizations and descriptions on an abstract level have to be
comprehensive enough to explain the various applications of the process
in particular situations and, at the same time, precise enough to illuminate
the activity of problem solving. Krech and Crutchfield (1959) recognize
this problem, and attempt to offer a four stage "classical" description of the
process of creative problem solving. They list *preparation, incubation,
illumination,* and *verification* as major steps.

Stages in creative problem solving are gross and abstract. Individuals, as well as groups, will struggle with a difficult problem and repeat stages

with almost compulsive regularity. The learning procedures of trial and error, insight, association, conditioning, and even autistic imagination are all a part of the process. The history of civilization is replete with examples of each type of problem solving or invention. The creative nature of problem solving has often been overlooked. Individuals and groups often display a singularly nonrespectful attitude toward the process of problem solving. Progress in thought is not easy. Experimentation, in order to establish principles, has often been conducted with rats, animals, and occasionally humans. The more complex the problem and the greater the number of variables, the longer and more difficult becomes the solution. The United Nations is a group trying to solve a problem. Peace has perhaps never been so simply described as an issue for mankind. All of us are familiar with the complexities and frustrations which are involved in such problem solving.

Duncker's (1945) analysis of problem solving is also presented by Krech and Crutchfield (1959), as a related view of the same issue. Duncker analyzes the process as a "related series of organizations" operating upon three levels. The earliest or beginning level is described as a "general range"; a "functional solution" is the second level, and the third is the "specific solution." These levels are descending in their level of abstractness and narrowing in their perspective. Duncker's views are complex, but closely related to the concepts of perception, differentiation, and complex relationships of figure and ground as presented by Combs and Snygg (1959, Chaps. 9 and 10).

Interaction phases

A research attempt to categorize the phases of group problem-solving behavior has been offered by Bales and Strodbeck (1951). These authors suggest and partially validate three major phases in group problem-solving behavior: *orientation, evaluation* and *control*. The orientation phase is concerned with asking questions and seeking information. The evaluation phase is marked by the expression by members of judgmental feelings, opinions, and testings of ideas. The control period is characterized by attempts of members to control "one another and a common environment." Positive and negative feelings on the part of group members are experienced in each phase, with increases in each type of reaction as phase transitions are experienced. As the problem is solved, the positive feelings tend to increase.

These research findings are helpful as the attempt is made to reveal the processes involved in group movement and progress. The authors are not certain that their concepts are applicable to all groups (Bales and Strodbeck, 1951, p. 638), and do not postulate a common process for all groups. Particularly significant is the stress on the *cyclical* nature of problem solving in their reports. The groups reappear, return, and seem to move in cycles which in turn move towards a final solution. Many group members are distressed with this repetitive, seemingly non-productive, movement process. These writers question whether or not this is not almost typical in group problem solving, as it is so frequently in individual problem solving.

Group stages—descriptive

The elements of group formation, structure, leadership and membership, communication, and motivation are all related to the stages, steps, or levels of problem solving and group success. Benne, Bradford, and Lippitt (1951) describe the step-by-step actions of most groups in discussion and group thinking. Nine stages are offered as characteristic within groups (Benne et al., 1951, pp. 68–84):

1. Clarification of group procedures
2. Building a feeling of permissiveness to have problems
3. Getting the problems out
4. Boiling the problems down and selecting a common problem
5. Developing and maintaining group direction
6. Maintaining "realism" in group discussion
7. How a group informs itself (obtaining facts and data)
8. Making group decisions
9. Evaluation of group progress

These steps are virtually self-explanatory as they are viewed against a background of the total process involved in the operation of groups. Although they are effectively descriptive, such phrases are not effective in clearly revealing the actual learning process which must undergird any problem-solving type of behavior.

Cyclical learning

Miles (1959) devotes an entire volume to the skills that can be acquired in the area of group work. His volume, *Learning to Work in Groups*, stresses the actual learning experiences which must be accomplished if skills of leadership and group membership are to be made a permanent part of the personality of the learner. In Figure 7.1 the diagram of the process of learning (training, to Miles) illustrates that his formulation is similar to the ideas of Krech and Crutchfield (1959), and Duncker (1945), while being descriptive in the tradition of Benne *et al.* (1951)

Perhaps the most original contribution of Miles in this area is not in the actual steps or stages he offers, but in the cyclical nature of the process. His diagram is circular, showing the completion of one process and the immediate entrance into a subsequent process. There is little question that within each cycle or circle of the experience there are subcircles of repeating, reversing action. Ancient astronomers invented the concept of retrograde motion. Such a concept was needed to explain observed phenomena of newly discovered stars and planets. The concept was not retained in the world of astronomy, except in theoretical form, but perhaps it can be effectively used to understand and to explain the learning process within group discussion methods.

Critical thinking

A final element within the over-all learning or problem-solving process needs to be highlighted. Desirably, learning is not a chance or incidental process. Groups are organized in order to provide conditions for effective learning to take place. Counseling experiences, vocational explorations, and even student government situations are all common within an educational environment in which learning is a goal actively sought. Future behavior depends upon previous acquisitions of knowledge; future accomplishments develop out of qualitatively superior past behaviors of a problem-solving nature. Critical thinking is a term which can be used to differentiate incidental learnings and qualitatively meaningful experiences. Critical thinking involves a future sense of time.

The problem-solving and adjustment processes of life involve experience of a primary level. To select out of this primary level of experience those elements, principles, and learnings that will aid in future problem-solving and adjustment processes demands thinking of a higher level of abstraction. Critical thinking is the process of drawing meaningful conclusions, generalizations and applications out of the present for future use.

Present experience needs to be organized, ordered, and interpreted

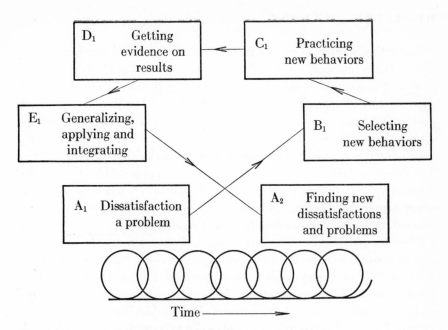

FIG. 7.1 *Steps in the training process**

so that it will effectively influence future experiences. Psychology has taught that man is not solely a rational being. Man is influenced by his hopes, fears, dreams, and unrealistic or realistic perceptions of himself. Reason or intellect is only one element within the process of critical thinking. Man as a totally functioning organism needs to solve problems with the best skills and talents which he can marshal. As man individually can accomplish the process of critical thinking, so then can groups begin to apply the principles of abstraction and critical thinking.

Groups can solve present problems; yet the quality of the solution needs to be tested against future problems of a similar nature. Critical thinking in problem solving demands that a solution or answer must be used or usable in future situations or the answer or solution can only be a specific or restricted concept. A group of students may evolve a particular method of studying or preparing for a scheduled examination. If this method is usable for future examinations in other areas and at other times, the solution is qualitatively better (involving critical thinking) than a specific solution usable for only one experience.

* Miles, M., *Learning to Work in Groups.* New York: Bureau of Publications, Teachers College, Columbia University, 1959, p. 38.

DECISION MAKING

Democratically-oriented groups must face the necessity of arriving at a decision. Often members believe that to take a vote is the most democratic method which can be found. Actually the voting process can be divisive in group action. Contrary influences have developed within the study of groups that have stressed the achievement of consensus, the agreement of all members with the proposed action or step. Consensus has frequently been offered as *the* method for groups to use as a decision-making process. The dangerous divisiveness of voting has been supplanted by the equally destructive concept that "men of good will agree if they talk long enough!" Many a group has been caught in the dilemma of avoiding a vote so as not to separate the group into subunits, while languishing in chaos and disorder waiting for consensus to occur (Kerlinger, 1954). Consensus and voting are but two of the methods which may be used in obtaining group decisions. Each of these processes needs to be understood, but not formally and inflexibly applied in group situations. Authority, compromise, and a "block-and-gap" consensus are additional methods of achieving decisions within groups. Each of these techniques needs to be examined in order to provide perspective within the process of group operation and problem solving.

Authority

The cartoonlike figure of the dictatorial leader imposing his decision upon the unwilling followers is a caricature of the authoritarian type of decision-making process. There is little question that this type of action deserves the opprobrium of all democratically oriented persons. However, there are appropriate times and appropriate methods for authoritarian decision-making which are not only compatible with democratic groups, but vital to their continued success.

The concept of delegation of authority, and the concept of authority appropriate to and commensurate with responsibility are basic within a democratic society. These principles give rise to a type of decision-making process that is related to a concept of compulsion or authority. The positive aspects of authority have not often been stressed within democratic groups. The dangers and evils of dictatorial methods are well known; re-emphasis on selected aspects of decision-making out of authority can clarify the meaning of democracy in groups.

A democratic society demands that many decisions be rendered by judges. There may be appeals, disagreements, even cries of dictatorship (the Supreme Court's decision on desegregation in schools), but members of a democratic society are compelled to abide by the decision until peaceful means are found to change the decision. The rubric of democracy is a commitment to peaceful change, and the repudiation of force as a method of problem solving. Congressional committees, peace officers, and officials of all types are delegated authority and responsibility to make decisions in our society. A group of bank robbers or a collection of sophisticated embezzlers in the city government are not allowed to take a vote or arrive at consensus before submitting to arrest. Similarly there are groups and units of our society that specifically delegate decision-making power to the leader of the group. The group could not function without delegated power and decision-making authority. Airplane pilots, orchestra directors, and similar task leaders have such leadership roles.

Decision-making power not only *can* be vested in a role or a position of leadership, often it *must* be. Democratic purists are quick to point out that "all who are affected by a decision must share in its making!" Otherwise, they state, no meaningful decisions and group action can result. La Fauci (1958), found that "good" decisions were accepted fully by members who did not share in making them; "poor" decisions were rejected, and a clamor was raised because of the failure to share in the developing of the decision. It would seem that democratic followers are not concerned about "good" decisions (those which worked) being completely "democratic." T. Gordon (1955) includes "delegating decisions" as a type of decision-making. Shared decisions are desirable, but not mandatory in a democracy.

The important issue in the context of authority-based decisions is the recognition of the necessity of such decisions at selected times. A reading group could spend several meetings discussing what book should be studied. The group might profit in terms of learning about discussion techniques and the difficulties of arriving at consensus. However, such issues are not primary and can contribute to the disintegration of the group. The leader, with or without consultation with the group, may decide to start on a particular list of readings. At a later date the group may wish to enter into the discussion and selection procedure. A beginning breakdown on process (what books can we read?) can destroy such a group. Similar group decisions may need to be made within the authority area. The principles of delegated authority and responsibility commensurate with authority are guiding concepts whenever leader-centered decisions are made.

Voting

Groups may approach all decisions as a time for voting. Youngsters, learning the voting process of democracy, reveal the divisive nature of vote-taking. A group of young children are discussing their choices for an afternoon's play; many possibilities are discussed and good-natured disagreement is present. A vote is taken and differences become solidified. Two camps are possible and each person is either for or against a project. Huszar (1945) reveals overdependence upon voting as a characteristic of an immature concept of democracy.

Groups who vote early and often open themselves for a type of "group one-upmanship." Skilled observers of parliamentary procedure have recognized that a positively worded motion, first on the floor, will more than likely be approved by the group. Knowles (1952) observes this process as he objects to the crystalization of the group on a particular proposal before additional methods or procedures may be discussed. The entire system of parliamentary procedures is often inimical to the effective functioning of a small group (Benne and Muntyan, 1951; O'Brien, 1956).

Voting is sometimes appropriate within a group. The leader and the members need to understand that a vote is a more irrevocable step than a tentative, temporary census which may later be revised. Groups recognize this problem as they take straw votes. The straw vote reveals the degree of difference within a group, and may aid in structuring the group's procedures in attempting to solve the problem and to make a specific decision. Wise leaders and groups avoid early vote taking that establishes a majority and a minority, except where final action or definite positions within the group need to be recognized within the group.

Compromise

Leader-centered authority and voting are not the only procedures open to groups in arriving at decisions. Compromise is an ancient and valuable tool in the group process. Benne and Muntyan (1951) caution against compromise:

> . . . this method of attaining common action leaves the minds, the outlooks, and the perspectives of the conflicting groups unreconstructed or at best partially changed. (p. 299)

Seldom, however, are the opposing sides of issues in groupwork as clear-cut as the "Blue and the Gray" of the Civil War. Complete agreement is seldom possible among men of even excellent will. A loyalty to the process of decision making within a group can surround compromise and provide a method of problem solving for the group. Compromise is not an ideal method, but can serve as a stopgap method of decision making prior to more complete agreement on the part of participants. A review of decisions and a restructuring of plans can always advance a group beyond the lines of original compromise.

Consensus

Consensus is an ideal for all problem-solving groups. Consensus is a decision agreed upon by all members, or action reflecting "valid insights and values of all parties" (Benne and Muntyan, 1951). These authors see consensus as a process in which a group attempts to isolate areas of conflict and disagreement through discussion. The group seeks to identify areas of conflict and then, through study, acquisition of common facts, discussion and other methods, to agree upon a common plan or decision (Benne and Muntyan, 1951, pp. 304–307).

The group which can achieve consensus is able to implement common goals, objectives, and methodologies. Consensus reflects the successful operation of groups, members, and leaders. There is no question about the desirability of achieving consensus; however, the difficulty of such a task has seldom been thoroughly understood. The size of a group affects the achievement of consensus. Hare (1952) found that a group's ability to achieve consensus decreased as the size of the group was increased from five to twelve. Varying conditions and varying conflicts are sometimes resolved through consensus and at other times decisions are not achievable (Guetzkow and Gyr, 1954). Guetzkow and Gyr found that as *substantive* conflicts were resolved, the groups had succeeded through emphasizing areas of agreement and building upon areas of consensus, not through an emphasis of what was in conflict! *Affective* or emotional conflicts were solved through reducing forces which caused the problem. The achievement of consensus is as complex as the total operation of the group.

Consensus is applicable as an ideal goal for groups. Disagreement exists as to the method of achieving consensus. Benne and Muntyan (1951) stress study of the areas of conflict; Guetzkow and Gyr (1954) stress the building upon common areas of understanding and agreement. What then can a group seek?

"Block-and-gap" consensus

The investigations of Guetzkow and Gyr (1954), as indicated, seem to provide a method of operation for groups of various sizes. Groups always can find areas of disagreement. Psychology reveals that each person is different from each other person. As differences are magnified, as disagreements are isolated, succeeding differences and disagreements can tumble pell mell after one another; disagreement breeds disagreement and difference. Common areas of belief and operation exist also between and among persons. Guetzkow and Gyr offer the conclusion that further consensus is achieved as smaller, simple common beginnings are stressed and collected.

A concept of "block-and-gap" consensus can incorporate such a finding. The entire problem area is surveyed and examined. Rather than isolating and highlighting areas of divergence or conflict, areas of agreement and common belief are selected from the context. Often, illogical steps seem to be resulting. Large gaps exist between agreements; only blocks of agreement exist. The rigid logician will be distressed by the lack of continuity and sense of such a method. However, out of early agreements can come later consensus.

Block-and-gap treatment of the idea of consensus reflects a realistic appraisal of the nature of human beings to be different. Conflict divides; agreement breeds consensus. Realistic problem solving in groups of large and small size demands that pure consensus be held as a goal and a stimulant to the level of aspiration of the members of the group and the leaders. Block-and-gap approaches to agreement allow for variations and differences in group size, structure, leadership, and problems.

GROUP PRODUCTIVITY

The new uniform and the overall sartorial splendor of the new first baseman on the varsity does not determine how he will hit or field. The new man on the team may be a "big hit-no field" or even a "good field-no hit." The applications of groups must similarly rest not on how desirable they may appear in theory, but on whether or not they are able to do the job. Leadership, membership, and group structure are all variables that affect productivity;

yet even under ideal conditions or under undesirable conditions, groups must face the test of productivity.

The early history of groups is filled with concerns of the success of the group as compared with individual productivity. Many classic experiments have been contradicted by later attempts to validate the results in similar surroundings. Research is beginning to catch up with theory and evidence has begun to accumulate in support of groups as productive organisms. The interrelated effects of leadership, membership, and the interaction variables of the group are beginning to establish consistent results as groups are studied. In many areas of early group study, simple faith was often placed in the group as naturally superior; simple faith has been replaced by scientific examinations of the forces, conditions, and environments which can produce effective groups.

Groups "versus" individuals

One of the early studies of the nature of the group in decision making and productivity was completed by Shaw (1932). Shaw found that the group was able to reject more incorrect ideas and hypotheses than an individual working alone. She also found that the group was able to develop more possible solutions to a given problem. Shaw's findings in these areas were confirmed partially by R. L. Thorndike (1938) who later showed the effectiveness of groups in conditions of varying problem complexity. Perhaps the most influential and widely known experiments on the value of the group as opposed to the individual in accomplishing a job were completed by Kurt Lewin during the period of World War II. Lewin attempted to change the attitudes toward buying, serving, and using readily available but unpopular food products. A skilled nutritionist lectured to groups of housewives on the use of beef heart, animal brains, kidneys, and other little-used foods. Three per cent of the group later tried the food. Another group of women were involved in a discussion of the problem by a discussion leader who knew little of nutrition and food values. Thirty-two per cent of the latter group were found to try these foods. Lewin summarizes these and other related experiments in his article titled "Group Decision and Social Change" (1947).

Various findings have since challenged Lewin's conclusions. Later experiments designed to test his conclusions have not always shown similar or even related results. Some writers were even inclined to cast doubt on the effectiveness of all group decisions. However, evidence continues to be collected that is supportive of Lewin's original concepts (Levine and Butler, 1952; Kipnis, 1958). Coch and French (1948) reported a study in which workers were involved in a change of work procedures. Three groups were established: (1) the changeover in work methods was handled in "autocratic" fashion, with supervisors explaining the changeover and answering questions; (2) the changeover was discussed with two representatives of the workers; and (3) the change was presented to the employees, and plans were established jointly for the new methods. The group that was handled in "autocratic" fashion showed a marked drop in production at the time of the change and never recovered the original level. The "representative" group showed a marked drop at the time of the change but slowly gained in productivity and surpassed its earlier level. The "participatory" group showed a slight drop at the time of the change, recovered rapidly, and soon reached higher levels than previously maintained.

Added evidence showed that the "autocratic" group, when involved in full participation for another change, could reach new high levels of production. This experiment is classical in its application and duplication in many industrial settings. Cartwright and Zander (1953, 1960) have offered it as an example of industrial reaction to group involvement in management action. Such involvement and respect for the participation of those who are to be involved in a decision is in the best tradition of democratic decision making and certainly in the tradition of the "Hawthorne Studies" (Roethlisberger and Dickson, 1939).

The sharing of decision making and the involvement of workers in the processes of management have been significant outcomes of the application of human relations skills and intergroup programs in industry. Dubin, Meier, Pigors, and Meyers are names of writers in sociology and industrial human relations, all of whom accept the principles of group involvement in processes of management and business, for productivity as well as desirable human relationships. Tannenbaum and Massarik (1951) typify the concerns of management with the worker. Their approach is a down-to-earth participation with workers, but not the abandonment of decision making power to workers.

Studies of conformity by Asch (1956) and by Crutchfield (1955) have demonstrated the influence of opinions of group members upon individuals. That "conforming" persons exist is not doubted, but many questions need to be raised about the reasons for the conformity (E. Hollander, 1960). Essentially the issue which must be faced as conforming persons are analyzed is that "conformity" is not a specific personality trait, but "a complexly determined output of interaction" (E. Hollander, 1960, p. 224).

Trends in group productivity

That many times the group has advantages over the individual in the process of problem solving is not seriously contended any longer. The important issue is concerned with the specific advantages which do attach to the group as opposed to the individual, and the applicability of the results. Also, investigators are now concerned with the question of research results arising out of "ad hoc" (especially established for research) as opposed to "traditioned" (naturally existing) groups (Lorge, Fox, Davitz, and Brenner, 1958). There is always the issue of transfer of results. Certainly the complexity of the problem to be solved (Thorndike, 1938), the strengths of the group members, the experience of the leader, are variables which must be considered in any report of group effectiveness.

Conflicting results continue to be reported in the literature. Hudgins (1960) shows clear superiority of group problem solving in arithmetic over individual efforts with no carry-over of group learned skills into later individual efforts. Lorge, Davitz, Fox, and Herrold (1953) stress the problem of complexity as they find that individuals are more effective than groups. The question remains, how and when can groups be most effective?

Oversimplified approaches may be the cause of the problem. As three and four-member groups are shown at one time to be superior and the next time to be inferior to individuals in the problem-solving process, the applied group worker becomes confused. Simpler problems appear to be resolved more effectively by groups; more complex problems seem to be best solved by individuals. Recent investigators have examined contributing issues and applied more sophisticated measures to the measurement of group productivity. Siegel and Fouraker (1960), in their investigations of decision making and bargaining, found that "level of aspiration" made a significant difference in the productivity of individuals in a group (two person) problem-solving issue. Fiedler (1958; 1960a; 1960b) has accomplished a series of experiments attempting to isolate factors of group productivity as they relate to a complex study of individual and group reactions. The leadership and productivity experiments at Ohio State University compiled by various authors (Fleishman, Harris and Burtt, 1955; Rush, 1957; Halpin, 1957; and Hemphill, 1957) also reveal more comprehensive and sophisticated measures of group productivity.

Interpersonal perception

Fiedler has investigated the productivity of a group in many situations (Fiedler, 1958): basketball teams, bomber crews in the Air Force, tank crews in the Army, open-hearth steel shops, and farm supply co-operatives. His research deals with the relationship of the leader with the group members. He does not offer a single independent variable which applies to all situations; rather, he postulates a complex environment of psychological distance between members and the leader.

Leaders can be effective as warm, accepting persons if they are able to maintain a degree of psychological and social distance from the group as a whole. Distant, non-accepting leaders can be effective as group leaders if they can establish close sociometric or social relations with members of the group. Also, leaders accepted by group members must possess the skills to solve the problems. Fiedler tests these hypotheses in all of the situations listed above. Variations exist in the results, but he concludes that the hypotheses are appropriate for all of the groups (Fiedler, 1958, p. 256).

The key to the success of the research by Fiedler would seem to be an awareness that various factors are able to produce similar results; productivity is the complex result of interacting forces. Fiedler offers the interpersonal atmosphere or climate which is established within the group as the key factor. He pleads for an understanding that such conditions can be established in varying fashions by different leaders and groups, as differing tasks are faced.

Situational analysis is related to the group perceptual field of Fiedler. The Ohio State studies in bomber crews, industrial plants, foremen behaviors, and supervisory attitudes were alike in concerning themselves not with single variables, but with patterns and continua of characteristics. *Consideration* and *initiating structure* were significant variables in several of these studies. Consideration was described as concern for others, friendship, trust, respect, and related characteristics in a leader. Initiating structure was offered as a pattern of behavior in which the leader actively organized the group, defined roles in membership situations, and clarified patterns of work. Aircraft commanders who were low in each of these characteristics (Rush, 1957) had crews which formed cliques and stratified themselves into subgroups. Industrial situations where leaders lacked these characteristics became almost leaderless group situations (Fleishman, Harris, and Burtt, 1955). Effectively productive groups in such various situations as aircraft crews and university faculties were marked by leaders who possessed all of these characteristics in an above average degree (Halpin, 1957; Hemphill, 1957).

These Ohio State studies are similar to Fiedler's work at the University of Illinois in their emphasis upon a total situational analysis. None of these experiments attempted to isolate single leader or member behaviors. Each series of studies (remarkably similar in design and procedure) stressed different aspects of the climate or atmosphere which existed in the groups. Productivity was related to the establishment of perceptions on the part of the members toward the leader and of the leader toward the members. The climate and atmosphere aspects of these studies leads one back to the early work of Lewin, Lippitt, and White (1939). These complex studies are attempting to narrow and define the meaning of the democratic group as first highlighted by the famous "climate studies."

Final answers are not yet available; however, group actions can be made productive through an understanding of the complex factors involved in the establishment and maintenance of understanding acceptance and co-operation within the group. Fiedler (1960b) raises the issue directly as he underscores the failure of so many studies to isolate traits of those who become leaders. He calls for an analysis of the effectiveness of leaders and groups. As understandings and working skills are revealed within productive and co-operative groups, it will be possible to identify the things which a leader must *do*, not what he must be before becoming a leader. Fiedler supports the view that however a person becomes leader, he must then prove himself through an ability to lead (1960b). Groups and their productive capacities thus turn back upon the effectiveness of the leaders and the establishment of a climate or atmosphere. Productivity has led back to the first issues of group work: establishing objectives, building climate, selecting leaders, analyzing how leaders lead, the motives of members, and the process of communicating with other members.

Diagnosing group problems

Groups may fail to progress, fail to agree, and disintegrate. Group failure may stem from many factors, but two major categories are always apparent. Either the group failed because it could not solve the problem (task or content), or the group broke down in its functioning (process or method of functioning).

Content problems in the areas of guidance, counseling, and education have not yet been presented; the content of groups, as they function in a guidance and counseling program, will constitute the entire portion of Part Three. Breakdown problems in process can be highlighted in a review of the major elements of group functioning.

A group planner or organizer, a leader, or a member can view groups and attempt to understand their operation from many perspectives. When problems begin to appear on the edge of the group's operation, prior to making a full-blown entrance, an analysis of the major categories of group process can assist in the determination of the causal factors associated with disintegration.

FORMATION AND ORGANIZATION.   How has the group been formed? What were the objectives in the minds of the members as they spontaneously organized themselves, or as outsiders worked to organize the group? Has the group been able to attract members? Are there features of prestige, accomplishment, or identification present within the group? Is there a sense of common purpose or of divided goals? Stable groups develop out of shared objectives and common tasks. As goals, objectives, and tasks have been isolated, consciously or unconsciously, have agenda procedures been completed? Are there too many "hidden agenda"?

LEADERS, MEMBERS, AND STRUCTURE.   How has the leader been selected? Does the leader fulfill an "office" or is he merely a figurehead or a person holding a "headship"? What type of leader does the group want? What type of leader does the group possess? Are members assigned specific roles? Are there divisive cliques among the members? Are members attempting to usurp the leader's role? Is there an "unofficial leader" rather than, or in addition to an assigned leader? Where is the locus of power in the group? Does the group fear or reject the authority of the "power figure"? Does the group meet the test of Thelen's "Least Group Size," or is the group too large to fulfill its stated function?

PATTERNS OF COMMUNICATION.   Are members of the group able to understand one another? Can the contributions of individual members be accepted by the group, or are there "breakdowns" of communication patterns because of emotional distortions? Can the group afford not to recognize each member of the group as a person, a separate personality? Are there two groups in operation, the informal and the formal group? Are problems of understanding and group success related to the particular nature of the group: student-centered, teacher or leader-centered, or task-centered?

MOTIVATION AND LEARNING IN GROUPS.   What are the motives of the leaders, the members, the organizers, the group? Are the frustrations of members translated into group frustrations, or is the group able to produce problem-solving behaviors which can lower the frustration levels of the members? What are the learning techniques which are used by the leaders, the members, the groups? Are elements of co-operation and competition used to enhance or to lessen learning within the group?

MOVEMENT AND PROGRESS IN THE GROUP.   Has the group recognized the steps or phases of the problem-solving process? Has the group bogged down at one of the phases or steps of the process? What are the decision-making procedures that have been used by the group? Are the methods of arriving at decisions—such as the use of authority, voting, compromise, consensus, and block-and-gap consensus—used properly, or are there distortions in the applications of the various methods of decision making? What is the quality of the solutions or answers developed by the group? What are the factors which have prevented movement and progress by the group? Are there readily observable forces operating within the group which can preclude productivity or the solving of the problems of the group?

SUMMARY

Movement and progress in a group result from the completion of problem-solving steps or phases. The specific elements in the problem-solving process may be viewed in several fashions. All descriptions of the process stress cyclical movement on the part of the group and its members.

Decision making provides the method by which movement is accomplished in a group. Decisions may be obtained through five methods: authority, voting, compromise, consensus, and "block-and-gap consensus."

Comparisons of groups with individual problem-solving actions provide equivocal results when research is examined. Group methods seem to be superior to individual approaches whenever the problems are non-complex and allow for co-operative efforts of group members. Productivity is related to group efforts in a complex rather than simple relationship. The perceptions of the leader toward the group and of the group toward the leader, as well as factors of consideration and initiation, are clearly related to productivity. A failure in the movement or progress process of a group can be related to many variables.

SUGGESTED READINGS

Cartwright, Dorwin, ed., *Studies in Social Power*. Ann Arbor, Mich.: University of Michigan, Institute for Social Research, Research Center for Group Dynamics, 1959.

de Huszar, George B., *Practical Applications of Democracy*. New York: Harper & Bros., 1949.

Dubin, Robert, *The World of Work: Industrial Sociology and Human Relations*. Englewood Cliffs, N.J.: Prentice-Hall Inc., 1958.

French, J. R. P. Jr., and B. H. Raven, "The Bases of Social Power," in D. Cartwright, ed., *Studies in Social Power*. Ann Arbor, Mich.: University of Michigan, Institute for Social Research, Research Center for Group Dynamics, 1959, 118–149.

Glanzer, Murray, and Robert Glaser, "Techniques for the Study of Group Structure and Behavior: I. Analysis of Structure," *Psychological Bulletin*, 56, 1959, 317–332.

Kerlinger, F. N., "Authoritarianism of Group Dynamics," *Progressive Education*, 31, 1954, 169–173.

Luszki, Margaret B., *Interdisciplinary Team Research and Problems*. Washington, D.C.: National Training Laboratories, National Education Association, 1958.

Meier, Arnold, F. D. Cleary, and A. M. Davis, *A Curriculum for Citizenship*. Detroit, Mich.: Wayne University Press, 1952.

Raven, B. H., and J. R. P. French Jr., "Legitimate Power, Coercive Power, and Observability in Social Influence," *Sociometry*, 21, 1958, 83–97.

PART THREE

Groups can be used in many areas of guidance programs at all educational levels. The applications of groups in the following types of guidance activities form the subject matter for Part Three:

1. Human Relations and Group Training
2. Student Activities
3. Articulation and Orientation
4. Psychological Testing
5. Educational Planning
6. Vocational Development
7. Counseling
8. Organized Guidance Classes

Each of these topics is treated as a single chapter in the pages to follow.

8. HUMAN RELATIONS AND GROUP TRAINING

American education, as the handmaiden of a free society that nurtures and protects it, is alternately vilified and praised by members of that society. The institution of education is charged with the task of constantly advancing the content of knowledge while concurrently training citizens to live within and to protect a free democratic society.

Vehement attacks by critics within towers of learning and by self-made specialists seem to score most frequently the failures of education in the content area. Yet, we are constantly building better submarines, bombs, and methods of destruction; our methods for achieving even peaceful co-existence lag pitifully far behind. The content and technology of our society is steadily improving; the process by which we solve our problems and live together remains comparatively primitive.

The existence of violent disagreement between society and education reveals the importance of effectively containing conflict while providing solutions to the issues. A democracy depends upon the open nature of its education; education must provide more effective means to aid members of a free society to advance and protect their free way of life.

Respect for human dignity and concern for individual welfare are primary characteristics of a democracy. Respect for the means of problem solving as well as for the ends or goals of a society is a protection of the fundamental meanings of a democracy. As citizens can learn to operate within a philosophical framework which includes these two demands, they can become full-fledged members of a democracy. The group is able to serve as a fundamental learning unit in education and in all of the operations of a free society. The interaction of personality with problem-solving and decision-making actions within groups demands skills that need to be learned and used at all levels of education.

Administrators, teachers, and all specialists in education are users of the group process as a tool in training persons in human relations at the same time that they master any academic discipline. Guidance persons, as they can use group procedures to aid students to solve their own problems and to aid students in learning, can affirm their own acceptance of the basic goals of education as the fundamental objectives of guidance. Jane Mouton (1957, p. 342) expresses this charge to guidance persons in direct fashion:

> One of the challenges of the future is to create learning situations as concrete and meaningful to students as counseling and psychiatric aid . . . focused not on the removal or control of personal defects, but rather on the expansion of an individual's capacity for adjustment within the social framework.

Citizenship training

Educators have been slow to accept the responsibility for the development of a society through education. Control is seen as a genie to be kept in the bottle or magic lamp. Yet, tyranny or freedom in a society can only be established and maintained through the instrument of the state—education. Education in a democracy is a force for freedom.

Harry Stack Sullivan has pointed out that the formation of personality and of the self of the child is in the hands of parents or other significant persons in the home. Further, "Personality can never be isolated from the complex of inter-personal relations in which the person lives and has his being" (Sullivan, 1947). Citizenship is similarly a product of the interaction of personality and school experiences that are assimilated within the educational system. An assessment of the role of education in a democracy and of the interrelated responsibility of guidance and personnel workers within education leads to the following statement by Melby and Reeves (1959, p. 23):

> More than ever the school must become the one place in the life of the individual where facts can be faced calmly, where people can differ with safety, where originality can be encouraged, rewarded and prized by others.

Schools are involved in citizenship training; human relations training is a part of citizenship training. The use of groups can become one of the major tools at the disposal of teachers, administrators, and guidance persons as they seek to achieve goals of human relations training and citizenship responsibility.

Human relations training

Feelings are facts that help to form patterns of personality. Further, feelings and personality interact within a social structure like that found in any school. A social structure of a school is thus a part of life and not merely a training ground or preparation for life to come.

Human relations skills can be taught within a framework of the curriculum, the guidance program, and the school program. Ojemann (1955) pleads for the teaching of such skills along with other subjects and for the practice of such skills in the classroom. A special course in human relations in the curriculum is most frequently not the answer to problems of involvement of students. Human relations are a part of all of the major elements of the school curriculum and the life experiences of the student of any age.

While specific courses in human relations may or may not be possible or desirable within a particular setting, it is highly desirable to be able to train students to be sensitive and aware of the feelings of others and to be capable of interacting effectively with all persons in different, variable environments. Group approaches can provide the means for achieving such goals.

The role of guidance

The importance of training students in human relations and in aiding students to understand and accept citizenship responsibilities is a vital task for education and for teachers; too frequently guidance personnel assume that such goals are no real concern of the counselor or the guidance director. Yet the *Personnel and Guidance Journal,* a major spokesman for all guidance persons, sponsored a series of articles on "Basic Approaches to Mental Health in the Schools." Samler and his associates (1959) have been offered the series in a special reprint booklet. Samler's final paragraph states the issue in clear form for the guidance person (p. 64):

> We seek a society that will counter the trend of our times, destructiveness, alienation, rootlessness, loss of personal identity, in total a loss of the meaning of life. The programs described [in the previous pages] facilitate the emergence of man's essential humanity and we have here the possibility, revolutionary in its implications, of the emergence of the competent and productive, tolerant and respecting, feeling and loving human being.

More and more the guidance person and the counselor have been urged to become concerned with human relations and the total goals of education. Lloyd-Jones (Lloyd-Jones and Smith, 1954) has long been willing to define a guidance worker as a "human relations specialist." Recent writings of Wrenn (1959 and 1961) show his concern for the beliefs *and the functioning* of guidance persons.

As the counselor and guidance person function as catalytic agents in a school situation (Salinger *et al.,* 1960), progress in the goals of education and human relations can be achieved on a more realistic basis. However, in Wrenn's view of the functioning of the guidance person, an acceptance of a series of goals is not enough; means and procedures for aiding students to better learn human relations and citizenship are necessary. Rogers (1958) has delineated the characteristics of the helping relationship in a counseling and therapeutic relationship; more attention needs to be given to the characteristics of the guidance person working with a normal population.

Some of the answers for the counselor and guidance person would seem to lie in the combined use of counseling and groupwork techniques. Human behavior is not restricted to growth in a one-to-one therapeutic or counseling relationship. The reverse side of the problem was shown by the case history of three group-trained sociologists working with teen-age gangs. Crawford, Malmud, and Dumpson (1950), in *Working with Teen-age Gangs,* point out that the forces affecting youngsters in antisocial groups are the same as those within approved social groups. These reporters stress the importance of a total knowledge of human behavior; they regret that they were unable to work with individual persons in a counseling relationship. In normal school settings is it not possible for trained counselors to understand and use group techniques so as to better help and assist students of all age levels?

Training in human relations for application in citizenship or in other elements of a school program demands that concrete and useful procedures be available to use with student groups. Programs and methods are now available. The practical issues often raised by school personnel are *when* and *by whom.*

Student personnel and guidance as a discipline has often been torn by a conflict in which narrowness is praised. The school counselor is urged to confine himself as much as possible to counseling and to forgo involvement in any other phase of the widely spread guidance program. Pierson and Grant (1959) defend this position and offer most of the standard arguments in its favor. However, most writers represent the responsibility for student activities, leadership, and human relations as being a part of the total guidance or student personnel program. If these program elements are to be a part of the work load of the guidance person, it is natural that he should also be responsible for the program of training in human relations and group procedures. In fact, such an assumption needs to follow if guidance persons are to undertake the broader tasks of aiding students in learning and living with a democracy.

Human relations and group training may be undertaken by many persons in a school staff. Whether or not the guidance person assumes a leadership role in the program is unimportant. He cannot escape the charge of concern and knowledge in the area; if others are not interested, the guidance person must initiate action and attempt to co-operate with others in accomplishing the task.

THE TRAINING PROCESS

Training in human relations and in group procedures may be included as a part of a "Leadership Seminar" scheduled for members of the student council and club leaders; in a social science class as an introductory unit of the course; in an elementary science class so that the students may discuss the presentations offered by a closed circuit television program; in fact, training to participate in a discussion and to differ while seeking answers is a part of the total educational process. This training may take place as early as the first grade and as late as graduate school. The program will need to be planned with a knowledge of the previous experience of the participants.

Elementary school pupils are apt learners in the group discussion process. The need for the teacher to attend to and supervise numbers of student groups puts an early premium upon teacher training of pupils in self-directing group techniques. If similar stress could be placed upon such behaviors in all the years of school, pupils would be able to build new learnings upon past experience. Too frequently, a program of group and human relations training is an isolated feature in a school program.

Wide experience in training adults and adolescents has been recorded by the National Training Laboratory of the National Education Association. Many publications and manuals by this group are available to aid beginning trainers. Their reports of summer workshops since 1947 and many training aids are available through the National Education Association. Community and adult groups have been the primary audience to which they have directed their efforts, but in 1959 and 1960 they began to be concerned with the training of educational leaders (National Training Laboratory, 1959) and student leaders (1960). Miles (1959) has prepared a textbook devoted solely to the training process.

The training process is a "learning through experience" program. Participants are placed in actual group discussions on various topics and they acquire an understanding of the elements of group functioning through firsthand experience with the actual raw material of personal involvement. The planning and implementation of a training program are complex, and will demand the best efforts of the leaders and the participants. Particular stress will be placed upon learning about the process of working in groups. The roles and responsibilities of participants need clear and specific planning.

Training in groupwork is not a cut-and-dried, didactic process. It is necessary to provide spontaneous and meaningful experiences. These responsibilities and performances are a part of the training process and make the program a new experience for the planners and the participants on each occasion, no matter how frequently it is repeated with different groups of persons.

A training program will stress technique and practical applications; emotional attitudes and reactions will be even more basic to the personal success of participants. Each person in training needs to deal with his own feelings and insecurities. Shephard and Bennis (1956) reveal the threat to the self and the high anxiety level that is inherent in training and learning procedures. Persons conducting programs of group training need to balance all such factors and recognize personal progress in varying degrees. Dependency-interdependency feelings, related forces of authority and intimacy, and even the factors of power and love all affect personal progress (Bennis and Shephard, 1956).

A training example

One elementary teacher, in a school where little stress was placed on the development of discussion skills on the part of students, was determined to aid her fifth grade students to become more skilled in leading and participating in a discussion.

> Miss Carver met with a group of pupils who had been selected through sociometric procedures with peers to be "first leaders." During a free reading period she met with the "Leaders To Be." She explained to the six leaders (five and a spare, for a class of thirty) that after a particularly provocative movie they were to see as a class, that the students in the class would be divided up into five discussion groups of six persons. Each leader was to serve as moderator for a group of six students. After the discussions were completed it would be the responsibility of each leader to summarize his group's conclusions to the class as a whole.
>
> Miss Carver took questions from the special training groups and announced that on the next day they would see, in advance, the special motion picture.
>
> While the class as a whole was engaged in library and other work, the "training leaders" and the teacher watched the motion picture. Afterwards the teacher played the role of the group discussion leader and helped the group to isolate the issues in the picture. After a short period of time the teacher stopped the discussion and asked if any of the group had any questions about their own assignments for the discussions following the presentation of the picture to the class as a whole. Several students raised questions about what they should do if. . . . The teacher immediately asked the student who raised the question to role play the "leader" of their little group. The student group, with the teacher as a "member" of the group helped the student to cope with the issue presented. Several other similar questions were handled in the same fashion.

The teacher then explained that the first leaders would be succeeded in turn by other leaders from the class in future movies and selected reading assignments. The next day she showed the motion picture to the class and held her discussion groups.

The elementary teacher demonstrated several principles of training in her attempt to involve her fifth graders in discussion groups. She had planned her activities carefully and had selected prospective leaders on the basis of peer evaluation. She met with this group in a private session while the class was involved in other activities. The future discussion leaders had an opportunity to assess their tasks and to learn in private about the problems they would face. The teacher gave them the opportunity to be well prepared by seeing the motion picture in advance, and to anticipate problems by role-playing the possible problems with her.

Several omissions were certainly intentional. There was no immediate evaluation of the leadership roles assumed by some of the students. She had planned to rotate the leadership roles among other students in future situations and only after several other situations did she ask the class to begin to structure the responsibilities of the leaders and of the members. Evaluation was indirect and pointed toward future effective leadership responsibilities. The class as a whole profited from the leadership training and the discussion skills of all students were improved.

Training activities involve several stages, regardless of the level of the participants and the design of the training. Planning is a first concern, then must come learning activities, and lastly, an evaluation and application period.

The planning stage

A training program will be the result of an idea or plan of one person or of a group of persons. Group planning can strengthen the final program. When the elementary teacher in the previous example attempted to arrange a training program, she might have been able to do a better job had she involved a small committee of the class in the planning of the program.

A planned program needs to be seen in its totality prior to the development of a detailed plan. The steps in the planning operation can be structured as follows:

1. Idea or design of the program
2. Formulation of a small committee to plan a program

3. Outline of specific steps to be accomplished
4. Intermittent evaluation and restructuring
5. Summation and conclusions.

The design of a training program needs to stress flexibility and variability. Many training programs are designed by a planning committee made up of teachers, administrators, or adults, and adequate representation of trainees. The planning committee remains in force (even with rotating membership) to re-evaluate and restructure the program as it moves ahead. Such flexibility and variability needs to be preplanned.

The following example of a planning committee's activities is drawn from a college-level program in leadership training (Harren, 1961):

> A joint student-faculty committee was established to plan for our Fall Leadership Workshop. There were two faculty members and three members from the student body. The design of the program was established in a series of committee meetings and a program mimeographed for distribution to the students who were to attend.

> We had planned to have an opening address and then to arrange the students into several groups so that they could discuss one of the two "current events" topics we had planned for the morning session. Leaders were arbitrarily selected. Following lunch we planned a demonstration of a "good" committee meeting and a "bad" committee meeting. The demonstration was to be put on by students from other parts of the university so that the attending students would not know any of the "role-playing demonstrators."

> Following the two demonstrations we planned to have the students ask questions and react to the demonstrations. Several guest faculty members were in attendance; a hurried meeting was called of the planning committee, and a decision was made to ask the faculty to comment on the demonstrations. Their comments were a high point in the program. After the demonstrations, the students were again formed into the same groups as had existed in the morning session. Discussions were completed on timely topics drawn from the problems of the student council of the college. After a closing summation the program closed.

Perhaps the committee learned more than the participants in this leadership training program. Certainly a spur of the moment decision can qualify as "flexibility"; the "intermittent evaluation restructuring" title would certainly be too grand a term to be used. Programs which run over a lengthy period of time, several days or two weeks, can be evaluated more leisurely on a free time basis between sessions.

PROGRAM DESIGN.   A basic question which underlies all planning steps is the issue of a program design. "What is the purpose of this training (leadership, human relations) program?" This question must be faced as goals and objectives are established for the program. The wandering, confusing discussions which often mark a planning session for a workshop or a training program are a sign of misunderstanding of the nature of human relations training. A program will not "just grow" like Topsy. Detailed planning and severe questioning of ideas and concepts are necessary if a meaningful program is to be built. A planning group depends upon the abilities of its leader and its members, as does any group. A leaderless group may ultimately answer the question of who *might* be the best leader, but in the meantime, it may be possible for the proposed training session to be lost in vague, purposeless discussion.

Leaders and planners need to apply the principles of group organization, structure, and operation in planning for the training of others. Leadership begets followership of the type that is demonstrated, rather than the type which may be talked about. Workshop programs and training sessions in classes or school programs depend upon informed, skilled leaders who can help others to become effective in human relations and group procedures. Beckhard (1956), Knowles and Knowles (1955), and Miles (1959) are sources for those who wish to delve more deeply into the subject of designing and planning a training session or a special workshop.

PLANNING DECISIONS.   The many decisions which must be made as a projected training design is contemplated may be summarized for planning committees. Miles offers basic decisions which must be faced as plans are developed. Many issues will not be a concern of the informal school planner in a classroom, but other larger workshop programs will need to face all issues (Miles, 1959, pp. 61–71):

1. Purposes	5. Physical arrangements
2. Costs	6. Content
3. Who will take part	7. Procedures
4. Time arrangements	8. Special roles
	9. Evaluation

The first five issues, already discussed, are concrete in their applications. Clarification of the four last topics will be included in the sections of this chapter to follow.

Learning activities

Training in the operation of groups must include experience as a member of a group. Firsthand knowledge of forces, factors, and even personal distortions of personal actions are not easily obtainable from vicarious involvement.

After the training director, workshop director, or other leader of the program has determined a program design with a planning committee, the actual procedures and content of the program need to be established. A program design needs to dictate the procedures and practices to be employed. A program planned for training leaders and group members in beginning discussion topics (such as the elementary school program illustrated) would be poorly served through an analysis of hostility and aggression levels between and among interacting members. Such an analysis is desirable and appropriate in some of the research programs described in Part Two, the analysis of the dynamics of groups, but it is not germane to a beginning experience concerning leadership and group member responsibilities of fifth graders.

Actually it is necessary to involve potential group performers in a thorough understanding of all of the group dynamics issues. Continued programming can provide for developmental learning in all areas. Program directors may wish to establish their own order of coverage; however, leadership and group member responsibility are valuable as starting points because of the familiarity of most persons with such concepts.

The following types of learning activities can be useful in reaching goals and objectives established for a program design:

1. Training (T) groups
2. Leader roles
3. Content recorders
4. Process observers

These types of activities provide opportunities for learners to understand and to use the principles of group operations. Learning activities need to involve future group specialists in the actual use of the procedures in a laboratory type setting; the "not for real" training atmosphere provides a sense of psychological security and freedom for experimentation and learning.

TRAINING (T) GROUPS. The use of small groups in the training process has long been one of the more stable elements in the process of helping persons to become skilled in group work procedures. A T group is simply a small training group in which persons may plan and experiment, and then evaluate their successes and failures.

T group use helps new group workers to center upon the *process* of a group rather than the *task* assigned to it. Members of a T group do have a task. They must work on something in order to examine their own behaviors, feelings and attitudes, but the *growth* of the group members is the primary emphasis in the group procedures that are carried on in the training program. Training-group members focus on immediate understanding and applications of skills and operating procedures. The purposes and applications of the group process and groupwork skills are important and significant, but the stress in T groups is on behaviorally based skills.

The goals of the training program will determine whether particular emphasis is placed on the skills, or the emotional and attitudinal changes that occur in the program. Bennis and Shepard (1956), whose approach to training was earlier examined, stress the emotional and attitudinal change elements within the person; Miles (1959) is more concerned with the skill factors. Each of these approaches highlights a different goal of training. There is no disagreement about the factors involved—the starting points and the procedures are different; the goals and outcomes are desirably similar.

Training groups can provide the stage for the use of role playing, sociometric analysis, leadership techniques, communication patterns, and even analysis of the motivational factors operating within group members. The examination and dissection of the process of problem solving in groups can also take place most easily in a training or T group. Bradford and Gibb (1961) have edited a collection of papers showing the many applications of the training group.

The significant value of the training group lies in the self-examining attitude which prevails within the group at all times. Tasks are completed, tasks are rejected, progress or lack of progress is a function of the group as a whole; the examination of the process which leads to the actual happenings is the crucial step which must be taken within the training group. The threat of the possible failures and skill inabilities of the group make it necessary for the members to establish a secure atmosphere for experimentation (Weschler and Riesel, 1959). The training group provides the first level of experience out of which learnings may be acquired, though it needs to be integrated with other approaches in the training process.

LEADER ROLES. Training programs are ideal environments for the experimental use of various leadership types. The combined use of role-playing techniques and different leader types allows group members to observe, to act out, to experience on a first hand basis the theoretical elements of leadership. Many critics or partial critics of group procedures, such as Gunderson (1950), are concerned with the many terms that are used in describing group operations. The neophyte often shares this concern in experiences in group training; the diverse types of experiences that are a part of all training programs soon demonstrates the need for words to describe the qualities of new feelings and learnings that take place.

Demonstrations of the classical leadership types, *authoritarian, laissez-faire,* and *democratic* (cf. Ch. 4), are frequently early activities in a training program of some length. Familiarity with these rather clear-cut leadership types provides a background against which new leaders may try out variations on a new theme. Kirscht and Lodahl (1959) point out that small groups select leaders who can contribute to the group through the activities of participation, problem specification, action suggestion, and by aiding groups to achieve decisions that provide for an integrating consensus. New leaders can practice such behaviors in the laboratory setting of the T group with less tension and anxiety about their performance.

The need for leadership in a group, or the dangers of laissez-faire type leaders can be intensely experienced as group members participate in leaderless type groups. Leadership roles and potentials can also be explored through the use of leaderless groups. Investigation of the dimensions of leadership provides a balancing element to be used in a well-designed human relations, leadership, or group dynamics training program.

FUNCTIONAL MEMBER ROLES. Many unusual learning climates can be established through the use of specialized group member roles. A *content recorder* can be selected in a training group to aid the group to maintain its focus on the task assignment. The members who play this role in the group soon learn that there is more to the responsibility than the usual performance that is expected of a secretary in a more common nongroup oriented organization. The leader can call upon the content recorder to bring the group up to date on its progress towards its specific goal, or he may use the content recorder to summarize and establish the problem-solving phase in which the group finds itself.

Another functional member role is that of the *process observer* who supplements and gives added dimension to the work of the content recorder in group training sessions. Following a report of the content recorder, the process observer may be called upon to clarify the methods and processes which were used by the group in achieving its current level of task accomplishment. The process observer's assignment is often rotated in a training group. Members need to learn to be aware of the process of a group while still participating as members of the group. The ultimate goal of the training process is to establish the principle that each member needs to function in the dual role of *participant-observer*.

The "Our Town" type of commentator and observer is a variation on the content recorder and process observer roles. The Our Town observer is not a member of the group, but he is able to stop the discussion at any time, to comment upon content or process, or to ask the group to repeat or to move ahead to other topics. This type of role is useful for the classroom teacher who wishes to involve an entire class in a training process. A training director or *resource specialist* is also free to help a group in this fashion. When the specialist is a stranger to the group, there is often more freedom for the Our Town role and more security for the group members since they will feel less threatened by an unknown visiting "fireman."

Concrete activity in specific group problems can also help a new group member to learn about significant issues:

> When we first met as a training group everyone was very reserved and even somewhat hostile to me. The leader ignored any suggestions that I made and accepted even the silly ones made by anyone else. More and more they conducted the meeting as if I were not there.
>
> My feelings of hurt were primary at first; anger and hostility soon supplanted my feelings of rejection. I finally jumped in and insisted that the group listen to me. When this didn't work I was ready to "chuck" the whole business. I didn't care whether the group succeeded or not.
>
> When the teacher stopped the group discussion and told everyone that the group had purposely ignored and rejected me I felt much relieved. I have never forgotten how vivid my feelings were; my hurt was real and my hostility extended to everyone in the group.
>
> There had been a "rejected person" in each of the small groups. After each of us told of his feelings and reactions to the rejection, we

resumed our first planning meetings. Everyone seemed more considerate of every member of the group following my experience.

First-level experience of the type described by the beginning group member in the preceding illustration is learning and growth to the marrow of the emotional core of the person. Secure and stable persons are needed whenever experiments of this type are conducted. Other group members can watch and learn; the experimenters learn on a firsthand basis. Creativity and a flair for the dramatic are useful characteristics for a training director, a teacher, or a guidance person to possess in planning and implementing a training program. Festinger (1954) lists many particularly attractive gimmicks and methods of motivating, encouraging, and involving both hostile and interested persons in the process of learning through activity in groups.

CONTENT IN TRAINING PROGRAMS

Many training programs are designed to use "group process" as content for T groups and other activities included in the group design. Group process thus becomes not only the method of the group in solving problems, but also the content or the task concern of the group. Other means of involving persons in the learning process about groups stress the use of usual content areas as "sample" or experimental tasks or content for groups in training. Case studies sometimes are useful devices for use in a training situation. There are advantages and disadvantages to all of these approaches. Each type of content will be examined to show its use in a training program.

Group process as content

There is little question that the use of group process as a content area for T groups in a program of training is efficient and effective. Group members are immediately introduced to the major concepts that contribute to an over-all understanding of group operation. The major disadvantage exists in the complexity of group process for younger students. Sometimes new group skills are confused and persons actually believe that group process is usable only when "laboratory" or "unreal" situations exist. Group procedures are seen to be appropriate only for training activities, not for life use.

Group process as a content for training may obscure the differences between *process* and *content* in group work. The age of the persons in-

volved in the training, and certainly, the sophistication and previous knowledge of the learners are vital factors. Younger school persons such as those
in elementary grades do not need to learn any of the labels and technical
vocabulary which could be used in a community human relations training
program, or in a training program conducted in graduate classes in sociology or psychology.

Decisions must be made whenever group process is used as a content
for a training program; group process seems obvious, and yet it is extremely
complex and detailed. Never in a small training program can all of the
elements of group process be adequately covered. Which of the major elements of group process should be included in a training session? A longer
program that is able to focus successively upon related topics needs only
to decide upon an order of study. Chapters 3 through 7 of this book are concerned with the major characteristics of groups in operation. Additional or
varying presentations of group process are also possible. The following
simplified list of topics could be included in a study of groups:

1. Leadership roles	7. Individual motivations
2. Member roles	8. Problem solving
3. Group structure	9. Decision making
4. Process and content	10. Power in groups
5. Group objectives	11. Evaluation
6. Communications systems	12. Research in groups

Each program of training needs to be structured and designed to
meet the needs, experiences, and aspiration levels of the persons to be
aided through a study of group procedures. Jeep and Hallis (1958) list
forty-six principles of group process that could serve as additional content
topics.

"Process on process," or the study of the process of group operation, is a rewarding but confusing approach to training. Skilled group
trainers and leaders will be able to apply those techniques from which analysis shows that the participants are able to profit. Other programs may wish to
start with simpler and clearer content and, in later sessions, move to a
direct examination of group process.

Case study problems

The development of illustrative cases, or the utilization of previously prepared case study books or sources (Allen, 1933 a and b; Andrews, 1953;

Cabot and Kahl, 1953; Freeman, 1952; Pigor and Myers 1947), can provide a useful approach to the study of group processes. The use of a case study provides a concrete, first-level situation for analysis and discussion.

The use of long and detailed case studies can provide a continuing source of data while a group takes time out to "study itself." The process of self-examination is time consuming, and a difficult case study can add to the frustration level of the members if it is never completed. Shorter case studies are appropriate inasmuch as they are within the scope of the beginning learner.

A series of case books concerning human relations problems and business issues is available from the Harvard University Press. The case method of study was pioneered at the Harvard Graduate School of Business Administration. Early techniques and trends have been developed further in many publications. A series of educationally oriented case study source books is available from the Bureau of Publications of Teachers College, Columbia University. Guidance workers can find case studies in several textbooks written for use at various grade levels. Many of these textbooks have been cited in previous chapters and are involved in the list of source books in the Suggested Readings recommended for group workers in education.

Guidance workers, teachers and administrators in public schools and in colleges may find that the most rewarding type of case study to use is one that has been prepared from an actual event or problem situation in a local school. Care is needed in order to protect the innocent and assure ethical confidentialness to students, teachers, and counselors.

Local issue and concerns

Problems or issues that have arisen within the environment are a ready source of content for the training group. Church groups may wish to grapple with the problems of budget, membership, or a curriculum for a Sunday School program. High school student councils may wish to use problems of their extracurricular programs, leadership training (nearly process on process), club fairs, or even dating, family, or study problems. Colleges may use problems of sociology, class content, the effective reorganization of honorary societies, or other matters common to all students.

The significant advantage of the use of local issues and concerns as content for a training program is immediately discernible; student or participant interest is high, and there is established motivation for the solution of the problems at hand. A disadvantage is the frustration and hostility that can arise as discussions of the content (task) are stopped in order to conduct a process analysis. The advantage of this combination of effort is that the participants are in a life-oriented problem-solving task. They may be better able to combine the joint skills of process and content when they are able to tackle such issues at the same time. Research concerning training and its success is beginning to be available; differential research results which describe desired content for a program are not yet conclusive.

EVALUATION OF TRAINING

Two types of evaluation of training activities can appropriately be examined. Programs of research into the "back home" effect of participation within a training program have been cited in previous chapters. Several studies (Fleishman 1953; Fleishman, Harris, and Burtt, 1955; Miles 1960) attest to the value of training, while indicating the problems inherent in its use and application. A second meaning of the term, evaluation of training, is the "inside" use of evaluation in the training program and in the T group. This type of evaluation is centered upon the actual performance of the person or the T group. Such self-examination is a type of ongoing evaluation that is a part of the actual training process. Several major techniques of self and group evaluation will be presented for an examination of their usefulness in the training design.

Group evaluations

Training programs of lengths varying from a morning or an afternoon to several weeks have long used a type of written total program evaluation. A variation upon this technique is having each of the training groups complete a separate evaluation of the work of its own group. Combinations of groups, total evaluations, and single-element analysis are always possible. One striking method requires each training group to complete a series of group evaluations at the end of each meeting. These results may be charted, graphed, or illustrated in a variety of ways to help the participants and other group members to profit from the experience of others.

Simple rating scales may be devised by training committees for use by training groups. Issues such as participation, freedom, congruity of individual and group goals, progress or movement of the group, presence of hostility, acceptance of others, and other concerns may all be expressed on rating scales maintained by the training group. Carter (1954) lists variations of these issues. Charts and graphs demonstrate the ebb and flow of group morale, productivity, and the other elements of group process. These approaches help to reflect a group's concern for process, and they highlight developmental changes within the group.

Individual logs

Members of training groups may be encouraged to keep "process logs" that are also developmental reflections of the progress of the group and reflections of the members' awareness of the joint issues of content and process in the training group. A distinct advantage of such logs is the opportunity for a training official or a teacher to examine and evaluate the reactions of the class or training group members. Oftentimes, confusion about the distinctions between content and process, and other factors of concern in a training program, will become clarified only through such individual methods.

Miscellaneous methods

The process observer can serve as a major contributing factor in the evaluation of a group and of the individual member's contributions to a group. The concept of feedback is actually a variation on the use of the process observer (Jenkins, 1948). The interrelationships of the group members may be charted through standard sociometric methods (Jennings, 1947; 1959; Gronlund, 1959), or variations of them (Gardner and Thompson, 1956; 1959). The effects of varying attitudes towards fellow members of a group can have a profound effect upon the performance of individuals and of the group as a whole (Stock and Thelen, 1958; Festinger and Huttee, 1954).

Various mechanical aids to training can be creatively used to aid prospective group specialists: a simple blackboard for diagraming a group's problem-solving stages or for making agenda obvious; a tape recorder allowing members to hear the group's confusion and babble at times, or perhaps an individual's domination of the group; and even a new device, an Opinion Meter. The Opinion Meter is a device providing for the simultaneous electronic hookup of all group members, each with a separate button. Determining responses to issues, or determining the degree of support for any given position regarding an issue before the group is possible.

The device may be wired to work with a small group or with a group including 300 persons. Little data is yet available upon the use and applications of the Opinion Meter.

FUTURE PROBLEMS

There is little question that group techniques can be applied in every area of education, business, and the community. The challenges of the future will be to demonstrate the most effective training methods. Too often, group procedures are viewed by many persons, even after they have had training, as "sure-fire methods of wasting time." Laing and Munger (1959) stress the importance of effective training and proper use of group methods. Yet there can be no substitute for involving persons in the frustrating trial and error of learning through actual experience. Gragg (1953) highlights this concept in his article, "Because Wisdom Can't Be Told." Persons need to have the "feel" of failure and success in a group before they will be able to tolerate the often distressing time issue in a democratic problem-solving process.

Training methods must improve and become more efficient in enabling persons to become skilled in the process of solving problems while concerning themselves with the value and dignity of other persons who lack skill. The problems are difficult and the progress is painfully slow at times; however, the task is a genuine concern of a democratic people.

SUMMARY

Groups are key factors in understanding the issues of human relations and the meaning of democracy within a society. Education can act only as an instrument and agent of the society within which it exists. Training for successful membership in groups is related to performance as a citizen in a democratic society.

There are various methods of training persons in the skills of group operation. The "learning through doing" concept underlying the idea of the training of the T group is basic to all training activities. Leadership roles, membership roles, and other concerns of group performance qualify as concerns for a training design. The content of a training program can be drawn from several sources. The use of "process on process," or studies of group process, case studies, and local concerns are issues appropiate for training content. Methods of evaluation, both of the process of training as a whole and of the performance of the groups and the persons in the training program have disadvantages and advantages.

SUGGESTED READINGS

Andrews, K. R., *The Case Method of Teaching Human Relations and Administration.* Cambridge, Mass.: Harvard University Press, 1953

Bradford, L. P., and J. R. Gibb, eds., *Theories of T-Group Training.* New York: New York University Press, 1961.

Brown, Francis J., and R. B. Anloit, eds., *Human Relations in Higher Education.* Washington, D. C.: American Council on Education, 1951.

Cook, L. A., ed., *College Programs in Intergroup Relations.* Washington, D. C.: American Council on Education, 1950.

————, *Intergroup Relations in Teacher Education.* Washington, D. C.: American Council on Education, 1951.

Gulley, H. E., *Discussion, Conference, and Group Process.* New York: Holt, Rinehart, & Winston, Inc., 1960.

Hawkins, Thomas E., *Reflections for Students.* Hampton, Va.: Hampton Institute, 1960.

Heaton, Margaret M., *Feelings are Facts.* New York: National Conference of Christians and Jews, 1952.

Lane, Howard, and Mary Beauchamp, *Human Relations in Education.* Englewood Cliffs, N. J.: Prentice-Hall, Inc., 1955.

LeFevre, Carl, "A Laboratory Course in Group Discussion," *Journal of Higher Education*, 26, 1955, 489–492.

Miller, K. M., and J. B. Biggs, "Attitude Change Through Undirected Group Discussion," *Journal of Educational Psychology*, 49, 1958, 224–228.

Passow, A. H., M. B. Miles, S. M. Corey, and D. C. Draper, *Training Curriculum Leaders for Cooperative Research.* New York: Bureau of Publications, Teachers College, Columbia University, 1955.

Trager, Helen G., and M. Radke-Yarrow, *They Learn What They Live.* New York: Harper & Bros., 1952.

Weschler, I. R., and J. Reisel, *Inside a Sensitivity Training Group*, Industrial Relations Monograph No. 4. Los Angeles: Institute of Industrial Relations, University of California at Los Angeles, 1958.

9. STUDENT ACTIVITIES

Although knowing a person's beliefs will not always help to predict his actions, actions can reveal beliefs. Education offers at least two arenas within which behavior and belief, and the results of each may be examined. (1) The classroom can be both a place for learning about living and an environment in which life proceeds. (2) Student activities, also, are a portion of school in which life may be viewed as something of the future or as the stuff of everyday living. Guidance personnel and counselors are a part of the life inside and outside the classroom. Counseling, student activities, and group problem solving provide tools for aiding students to achieve a total education.

What are the beliefs and the philosophical premises upon which school personnel operate? So often philosophies and principles are treated as museum articles to be displayed and viewed, but never sullied by actual use.

The application of groups in the area of student activities focuses an intense light upon the issues of philosophy and practice in education. The practices must follow philosophy or else reveal the compartmentalization dividing belief and practices. Guidance personnel are not free of the charge that persons must be known by their actions.

THE QUESTION OF PHILOSOPHY

What is the philosophy that governs student activities and their role in American education? Herbert Stroup (1956) attacks this problem in his article, "The Intentions of Student Activities Systems," and pessimistically offers three major operational views: conformism, anarchism, and ritualism. Guidance and activities personnel will recognize all except anarchism. Stroup labels the open-ended (whatever comes out) to be a result of the laissez-faire political and economic fare which has been offered to western civilization. He even adds Carl Rogers and the "non-directivists" to his collection of anarchists.

Many charges are appropriate to the activities scene in American schools. Since practice can reveal belief, elements of the current scene need to be presented along with an analysis of the reality of student activities and a positive view of an activities philosophy. American education does possess a philosophy of student activities and the educator's responsibility to students.

The black pit?

The number of American schools and colleges that profess an attachment to democratic values and yet fail to operate upon them could lead one to believe that a blatant hypocrisy exists in our school systems. Many elementary and junior high school principals and teachers take the position that student government is beyond the capacities of their pupils. Many high schools and colleges make no pretense of having any form of student government (perhaps more honest than some systems). Wood (1953a) reports that thirty per cent of the schools surveyed in the National Association of Student Councils study provide for no system of open student elections. Miller and Dahl (1952) report in a North Central Association study of secondary schools that only three school systems had election procedures where appointment by the faculty was not a major element.

The reports on the training of football players in sportsmanship and school spirit have graced the pages of many publications, including some with national readership. Certainly the schizophrenic patterns of behavior in college and sometimes in high school athletics need no documentation in these times. What values are learned in such student activities? What is the answer of education?

Sports Illustrated often answers the charges against athletics in education. Its argument is that many outstanding athletes are also outstanding students. No one would deny that the athlete in education is a strange and uncertain person; according to individual and environmental factors, the athlete may be the bum or the prince of the campus. School activities of all types possess similar inequality and non-integrative characteristics. Amoral practices and outstanding democratic citizenship training exist side by side in school systems. Perhaps the anarchism charge of Stroup is appropriate?

The challenge to educators arising from the stress on athletics and student activities of all types is similar to the issue faced by contestants in the famous quiz programs with the attractions of quick wealth and fame. The question is seldom whether a particular practice be condoned; the significant factor is the personality of the person in action—can he resist the pressure?

The school principal who is fearful and insecure is unable to share his power of decision. The college administrator who is unable to discern the question of moral value is frequently responding to the pressures of personal security and acceptance by alumni, trustees, or even society in its nameless and formless strength. Rezler (1960) has shown the connection between values and achievement in straightforward academic work. Benezet (1955) makes a plea for educators to see the relationship between practice and values in the area of student activities. The hypocrisy of giving decision-making authority to a group and withdrawing it under stress is a comment upon the lack of clarity in understanding the shared responsibility of students, faculty, and administrators in the overall conduct of any educational institution. Perhaps an answer lies in the fact that respect for personal dignity and integrity while people learn to differ is a hallmark of a philosophy of education that can govern student activities of all types. Educators are needed who have the talents, strengths, and personalities to live within a democratic system designed to build upon the contributions of all participants. The failure of a system cannot be demonstrated; however, the failures of persons and the failures of integration of belief and practice surround us all.

I'm not one for a lot of this gobbledygook. We shouldn't always be pampering and building up the students. After all life won't. Let's be truthful with them. Don't tell them they have free rein, when you know very well you'll have to check them many times. Students see through people easily—and the people who work with them are a mighty important influence. We have to develop a combination of ease, co-operation, and respect. (Eddy, 1959, p. 78)

The faculty member quoted by Eddy in his widely read survey of the influence of college upon student character faces several truths. One could quarrel about what constitutes "pampering and building up" students; however, this faculty member combines an earthy respect for the world of reality with an insight into working with students with "ease, co-operation, and respect."

Education texts have long taught that student *self*-government is a "pernicious" phrase. Pure "administrative government" is equally destructive in a school system. Still, many activities persons and administrators of all levels seem unable to face the fact that neither students nor administrators can make all decisions in isolation. The school principal or college president who must decide the shape of the butter pats at the banquet for students is an extreme example of one side of the coin, while pure student government is the other side of the same counterfeit coin.

There are school areas within which student decisions can be final; there are other areas where student involvement in the decision-making process is neither desirable nor possible. A wide area of shared responsibility exists wherein mutual respect and exploration must precede the establishment of methods of decision making. The task of determining a workable philosophy and practical set of operating procedures is a constant challenge to every educator. Democracy is freedom within limits rather than license for anarchy to any group. This fact is a part of the challenge of providing education for citizens within a democracy.

Ruth Strang, a person long concerned with the promotion of group and student activities in education, lists fourteen major reasons why activities can fail (1958a, pp. 41–42). Many of these failures may be traced to the inability of the faculty and students to face directly the questions of power, authority, and decision making. Virtually every reason for failure is clearly related to improper use of the dynamics of groups in educational practice.

Programs of activities in schools and colleges have provided some of the most striking success stories in all education. Failure is not the common experience when secure, creative, and skilled leaders and students are brought together; meaningful and valuable experiences have arisen from student involvement on the playing field, in the dormitory or the fraternity house, or in any of the activities that concern students outside of their classrooms.

Several surveys of the student in his natural habitat (Eddy, 1959; Jacobs, 1957; Wise, 1959; E. A. Greenleaf, 1957) have revealed the seriousness of students as they examine their own values and responsibilities. No single view of reality is correct for any single student or even for any small collection of students. However, Eddy offers a quotation representative of the hundreds of comments he heard in his many interviews. Certainly a prevalent attitude deserving the concern of educators is the student's statement:

> Let me put it this way: where I found weakness, I took advantage of it; but where I found strength, I respected it. If I'm allowed ever to slip by, I'll do it every time. But if I'm really expected to perform I'll come through or go down fighting. (Eddy, 1959, p. 9)

Strong, skilled, free educators are needed to produce students who understand democracy as well as the tools and disciplines of a free society.

Activities and education

Democratic values in education not only permit, but demand that principles, philosophies, and beliefs in the dignity of the person and of the reality of problem solving will create conflict, unresolved issues, and the integrity of a defended principle or value. Educators must be strong in belief and free in methods of operation; students need opportunities to be able to learn to live and to solve problems. Group procedures provide the tools for student activity learnings.

The values of student activities are irreducible. The school must provide the crucible of learning for democratic ideals and operations. Student activities are neither extracurricular nor co-curricular. Student activities are an added dimension of the educational process in which *different types* of learning experiences are possible. Creative and democratic leadership can provide students with opportunities to learn through failures and successes. The world of life is not outside the school; life is within the school, but in a form that is not the same as life outside of school. Teachers, counselors, guidance workers and educators at all levels are helpers, guides, and co-experiencers with students. Respect for the dignity of ideas, persons, and the values of democracy that are not relativistic can cultivate within an activities program a laboratory for learning and living that is as different from the classroom as a wheel from an engine, yet as important to education as both a wheel and an engine are to the movement of an automobile.

LEADERSHIP AND GROUPWORK

The quality of a program of student activities is dependent upon the interactions of students, skilled educators, environmental circumstances and the tools available for co-ordinating these varying elements. The use of group procedures within a student activities program is demanded because of the vested interest of students in their own planned activities. Classroom procedures and other more formal learning situations may or may not include the use of groups of students. However, when a student activities program is planned or implemented there is need to respect the interests, desires, and talents of the students.

Students may succeed or fail in their attempts to help themselves in planning and implementing student activities. Guidance personnel concerned with students need to recognize the need for trained leaders and an informed body of students. The final quality, as well as the quantity, of the product arising from a program of school activities can be raised considerably through the use of training activities.

Identifying leaders

The issues of leadership are complex and not easily resolved in the practical environment of the school. Many reviews of research and of leadership literature have failed to demonstrate clearly the qualities of personality and behavior that are characteristic of leaders. The many environments in which leaders must work have a definite bearing upon the particular characteristics that are appropriate for the group leadership task to be undertaken. The clarification of leader and group roles is an important element in the functioning of groups (Lippitt and others, 1947).

One of the principles of the National Training Laboratory in Bethel, Maine, has been the belief that leaders can be trained to fulfill the tasks of the group in specific situations. Benne (1948) clearly defends this position; he is concerned with the concept that "leaders are made and not born." Other writers are more inclined to take the position that although leaders may be created for specific situations, particular characteristics can be isolated that are related to leadership (see especially Stogdill, 1948 and Mann 1959).

The person concerned with the selection and training of leaders is not interested in the determination of the sources of leadership. The practitioner must select potential leaders and attempt to make them effective in the program of the school. Many involved research studies have attempted to select potential leaders on the basis of data collected from psychometric sources. A recent development in research has promise for use in school programs in the selection and training of leaders. The Leadership Potential Inventory developed by Hayes (1961) is designed for selection and training purposes.

The leadership prediction instrument of Hayes is related to a similar tool prepared for school workers in the area of juvenile delinquency. Kvaraceous (1952) established a Delinquency Proneness Scale that attempted to determine which students would behave in a particular fashion in the future. The Leadership Potential Inventory concentrates on personality characteristics and environmental forces, and the combinations of these variables. Hayes demonstrated the validity of his instrument and its applicability in various types of educational programs.

Leaders may also be selected in pragmatic fashion by pupil personnel workers as they conduct sociometric leadership searches or review the data on file for students. Election, appointment, or the assumption of a leadership role in the past is a partial predictor of performance in the future. Many school leadership training programs are planned for all of the members of the student government, club presidents and officers, athletes, and even the faculty sponsors, and advisors. The particular program of leadership training and activities programming will need to determine the selection of potential leaders for training.

Significant improvement in the performance of the role of follower is often an outcome of leadership training. A well-designed program of training will stress all of the roles in a group organization. The potential leaders will then become more effective members in all of their group performances. The rotation of leadership roles in many schools creates opportunities for students to learn all of the responsibilities inherent in the functioning of groups in a democratic setting.

Training leaders and members

The establishment of a training program for leaders and members within a school system will frequently follow the general outline of training offered in the previous chapter. The necessity of planning and implementation by a joint committee of faculty and students is clear in a program of leadership training within a school setting. Faculty members often need help in acquiring the same skills that are being offered to students. The joint nature of responsibility for student activities offers an excellent opportunity for the involvement of faculty in a program. The threat that new knowledge is being offered because of ignorance and failure is absent whenever students and faculty co-operate in the development of a training program.

Reports of training programs in many types of school activities reveal variations in procedure and scope of training; nevertheless, essential elements of training remain:

> Our representatives to the regional and state meetings of the organization of the student councils came back with a clearer understanding of their roles as leaders within our student council. They had participated in discussions about the responsibilities of presidents, vice-presidents, secretaries, treasurers, committee chairmen, and similar topics that were most helpful to them. (High school student council sponsor)

> The director of guidance in our school has a meeting of all candidates for election. The meeting is devoted to a presentation of the responsibilities of office and the opportunities for learning through participation in a total program of student activities. (Junior high school)

> Our college conducts a leadership meeting in the fall and in the spring of the academic year. The administration underwrites the expense of the fall program and the student council pays for the spring conference. The program varies within each year and from year to year. A planning committee is established each year with members from the student personnel staff, faculty, and students. The students assume the major responsibility in all committee planning and implementation. (Junior college)

Many publications have been prepared for the use of student leaders. These books, many of them in paperback form, are useful in aiding students to develop skills of group process. Desirably, such publications can support and extend a training program. Other schools use the books on a "biblio-training" basis. Certainly such use may or may not be effective; the involvement of students in an actual experience of skill use is valuable in providing opportunities to apply the techniques covered in such books. Printed sources are represented by such books as *Successful Leadership in Groups and Organizations* by Wagner (1959) and *So You Were Elected?* by Bailard and McKown (1960). Many schools produce mimeographed handbooks and resource material about the activities carried on throughout the year. Such items can strengthen and localize a training program.

Leadership is sometimes taught in a classroom by subject matter specialists or personnel workers. A class for leadership or for student council performance is another form of training and its effectiveness with students will depend upon the variables listed above for less formal situations. Reaves (1956), Wood (1953b), and Wester (1956) describe such classroom approaches.

SCHOOL GOVERNMENT

Many titles have been used for the government organizations that exist in schools from elementary to graduate levels. Government Organization, Student Council, and Community Government are among the more common. The names reveal the philosophical differences that exist in the sponsoring institutions. The dangers of the "student self-government" and of the "administrative fiat" have funneled current practice into a more democratic governmental organization. Community governments have often made a fetish of representing the custodial staff or the cafeteria personnel. There is no question that the janitor and the dietitian are a part of the school program; the question is whether their interests might not be better served through respectful consultation by a student group on specific issues rather than through continued representation in meetings where few if any issues affect them.

School governmental organizations are inherently effective environments for democratic learnings. Faculty, administration, and students are able to learn together lessons of value in the manifold experiences that are a part of an appropriately functioning student government group. The administration of the activities program of the school, the supervision of student group finances, the problem-solving work of committees, and the training experiences that can be utilized in the future make student government a central aspect of any program of student activities.

Group activities involving students, faculty members, and administrators in joint problem solving often provide concrete learning experiences for all participants.

> Our student council committee had been working for several months on the preparation of a revised constitution for the school. We worked with three faculty members and the faculty sponsor of our council. Finally we had all agreed upon the basic premises of the revisions and planned to submit it to the principal of the school. Prior to the meeting with the principal, a faculty member—not a member of our committee—visited our committee and began to put the "pressure" on us not to submit it as planned. We were amazed. The faculty member was obviously a "representative" of the principal, but we couldn't figure out why such direct force had to be used in order to make us change our proposed constitution. We had been willing to meet with the principal and revise it according to the ideas of our group and of course, according to his views.

> We changed the constitution according to the wishes of our "new committee member." All of us wondered why the principal chose to co-operate with us in such a way. Our constitution was then presented to the administration and we were praised for our "fine work." Our accomplishments seemed a little flat after the pressure tactics he had used on us. Also we would have preferred to deal with him openly on whatever his ideas had been. (High school student council member)

Functional co-ordination and control

A school government organization is in a central position to effect a co-ordinating and controlling force on all aspects of the non-academic and non-business life of an institution. Many sources have outlined the broad scope of student activities on all levels of education. Hand (1938) was one of the early sources in offering an educational view of activities. More recent treatments of the total program of activities include Gruber and Beatty (1954); Miller, Moyer, and Patrick (1956); and Strang (1958a).

The formation and approval of student organizations rest traditionally in the hands of a student and faculty government group. The regulation, budget approval, suspension, and continued control of such groups are normal functions of school legislators. Guidance persons have aided in such programs and have even developed a specially trained budget personnel worker who serves all campus organizations (College of the City of New York and Boston University are examples).

The elements of activity that are within the scope of a school organization must be determined through the combined efforts of those who are present on the local scene. The philosophical bases and the methods of the program are dictated by the educational philosophy and its effective utilization by the educators working with students.

FACULTY ADVISORS AND SPONSORS.   Faculty and administrators who are co-operatively responsible with students for the functioning of a school government may assume many roles as local problems are solved. Many different patterns of operation are appropriate and successful. The faculty members who sit with students and assume equal voting privileges and responsibilities must recognize the psychological unreality of their role playing. Students and faculty (or administrators) are not "equal" in a school government regardless of the adopted ground rules of the organization or the provisions of the constitution.

Related problems occur if students are assumed to be free and independent in determining solutions to problems of activities control or those of judicial action in regard to discipline issues. Students are frequently more rigid and less willing to understand the delicate and varying psychological factors motivating fellow students. Such failures are to be expected; if students were as knowledgeable as faculty members in the solutions and adjudications of such problems, there would be some question about who was the teacher and who was the student.

Sponsors and advisors need to determine roles and participation patterns out of a knowledge of group process and a philosophical freedom to face reality and power forces in student activities. "Resource Specialists," "Limit Determiners," "Motivation Specialists," and similar roles are often appropriate for sponsors and advisors. Supervising roles and initiating leadership roles are freqently mixed as sensitive sponsors work with student groups. Sponsors and faculty representatives are also needed in a teaching role as specialized subject matter topics are faced by student groups. Parliamentary procedures are poorly understood by many faculties and administrators as well as students. One eastern school has appointed the faculty sponsor to the student council as parliamentarian to the faculty!

COMMITTEE "WORK." Committees can be established for almost every conceivable problem area in a school. The pros and cons of a point system (Henry, 1958) can be thrashed out by a student-faculty committee. A determination of new sources of revenue (Stout, 1948) is often mandatory for committee groups. The committee system in student activities is often the most maligned element within a total program; however, there is unequivocally no better environment for the learning of democratic skills. The charges against committees are legion within student and faculty groups. "An organized way to waste time," "A way to keep faculty members unaware of their low salaries," and even the charge that a "Camel is a horse put together by a committee," is standard patter in any school. Johnston (1952) rightfully rues the discrepancy between potential and performance in student activity programs. The charges by Major Mayer, Army psychiatrist, in his explanation (1956) of why so many American soldiers were capable of being "brainwashed" in Korea by the Communists, relate susceptibility to brainwashing to the diffuse and distorted view of democracy that so many students obtain in their school systems. Major Mayer is not indirect in his charges; he lays a major failure on the doorstep of American educators.

E. A. Greenleaf (1957) brings up the problem that as enrollments in schools rise, the proportion of student leaders and resulting opportunities for training will decrease. The red tape of democratic activities needs to be cut, and students need to be provided with opportunities to profit from experience and accomplishment.

The student council had appointed our committee to plan and to co-operate with the club sponsors in the presentation of the "Activity Fair" early in the school year. All school club and special interest groups were to present a booth at the Fair. We were going to use the gymnasium for two days and students from all study halls were to be allowed to visit the Fair whenever they were in study periods.

We first met in the late spring of the previous school year. We elected our own chairman and appointed the members of the committee to be chairmen of all of the subgroups in charge of the planning and carrying out of the project. We set up committees on publicity, physical arrangements, financing, tickets, entertainment, and the combined job of decorations and clean-up. Each subgroup chairman selected his or her own committee and developed plans for the "Activity Fair." Before the end of the year we had approved most of our plans, and at a final meeting there were over thirty-five committee members present and representatives from approximately thirty school clubs and interest groups. I was chairman of the publicity committee and we had a large number of posters placed on the bulletin boards before graduation.

Everyone was looking forward to the Activity Fair's being a big success immediately after the opening of school the next fall. The seniors were a little sorry that they would not be back and that they had been unable to work on the project. Many said they were planning to visit the exhibits and take in the Fair if they were in town. We were all sure that our club program would be a better one after the Fair than it had ever been before. (High school student)

Applications of learning

There have been various studies concerning participation in activities and its effect upon life after school. Several studies (Roskens, 1960; Krumboltz, 1957) show the positive relationship of college activity and after-college leadership. Leadership in high school is not as clearly related to college or after-college leadership, but the variables are more complicated in high school than in college. The satisfactory or above average academic records of activities leaders have been substantiated through the years in many studies. Research on the value and application of school leadership and membership in activities is needed in order to emphasize to school administrators the importance of the planning roles of the guidance and activities directors. Research in other applications of group procedures and leadership techniques were examined in Part Two. Research designs that can provide for a clear-cut application of group process upon educational issues are rare. Willerman (1959) has shown the value of such applications in aiding students to understand and accept university control of certain fraternity functions. Additional data are needed.

IMPROVING STUDENT ACTIVITIES

If student activities at all levels of education are to be a contributing factor to democratic outcomes for students, there need to be patterns for improving the productivity of qualitatively valid programming. Student behaviors are not simple and are not easily changed. The behavior of students in a school situation is similar to the behavior of adults in their worlds; behavior is the product of the many diverse variables of motivations, values, learning, and environments. Too frequently a mechanical approach to student learning in leadership and activity performance overlooks the emotional and personal factors that are intimately bound up with any change of behavior.

Earlier examinations of the emotional and personal factors present in any training program (Shepard and Bennis, 1956) only highlight this entire problem. Guidance workers belong within the pattern of student activities and student learnings because of their special knowledge of the elements of emotions and motivations. Counseling makes constant use of the principle of behavior change being a complex and intimate experience for all students. The assumption of responsibility by guidance workers for student behaviors and learnings in groups as well as in individual counseling sessions can provide a major strategy for improving an activities program. A second approach may be derived from some of the recent research findings showing the importance of group process upon human behavior and learning.

Counselors as activities persons

A guidance or personnel person must possess counseling as a first-level skill and performance ability. If this premise is accepted, a second necessary step is to place counselors in charge of activities programs. The demands on a director of student activities are intense and time consuming. A counselor has similarly harassed days, weeks, and months. The combination of the two tasks is certainly designed to make life complex for the guidance worker, and yet it seems inescapable that the "unrelated" activities program is one of the major causes for the development of hurtful or even nondemocratic learnings within a school program. A stress upon learnings that are surrounded by a joint understanding of the skill and the emotional factors involved demands that counseling training be a part of the background of the activities director. A time arrangement needs to be carefully developed to prevent a man-breaking job. The talents and skills of activities persons similarly contribute to the future counseling skills of the guidance worker who has such a dual assignment.

The issue of the counselor versus the guidance worker is here appropriate. If a counselor is to be concerned solely with one-to-one "in the office" counseling, there is little opportunity for a counselor to understand or to be prepared for the demands of a group specialist. However, as the counselor (and even the therapist) is forced to develop a knowledge of group process in order to work within a framework of group counseling and group therapy, the activities program would seem to be a bystander with no involvement, but with a ready-made profit.

> The editor of our school paper had not been invited to the leadership training program for the fall. The student government committee had selected the managing editor and another reporter to represent the paper. She was very upset and had burst into my office when she had seen the invitation list.
>
> There was no question in my mind that there had been a clash of personalities in this issue and that it was not going to be easy to unravel. She spent about an hour with me, discussing her feelings. She had started on the issue of the leadership conference, but had soon moved into the threat that the rejection had posed for her. After only a few minutes with her, I had been placed in a counseling role. She was able to clarify her own meanings to the rejection and had explored her relations with her parents that had definitely predisposed her to over-react to the missing invitation.
>
> Sue was not assigned to me as a counselee and after our conference I requested her permission to share the contents of the session with her counselor. She agreed, and it was the basis of a continuing relationship with her regular counselor. She had improved considerably by the end of the year.
>
> Many times I need to function as a counselor with the students that are active in the school club program. I have some students who can relate to me more easily than to their regular counselors. The students are around my office a lot and I see them in a different light from the other faculty members or counselors. (Director of student activities and counselor)

Lloyd-Jones (1940; 1954) has long stressed the importance of the social nature of students and the responsibility of student personnel workers, counselors, and educators of all kinds to be concerned with the total student. More recently, L. F. Allen and others (1954), Trueblood (1951; 1960), and Harvey (1951) have attempted to outline the joint responsibilities that fall upon the counselor-activities person. The concept of education possessed by a counselor or a guidance worker is the significant factor in the determination of interest, involvement, and developed skill. The principle that the building superintendent and the cafeteria staff are involved in the educational process is recognized by educational theorists. Can the counselor only remain behind shuttered doors alone with a counselee; can the dietitian state, "I only make peanut-butter sandwiches"? The counselor is a part of the total stream of education as is every person who is a part of an educational system.

Individual and group goals

The formation of a group is dependent upon an objective that has been decided upon by an individual or by a group of persons. Student activities are often the result of ideas and assumptions by faculty members or administrators that such and such would be a good plan. Students as leaders are similarly prone to push a personal plan or idea to the exclusion of the concerns of other students. Recent findings concerning the congruence or shared agreement between individual and group goals have reinforced many of the earlier findings of Lewin and other workers.

When group members understand clearly the goal of the group, the path that must be followed to reach that goal, their own tasks, and others' responsibilities, a group is more likely to succeed and group members are better able to contribute to the success of the group. These hypotheses were tested by Raven and Rietsema (1957), and related results were obtained in similar experiments by Smith (1957) and Gerard (1957).

The confusion and uncertainty that surround many student programs is directly related to poor planning and poor use of group process. These factors breed a lack of congruity among members of a group. Faculty sponsors, sensitive to students' personal needs and to the natural enthusiasm of young persons, are capable of recognizing the symptoms of failure early in a student program. Similarly it is often necessary for students to learn for themselves through failure and the heartbreak that can accompany failure. Hopefully, such failure can be accomplished within limits and within the supervision of faculty members working with students.

Our elementary school team group had decided to sponsor a book fair for the entire school. We set up committees and began to advertise the book exchange plan and to ask students to bring in their books for exchange or sale. We got off to a flying start, but chaos soon took over. The children were entranced with the idea of exchanging or selling their books to other students, but were unable to realize the need for planning, time, merchandising principles, and other too numerous details.

The books started to come in and we soon had a big pile on one of our tables. Our students were unable to resist the temptation of exchanging their own books prior to the sale. The committee became the buying public and our fine plan soon broke down completely. We had to abandon the book fair.

Another year saw our plans developed more carefully. Our committees were established and we worked out the details of the program in advance, prior to the collection of any books. The children soon came to realize their responsibilities as managers and as "entrepreneurs." At the actual book fair they took turns fulfilling their responsibilities and yet were also able to take their turns in exchanging and buying books. (Elementary school team co-ordinator).

CREATIVITY AND TRADITIONS

Custom and tradition play important roles on the college campus, on the high school football field, and throughout all grades of public and private schools. The tradition-laden ceremony of graduation and perhaps the half-step march to *Pomp and Circumstance* have meaning for the students, the school, and even the faculty. White graduation robes for kindergarten children completing their first school experience may be designed to tickle the emotional ribs of parents and friends, but little seems to accrue to the children. Conant (1959) raises such issues about other levels of graduation. The problem is to keep the traditions that contribute to the security of the students and to the meaning of the educational experiences while avoiding the exploitation of human personality.

Traditions can become anachronistic and empty forms. An ancient, honorable idea may be retained beyond its functional application in even an emotional sense. Again, a guidance person working with some near-retirement faculty members may be effectively prepared to help students to maintain traditions while avoiding meaningless obeisance to time past. There needs to be feeling and emotion in an education which appeals to the spirit and the mind of the student.

The *creation* of traditions is similarly an important issue in any school and sometimes crucial in a new school. Time has meaning for those who are insecure within their own period of existence. A new school with no tradition is often threatening to the student who feels bare and exposed to the things that he may fear because he does not understand. The student activity program within a free educational system is appropriately charged with the creation of meaning within the form of learning. The use of group process, within which the ideas and creativities of many can be harnessed, is a creative process that can contribute to education. Whether one attempts to use the ideas of "brainstorming," the attempt to create ideas while the critical or evaluative skill is turned off (Clark, 1958), or to hammer out a better way of doing an age-old task through the group process, democracy and education need to face the challenge of freedom—creativity.

SUMMARY

Student activities are a portion of the educational scene and provide an arena for learnings to occur that are different from but as significant as the academic and textbook data. The variegated, almost schizophrenic current scene of activities in education demands that a philosophical perspective be available to any group worker within the activities field.

The selection and training of leaders and skilled members is a task and a responsibility for an activity program. The quality and quantity of learning experiences within a school are dependent upon student skill in democratic problem solving.

School government is a co-ordinating, controlling, and central force in all student activities. The responsibilities of students, faculty members, and administrators are complex and demanding in school government, but necessary to the success of learning through performing.

Student activities of all types can be improved through the supervision of guidance persons whose training in counseling provides a balanced view of the skill and emotional factors in learning.

Traditions and the need for creative ideas are related aspects of similar problems in student activities. The privilege to be free and open in problem solving dictates that higher levels of operation be created through individual and co-operative effort.

SUGGESTED READINGS

Bellows, Roger, *Creative Leadership.* Englewood Cliffs, N. J.: Prentice-Hall, Inc., 1959.

Davis, Keith, and W. G. Scott, eds., *Readings in Human Relations.* New York: McGraw-Hill Book Co., 1959.

Freeman, G. L., and E. K. Taylor, *How to Pick Leaders.* New York: Funk and Wagnalls Co., 1950.

Gruber, F. C., and T. B. Beatty, *Secondary School Activities.* New York: McGraw-Hill Book Co., 1954.

Jones, Barbara, *Bennington College*. New York: Harper & Bros., 1946.

Kelly, J. A., *College Life and the Mores*. New York: Bureau of Publications, Teachers College, Columbia University, 1949.

Klopf, Gordon, *College Student Government*. New York: Harper & Bros., 1960.

Knowles, M., and H. Knowles, *How to Develop Better Leaders*. New York: Association Press, 1955.

McKown, H. C., *Extra-Curricular Activities* (3rd ed.). New York: The Macmillan Co., 1952.

Miller, F. A., J. H. Moyer, and R. B. Patrick, *Planning Student Activities*. Englewood Cliffs, N. J.: Prentice-Hall, Inc., 1956.

Newcomb, T. M., "The Cognition of Persons as Cognizers," in R. Tagiuri and L. Petrullo, eds., *Person Perception and Interpersonal Behavior*. Stanford, Calif.: Stanford University Press, 1958, 179–190.

Tead, Ordway, *The Art of Leadership*. New York: McGraw-Hill Book Co., 1935.

Tompkins, Ellsworth, "Evaluating the Work of the Student Council," in *The Student Council in the Secondary School: A Handbook for Student Councils and Their Sponsors*. Washington, D. C.: National Educations Association, 1955.

Weschler, Irving R., and J. Reisel, *Inside a Sensitivity Training Group*, Industrial Relations Monograph No. 4 Los Angeles: Institute of Industrial Relations, University of California at Los Angeles, 1959.

10. ARTICULATION AND ORIENTATION

"... and 'til then I had never actually thought about why I was in school. You know ... to wonder about why you are in school is very different from thinking about the what, how, when, and where. ...." The student who spoke these words, in a counseling session long after the opening of school, revealed an inquiring, active mind. Too frequently a concern about education does not exist in the complacent, happily adjusted student who has pat answers for all questions. Occasionally, some faculty members are even confused and concerned when they are asked, "Why do you teach?"

Education and learning can be exciting and rewarding ventures for students and faculty members. Young children are eager to enter kindergarten or first grade. They will vie for the right to play teacher and to conduct classes with their friends. High school students as well as college students are often jaded, blasé, and unconcerned about education and learning. Somewhere within the years of school a spark of fire has been lost; students wish only to endure and to be "taught."

The processes of orientation and articulation are designed to explore the meanings of education and to link into a meaningful whole the particular experiences that are education. Articulation is a more comprehensive concept, since it covers ending, beginning, and the in-between transition, while orientation is usually planned to help beginners.

Groups are practical and efficient tools for use in the process of exploring the meaning of education and the elements that comprise education. Group procedures may be used for various purposes and in startlingly different fashions according to the educationally constructed umbrella that covers the applications of groups. Various concepts of orientation and articulation that provide a foundation for the applications of groups in these areas need to be explored.

CONCEPTS OF ARTICULATION AND ORIENTATION

Climate is an important variable in learning. Pressures from psychological origins can be joined by uncertainties of a physical, mechanical, sociological or emotional nature to produce frustrations and blocking of the learning process. A free and open atmosphere for learning is the essential objective of any program of orientation or articulation. Groups within the educational process reflect the forces and pressures active in education and society (Olmstead, 1954). The educational environment and that of the surrounding society have impinging climates and pressures. Groups designed for learning may transmit such pressures; on the other hand effectively designed groups in education may provide a secure and accepting atmosphere and climate for effective learning.

Physical and mechanical concerns

The location of "cubbies" in kindergarten, or of lockers in a high school or college often seem to be the dominant worry of administrators and even guidance personnel in many schools. Added to these important elements of orientation and articulation are the problems of keys, combinations, gym suits, seat numbers, lunchroom assignments, and bus schedules. Strangely, it is true that academic schedules are also mechanical passes to the completion of a day in school. Without a schedule and a place to be at all times it may be possible for students to be unoccupied and untended. There is no question that many of these concerns and problems can be handled effectively through the use of groups. The waiting in line and the individual frustrations that seem a part of all institutional living are often reduced through the imaginative use of large and small groups to speed the administrative process.

The school personnel and students who are caught up in the tiring and unrewarding process of mechanically caring for hundreds and even thousands of students at the beginning of a school term are well aware of the importance of the little and large problems of accommodating a vast array of human beings for successive school terms. However, such concerns should not blind the educational staff of any school unit to the "Act of Faith" that is represented in the beginning of each academic year. School is the promise of society for the future, and its pledge is renewed on an annual basis.

Learning the culture of a world and inducting each student into the process of advancing that culture is the task of every school and of every teacher. The academics of any course and of any discipline are the means and tools of education. Certainly the impedimenta and technical elements of education need to be put in proper perspective at all times, particularly at the beginning—the time of reassessments and redirections of faculty members and students. Europeans often comment upon the "refrigerator and toilet" culture orientation of Americans; within the schools of a society roots should be established for the things that are truly significant.

Psychological and sociological concerns

Redl and Wattenberg (1959, p. 279) report upon the use of a small group for orientation purposes in an elementary school. A young child goes to school for the first time and is placed in a small group to enable him to respond to an atmosphere of freedom and understanding. The teacher, summarizing the boy's growth after a period of time in the group, commented upon the boy's good potential for the future if teachers could "cope with a very sensitive nature."

The mixture in American public schools of children from "across the tracks" with the children from "the hill" reveals vast gulfs between them in previous experiences and attitudes towards learning and education. Similarly there exists within each child from any subculture a potential to overcome his heritage and enhance himself, his parents and family, and even his neighborhood. The differences among children make every planned class of similar children a theoretical mockery. Yet, education must deal with groups of children that are similar in selected features or characteristics of personality, training, or capacity, or else education would need to be a process of individual tutoring.

Learning and education are emotional as well as intellectual operations. There is no question that guidance personnel as well as teachers must recognize the intimate and personal nature of changing behavior and acquiring knowledge. Education must also meet the challenge of the student who states:

> Our energies were drained by a week of singing, shouting, and security-making. And then they expected us to start classes with vim and vigor for learning (Eddy, 1959, p. 19).

Education and learning are not simple processes. The learners are as different from each other as the educators. The end product of education represents the integrated efforts of the partners in the process.

Education and learning

Orientation and articulation efforts must operate on the premise that learning and education are first values. Programs need to be supported and advanced with an awareness of psychological and sociological forces and made efficient through proper administration. Early views of education and learning stressed a rigid and cold view of the learning process. The rebellion against this concept fostered the development of orientation programs designed to promote psychological security and group morale. For many years it appeared as if there were to be no other concerns than the feelings of warmth and acceptance; academic concerns were almost forgotten.

Faculty members, students, and guidance persons have returned to an awareness of the importance of learning and of the academic curriculum. Orientation and articulation programs are now jointly concerned with the total learning situation as it exists on any educational level. The mind is not a muscle as some classicists had hoped; the student is not pure emotion as some reformers seemed to profess.

PREPLANNING AND ORGANIZATION

The quality of an orientation or articulation program is dependent upon the nature and the validity of the planning stage that must precede any actual programming. Administrators, faculty members, parents, student leaders, and the student body at large all have vested interest and must all be involved in a program of activities. A school guidance effort of any size and scope needs to take into account the variables of time, personnel, and integration of effort. Such concerns are involved in all levels of educational practice, from the elementary school pattern to the college program.

Time

The early part of the school year, the period when beginning experiences are still fresh and meaningful in the minds of students, is an effective period for the establishment of the orientation and articulation program for the succeeding year. New students in the seventh grade are still aware of their feelings as sixth graders looking forward to entering junior high school. Ninth graders in an eight-four system are similarly alert to problems. At all levels there are remembrances of problems, questions, hopes, and fears when a new school unit is entered.

The first steps of initiation of a program of orientation and articulation may be suggested by students, perceptive faculty members, or thoughtful administrators. School systems where records are not passed from school to school may have to begin by discussing even more fundamental issues. Parents are frequently involved in the confusions of relocation. The initiation efforts need to be supported by the guidance personnel within the school regardless of the source of the ideas. Guidance persons can similarly attempt to aid other persons within the system to recognize the problems that need to be faced and solved.

A single study group, or even a large number of study groups composed of representatives from many sources, can begin to explore problems and to develop partial ideas for their solution. Free exploration of potential activities is possible in a study group not charged with the development of detailed plans. The early appointment or election of such a study group can strengthen its potential for usefulness; a study group will feel pressed for time if there is a demand for an immediate, detailed report.

A planning committee can follow up the work of a study group. The study group will often recommend the make-up of a planning committee according to the ideas developed. The planning function in orientation and articulation is similar to the early stages of developing a training program. Decisions about a particular design, the specific activities that will be needed in order to implement a design, the selection of personnel, and other details will need to be determined. The planning phase is an outgrowth of the assessment period and it can merge with the early activities of articulation at the end of a school year. The orientation phase is the opening period of the next school year and in turn is followed by an evaluation and assessment period that leads directly into another planning phase. The cyclical nature of orientation and articulation is a strength that can aid in a smooth transition in the induction of new committee members and a rotating faculty representation.

Personnel

Students, parents, alumni, teachers, guidance personnel, and administrators can all be effectively employed in the development of a program of guidance in articulation and orientation. Fitzpatrick and Plattor (1958) describe a comprehensive program that involved all of these groups of persons. The plan, developed in the Plainview, New York, School District, provided for the seventh grade counselor to visit with the sixth graders in eleven classes in four elementary schools. Following these visits the guidance department of the district developed the detailed plan listed below as Phase I:

    1. The organization of meetings with the administration, faculty, students, and parents of both the elementary and junior high schools in order to determine needs, enlist support, develop ideas cooperatively, and prepare a series of classroom orientation activities.

    2. The composition of a handbook for sixth-grade students prepared with the co-operation of the art and audio-visual departments, the student council, and all interested faculty members and students.

    3. The creation of a handbook of study skills to be used in a series of lessons on study techniques in an effort to prepare the sixth-grade students for secondary school.

    4. The organization of a panel composed of junior high school students and the seventh-grade counselor to discuss the junior high school at assembly programs in the elementary schools.

    5. The preparation of an evening orientation meeting for parents of sixth-grade students.

    6. The initiation of an orientation program within the junior high school, utilizing the following techniques:

a. Visits by each sixth-grade student to the junior high school
b. Buddy system of visitation using seventh-grade students as guides
c. Conferences with groups visiting the junior high school to determine reactions
d. Group tours of the junior high school
e. Follow-up activities in June and September of the new term
f. Faculty meetings to establish class placement of sixth-grade students in the junior high school
g. Evaluation reports by teachers and students. (Fitzpatrick and Plattor, 1958, p. 155)

The community was so pleased with the program planned and carried out with the sixth and seventh graders that a second phase was developed for use with eighth and ninth grade pupils. The objectives of Phase II were stated as follows:

1. Assist pupils and their parents to understand the importance of considering each youngster's capacities, interests, and aptitudes in planning the high school program.

2. Familiarize the pupils with course offerings in the senior high school.

3. Plan tentatively a full four-year program for each individual pupil as well as select the ninth-grade elective courses in order to make goals clear and realistic.

4. Assist the administration to organize curricular and extracurricular offerings to meet individual needs. (pp. 158–159)

Specific orientation and articulation plans were developed to meet these objectives:

1. The organization of a program of group guidance in the eighth-grade classes

2. The composition of a handbook for eighth-grade students, describing course offerings and defining terminology used in planning a high school program

3. The preparation of an orientation meeting for parents of eighth-grade students

4. The provision for individual interviews to be held with each student and his parents for scheduling (p. 159)

The utilization of personnel from all levels and all sources is notable in this illustration of orientation and articulation in operation. Local newspapers co-operated with the program; parents, after being extended handwritten invitations, were enthusiastic supporters of all portions of the program. The authors who describe all of these activities considered the effort to be most worthwhile.

> The program has met with a tremendous degree of faculty, student, parent, and community support. (Fitzpatrick and Plattor, 1958, p. 161)

Integration of effort

It was evident in the description of the program of guidance at the Plainview School that virtually an entire pupil personnel program was constructed around the attempt to provide a meaningful unit for orientation. Counseling, testing, curriculum selection, vocational planning, classes using groups, large orientation meetings, and small group discussions were all co-ordinated with the major program. No mention of Phase III was made in the article, but an extension of the principles of the "inside" program was in a developmental stage so as to help bridge the gap between high school and college.

Many schools and colleges will be unable to provide such an extensive and thorough program for their own students. However, a significant element in any program will be the degree of internal consistency and integration of effort. Too frequently the effects of a dynamic, although small, program, are vitiated through an isolation from the remainder of the personnel or from the educational program of the school.

PROGRAMMING WITH GROUPS

A familiarity with the many variations of groupwork applications can provide for distinctive programs of aiding pupils to adjust to a change of school. The elements of a school program are diverse and offer many opportunities for creative planning and implementation. A cross section of a school program of any level would show activities that could be classified as follows:

1. Need assessment
2. Formal presentations
3. Psychological testing
4. Academic registration
5. Social activities
6. Parental involvement
7. School government efforts
8. Faculty-student activities
9. Academic orientation

Each of these areas will be examined briefly; specific suggestions for program planning and group utilization will be offered.

Need assessment

Earlier reference was made to the importance of allowing all students, particularly the new students, to participate in the planning and construction of an orientation program. Student ideas can be more authentic and literal than the second-level perceptions of teachers or administrators. Students need to have the freedom to express themselves without the fear of adult misunderstanding. Group discussions, particularly study groups in which evaluation is not stressed, are appropriate and effective in the assessment of student needs in any school. Seventh grade pupils often remind guidance persons of the importance of reaching down into the elementary school to work with sixth graders.

Homogeneous groups of students with student leadership, faculty groups with faculty leadership, and guidance personnel with counselor leadership can often tap problems that are not uncovered in heterogeneous assessment groups. Each pattern may be appropriate in a particular situation.

Formal presentations

Seldom is it possible to begin a school year without a greeting, an address, or a formal assembly to welcome, instruct, or to enlighten a group of pupils of any age level. There is little question that a large group meeting can be effective and contributory to the over-all objectives of a school program. However, well-trained speakers or specific group techniques are needed in order to provide a useful experience in many situations.

Panel presentations may serve to break the monotony of meetings with individual speakers. A panel, with a definite time limit, also helps to keep speakers of any administrative level more brief and to the point in their presentations. Written materials are often a proper substitute for formal meetings. A speech instructor of the author once said, "If it's so important that the audience cannot miss a word, it should be in written form so that it can be studied with leisure."

Audience participation is often a valuable addition to a formal meeting. The usual question and answer technique may be made more effective if audience members are provided with small three- by five-inch cards to write down the questions. Many a potential question has been lost because of the timidity of the questioner. The speaker may also screen the questions and spend his major effort on common issues. Buzz or "66" groups may also be employed to involve the audience in the questions at issue (Vinache, 1957).

Formal presentations are frequently more meaningful towards the end of a program. The participants have had an opportunity to experience what they have been told is "ahead of you." The actual completion of the program may make an audience much more receptive to the points to be stressed by a speaker. Conclusions and summaries are valuable and underscore the essential experiences after the fact, when meanings are more clear.

Psychological testing

Orientation usually means long hours of test taking for pupils entering a new school. The scientific demands of standardized conditions often blind the test administrators to the need for proper rapport with a large or small group in "test conditions." A simple and direct explanation of the purposes of the testing, the uses to which the results will be put, the values that will accrue to the students as a result of completing the tests, the relationship of the testing to the counseling and guidance program—these are but a few of the many issues that are important to the test takers. Simple courtesy and consideration for the feelings of pupils demands that such presentation be a portion of all test conditions.

Social breaks are important at the time of testing. The anxiety level of many students is very high during any testing, in spite of the efforts of the test administrator. A straightforward recognition of this fact suggests that test periods be spaced around and within other types of activities, particularly social activities.

A particularly valuable technique, one that helps to tie a testing program into a counseling and guidance program, is to involve the pupils in a questioning group session immediately after the conclusion of the test taking. Small discussion groups are organized on an arbitrary basis. Each group is charged with the compilation of questions and concerns that they may have as individuals and group members. The testing program usually taps a variety of student behaviors and the questions that arise are valuable for future class meetings, counseling sessions, or even student council actions. Reports may be taken in oral, written, or combination form.

> We organize leaderless group discussions immediately after our last testing session with the new sophomores. A recorder is selected arbitrarily (first or last person in alphabetical order), and we instruct the group members to list the questions they hope to have answered in the future. The groups are noisy, the climate confusing, but the students always release a lot of tension and anxiety in the process. We use the questions in later class sessions and the students always remember their feelings experienced during the testing period. (Director of testing, high school)

Academic registration

The feat of registering a pupil for a series of courses in high school is viewed by some teachers and administrators as similar to the feat of Frank Buck caging a Bengal tiger in the wild. The student may feel as if he had been staked and tied by the school. A large urban university once studied the number of times a student was required to write his name in four years of college—the resulting number was over three thousand! Doubtless the largest number of signatures was collected at registration time.

The long lines at colleges and universities are matched by the legal-appearing papers often signed in high school by parents and pupils and witnessed by a duly constituted administrator (and counselors?). The contrast is startling when such practices are compared with the following experience:

> My class in guidance in the eigth grade stressed the joint problems of self-assessment and curriculum choice. We studied abilities, interests, values, and the courses available in the last four years of high school. Each subgroup of pupils in the class was studying one of the curriculum choices available in the high school. The students were particularly interested in exploring the ultimate applications of the courses they were to choose at the end of the year. Their group

discussions were often spirited and I was needed to help answer various questions.

The student and parental conferences toward the end of the year were a revelation. . . . For the first time it seemed as if we were intelligently establishing a plan of education rather than filling in forms! (Eighth grade teacher)

Each faculty member was assigned to work with several small groups of students prior to the time of registration. We had staggered our registration period and it provided for the needed time for faculty members to meet with the groups of eight to ten new students. Sophomore students were used as "assistant leaders" and were very helpful to the faculty.

Our entire registration period was less rushed, frantic, and mechanical. The faculty reported that the new students were very interested in discussing their prospective programs. The sophomore students helped to link the new students and the faculty members together. We plan to use a variation of this technique in our forthcoming "pre-registration" process with upper class men. (Dean of students)

Our counselors are assigned to approximately three hundred incoming sophomores. Each counselor follows the group of students for three years, until graduation. The counselor is on a reduced teaching load for the sophomore and junior years and has no classes in the senior year. Course planning is covered during the group meetings in the sophomore and junior years.

The counselor's plans usually provide for homogeneous groups of students from each of the curricula available in the high school. Several counselors have experimented with mixed groups, groups with pupils drawn from all of the curricula. We do not insist on either method, but rather allow the counselors the freedom to develop their own plans. Some will bring in faculty members to discuss future courses; some will bring in persons from the community to help to place the courses in a vocational perspective. Our goal is the smooth and meaningful development of "plan sheets" (course programs) for each student. (Director of pupil personnel services; two high schools with over two thousand students in each school)

The examples cited could be duplicated, or variations could be presented according to the locale of the school, the educational level involved, and the creativity present in the planning group.

Social activities

An informal coffee hour, a coke and cookie period, a punchbowl hour, or even an "ice water" break can add a distinct dimension to any crowded program of school activities.

The Graduate School of Industrial and Labor Relations at Cornell University once boasted of the centrally located "coffee-break period room." Students, faculty, even visiting labor leaders from foreign countries, were to be found in the room at all times of the day and night. A college sociology department, unhappy in their academic lot, once advertised in a humorous fashion, "have coffee pot, will travel."

Specialists in human relations have often written about the value of an informal social period wherein persons of all levels of importance and status may be together. The break in time and the increased opportunities to know and appreciate other members of a joint enterprise are the values attributed to such activities. The actual coffee or soft drinks are incidental. They serve as a cue to relaxation or a more informal atmosphere. Conversation, particularly in groups with new members, is easier under these circumstances.

The large insurance office or manufacturing concern that brings coffee in to the worker and yet wonders why the workers still stop to talk together and wander around visiting, have missed the essential psychological meaning of the coffee break. Higher echelon directors complete their business at lunch—or long coffee breaks; human relations business is accomplished in any planned, supervised, and well-designed social break.

Sociability, learning to know new classmates, or sharing a last hot dog or formal dinner are all significant elements in an orientation or articulation program within any school. The personal nature of all learning, particularly between student and faculty persons, underscores the importance of socially based interactions. Program planners need to create "coffee break" periods in which faculty members, students, and administrators can participate.

> Our college orientation program has always started with a "coffee and cocoa hour." The students are invariably somewhat shocked by the opportunity to share a cup of coffee or cocoa with their future teachers. They learn to know the faculty members as persons. The same faculty members often "pour it on" in the first class with a heavy assignment. The students learn to realize that faculty members are human and yet are also taskmasters. (College dean)

High school and elementary school faculty members are more hesitant to meet their students on equal social footing. Elementary school teachers often will complain about "lunchroom duty" and plead that they eat often enough with their students. The essential feature of a shared social hour is the equal status nature of the contact. Planned luncheons, cookie breaks, afternoon teas, morning coffee hours and similar activities are possible from the first grade upwards. The creative kindergarten teacher is very willing to share a "tea party" with her students, and will angrily attack anyone who denies that she enjoys it and says that she is not on an equal status with her pupils. The college instructor and the kindergarten teacher are willing to assume equality with students on a social basis. Perhaps teachers at other levels may find it both profitable and fun to come out of the teachers' dining room and sit down together or stand up together with students. Daily practice is certainly not desirable; the beginning and the ends of the academic year are particularly appropriate times for invitations.

Parental involvement

Parents' night at the local school is a tradition in many schools. The opportunity to visit the classroom, sit in Johnny's or Sally's chair, listen and watch the teacher, are valuable contributions to school community morale. Some colleges provide for parents to attend a day's classes with their freshman sons and daughters. The Plainview School District emphasized the role of parents in a comprehensive plan of orientation and articulation. MacKay (1958) describes a specific plan for including the parents in the process of a senior high school orientation program. He used group discussions designed to provide information and understanding about the curriculum, vocational and educational opportunities, and other school activities. Parents reported very real satisfaction with the opportunity to become informed. Other examples follow:

> Our college established a series of parent-student conferences with a guidance counselor prior to the opening of college. Seven to ten students were invited and required to bring one or both parents to the conference. The results were very rewarding. The counselors, the students, and particularly the parents were pleased with the outcome. (College counseling bureau director)

The parents in our high school responded with tremendous enthusiasm when we invited them to attend a series of college planning sessions with their sons and daughters. We tried to "section" the parents and students according to their selections of a potential college, technical school, business school, or other type of post-secondary institution, but . . . we had problems. One mother unintentionally crushed a father when she politely asked, "Where is Harvard?" We hope to iron out some of the "bugs" for our next year's program. However, we believe that it is very desirable to bring the parents in on the total planning. (Director of guidance, high school)

Our college prepares a "handbook" for parents. The problems of adjustment in college are often complicated by parent-child relations. The handbook helps students and parents. (Urban university)

Student government periods

The officers, members, and committee personnel within a student government all welcome an opportunity to participate in the program of orientation and articulation. Relegating to students the somewhat obsequious roles of guides and traffic officers denies the realistic contributions that are possible from a student-sponsored presentation.

Certain church groups start the younger children on a speaking career very early in their lives. A portion of the church period is devoted to hearing their reports and contributions. With training, school pupils of all ages become capable of presenting ideas, rules, procedures, advantages, and dangers of school activities.

The importance of speaking to the incoming, the outgoing, or even the returning student body is a major thrill for any student government officer. A panel of committee chairmen can stir a considerable degree of initiative and drive in new students for a school activity program.

The essential item in aiding students to help students is preparation for the actual meeting. Students need to be free to construct their own concepts of what is important and what needs to be offered. Faculty aid, with the light touch, is needed, but not faculty domination and control.

Faculty-student activities

The social activities periods recommended earlier are possible and desirable in student affairs, joint student-faculty programs, or even student, faculty, and administrative mixing. The importance of the faculty-student relationship in the learning process also puts a premium on the early establishment of a serious working, interpersonal relationship. Brief tryout courses reached a peak of popularity in the late 1920's or early 1930's. More effective relationships depend upon long-term mutual concerns of students and faculty.

Pupil personnel workers or counselors recognized the need for them to report a week before the opening of school and to remain a week after school closes. College personnel persons often are on eleven-month contracts because of the nonclass needs of students. The opportunity and even the necessity of bringing in regular teaching faculty members to meet and talk with students before and after the regular school period is not simply a desire to make others sacrifice their own time. The efforts of the entire school or college are needed in beginning or ending a school year.

Small group discussions between new students and faculty members are profitable periods for all participants. The new students respond to the informal, nonacademic nature of the meetings; the faculty are able to greet new students and to explain the rationale and nature of the courses that lie ahead. Upper class students can serve as assistant leaders and are valuable in conducting their own orientation of new students.

> Our school schedules small faculty-student orientation conferences for an hour during the week before school opens. All of the subject-matter teachers are involved in the program and meet with four to five groups. Each faculty member is involved for a total period of approximately a day. Their initial reactions were those of protest because of the extra time and the need to come in for a special day. They have responded very well to the program in recent years and have come to expect that they will be asked to participate. (College)

Many school systems have an integrated program of visits from upper level schools to lower grades and to separate (elementary or junior high schools) school units. Colleges often employ special visitors and traveling counselors. There is no question that proper design of programs of recruitment or admissions interviewing within high schools is a needed guidance function. Certain colleges employ a huckster type of traveling salesman, but most high schools frown on such practices.

Career days and nights are beginning to lose favor in most high schools because of the high-pressure nature of some programs. Even in well-designed events there is little time for careful exploration and assessment on the part of the college or the high school. More effective practices are replacing these fading programs in most communities. High schools are scheduling, on a continuing basis, group sessions to coincide with the visits of admissions interviewers, employment personnel, and other post-secondary school representatives.

Colleges, technical schools, employment interviewers and other representatives of nonpublic school institutions recognize the public relations values and actual importance of "extension-type" guidance practices. Public high school and junior high school guidance personnel may well observe and recognize the same need within their own school systems. Administrators in a co-ordinated educational system will perceive the need to smooth the transitions in enrollment and to match more effectively pupils with school programs. When a school system retains permanent records in elementary or junior high school, it may be unrealistic to hope for a planned program of faculty-student conferences between school units, particularly at the beginning of a school year. Such programs are, however, practiced in many outstanding schools, attesting to their value and practical nature.

Academic orientation

Programs for aiding students to acclimate themselves more effectively to the academic requirements of a school are not new. Alltucker (1924) describes a plan of counseling aid to bridge the gap between junior and senior high school that contains features still applicable and practical in today's schools.

Recent efforts at "freshman week" or periods of orientation on any level have often been inclined to ignore the essential importance of the academic attitude in any guidance or orientation program. Older philosophical concepts stressed that, "Guidance would deliver the student to class, ready to learn!" The academic aspect has more recently been recognized as the vital force in any program of orientation and articulation. Guidance personnel need the aid of faculty members in orienting students.

Efforts of departments, such as the English department (Whalen, 1946), the physical education department, or even the solitary efforts of a principal or a superintendent are inadequate to the task, just as the guidance department is unable to succeed in isolation. The flavor of a total school effort may be obtained from the following brief reports of practices in two different situations.

The elementary school team for the fifth and sixth grades made the most outstanding contribution to our academic orientation efforts.

Our "team group" included a "career teacher," two regular teachers, a new teacher, and a nonprofessional teachers' aide. This group was assigned to 120 pupils. The team, as a group, planned and carried on three days of "academic orientation."

The total group was scheduled for a series of major presentations by three of the teachers. Following each of the three presentations (on three different days) there were class periods in which a series of small group discussions were supervised by the teachers. Other activities included: motion pictures with question and answer periods following; panel presentations by selected and prepared groups of sixth graders to the fifth graders; and demonstration of much of the academic work that was to be covered in the succeeding terms. (Elementary school)

Efforts such as this in an advanced school program are aided by the availability of newer type buildings, creative administrative patterns of education, and dedicated, skilled teachers. Variations may be seen in many schools that are attempting experimental approaches to learning and education (Clinchy, 1960a, 1960b).

A simpler and perhaps more easily accomplished scheme was completed by a college faculty on a school-wide basis:

The faculty voted to schedule a two-week orientation and introduction unit in each department for all freshmen. Every department established a two-week introductory unit designed to show the students in the course the importance and meaning of the subject matter. The interrelationships of all of the courses were stressed and no department attempted to sell its own program "long" and others "short."

The program was very uneven on the first attempt. Some departments dragged their feet and others were too ambitious. The most valuable portion of the program was the stress placed upon the interrelationships of all of the courses. The students reacted most favorably to this element of the orientation period.

Since the first year, we have kept the concept of college-wide orientation to the curriculum but we have reduced the time to about one week, two or three class meetings.

PATTERNS OF PROGRAMMING

School systems as well as colleges and universities will vary in the particular pattern of orientation and articulation presented. The uses of groups in each pattern will vary and follow the basic decisions that will be made in terms of total design. Three major types of programs are common in all levels of education:

1. The "Big Push"
2. Extended Courses
3. Integrated Learnings

The "big push"

The overwhelming popularity of the concept of "Freshmen Week" on the college level has dominated the orientation practices on all educational levels. The idea that all problems could be solved within a few days was most appealing, even to elementary school personnel. Formal greetings, speeches, psychological testing, social activities, faculty-student conferences, even leadership training programs, have all been crammed into a few days in many school programs. The reactions of students have finally influenced administrators in taking a second look at the problems. The mental, physical, and emotional exhaustion that accompanies such programs has been greatly underestimated.

New practices have been reported by several sources (Greene, 1954; Froe and Lee, 1956; and Hoffman and Plutchik, 1959 a and b; Drake and Remy, 1955; and Fitzpatrick and Plattor, 1958). Psychological testing has been spread over a much longer period of time. Academic orientation and a concern for the basic issues in education has taken precedence in many schools. The small group discussions between students and faculty members have been a more successful approach to orientation problems. The low key or informal atmosphere that can exist in small groups along with meaningful learning experiences are among the primary reasons for the more extended use of such techniques. Grier (1951, 1954) outlines the use of such groups and the integration of them with individual counseling. Lloyd-Jones stresses the educational values of such an approach in Hoffman and Plutchik (1959) by saying:

> Orientation through small-group development . . . is, in reality, higher education in some of its more creative aspects. (Lloyd-Jones, 1959, p. x)

Student involvement in school opening procedures has often helped to build effective programs. Student government committees have taken over the task of writing to students during the summer months and often have assumed responsibility for the assignment of an upper classman to each new lower classman. These schemes are certainly related to the older concept of the "big brothers and big sisters," but are considerably more flexible, sophisticated, and appropriate. Also, creative development is encouraged by the freedom given students to pattern their own programs.

Extended courses

The unsatisfactory nature of the intensive period of orientation at the beginning of the school year led to the development of orientation through individual courses. Subject-matter courses and special orientation courses spread throughout the first half-year have been scheduled in junior high school, senior high school, and college. Similar college problem courses, under the titles of sociology, family living, or life adjustment, have been offered across the country. Borow and Lindsey (1959), Martinson (1959), Hoffman and Plutchik (1959 a and b), as well as Glanz and Walston (1958), are variations of these patterns on the higher educational level. Nelson (1942) evaluated the college programs almost a generation ago. The problems he found have been solved in many cases, yet some of the same student problems still exist.

The line between an orientation course and a guidance course is a very difficult distinction to make. Chapter 14 will examine this problem in complete detail.

Integrated learnings

An approach to orientation and articulation that has much to commend it has been the integrated core program or, as it is more commonly known today, the team approach. Groups of from seventy-five to one hundred and fifty students have been organized within one grade level and from several different grade levels. Learning is allowed to progress as a more natural process. Students are free to progress more in accord with their abilities and interests rather than being bound by artificial grade barriers.

Team teaching has additional strength in the decentralization of responsibility and authority for orientation and articulation. The individual teams have often been given much freedom in constructing and organizing the beginnings, ends, and often even the units of the courses. Foundations have been generous in their support of such projects; the results are beginning to be available from all levels of educational operation. The future appears even brighter in this area than in any other.

SUMMARY

Orientation and articulation in education may be viewed as problems of physical, mechanical, psychological, sociological, or educational adjustment. A comprehensive view of these problems is basic to a meaningful beginning for all students.

The planning and organization of an orientation and articulation program is fundamental to its ultimate success. Group construction of a program design can provide for the total contribution of all concerned persons.

Group procedures in any type of orientation and/or articulation may be programmed according to local needs. Specific group methods can be used in formal presentations, psychological testing, academic registrations, social activities, parents' programs, student government contributions, joint faculty-student activities, and academic course introduction. Principles and examples of practice are offered in each of these areas. A broad summary of various programming patterns closes the chapter.

SUGGESTED READINGS

Alltucker, M. M., "A Counseling Plan for Bridging the Gap Between the Junior and Senior High Schools," *School Review*, 32, 1924, 60–66.

Cortright, R. L., and G. L. Hinds, *Creative Discussion*. New York: The Macmillan Co., 1959.

Dixon, F. B., and O. G. Thompson, "Freshmen Orientation Practices," *School Activities*, 16, 1944, 3–5, 20.

Eddy, Edward D. Jr., *The College Influence on Student Character*. Washington, D. C.: American Council on Education, 1959.

Hoffmann, R. W., and R. Plutchik, *Controversy*. New York: G. P. Putnam's Sons, 1959.

Kelley, Janet A., *College Life and the Mores*. New York: Teachers College, Columbia University, 1949.

Koos, L. V., *Integrating High School and College*. New York: Harper & Bros., 1946.

Sharp, O. Louise, ed., *Why Teach*. New York: Holt, Rinehart & Winston, Inc., 1957.

Voeks, Virginia, *On Becoming An Educated Person*. Philadelphia: W. B. Saunders Co., 1957.

Wells, H. G., *Babes in the Darkling Wood*. New York: Alliance Book Corp., 1940.

11. USE OF PSYCHOLOGICAL TEST DATA

Psychological test data provide one of the major sources of information for use in a guidance and counseling program. Test data are used at every level of educational practice and few, if any, educators are uninvolved in the application of tests in education. The prestige and status of tests in psychology and education veil some of the basic questions which need to be faced and resolved as any test instrument is used in a school system.

Many counselors and guidance persons, as well as parents, teachers, and administrators, have often felt that psychological test results are much less useful than they are supposed to be. The test data may frequently help the teacher, the counselor, or the principal; however, they may be of little value to the student. Rothney (1958, p. 90), after a detailed eight-year developmental study of guidance procedures, concludes:

> Observation of the problems . . . in this study suggested that tests are of considerably less value than publishers would have us believe.

Rothney seems unafraid of saying, "The Emperor has no clothes on!" There is no question that tests have uses other than helping students; however, the cost in terms of time and money would seem to dictate that tests ought *also* to be valuable to students.

Conflicting views about the application of psychological test data are widely known but seldom admitted in many school situations. An examination of the representative views of several writers can help to isolate and reveal the problems. Cronbach (1960) is a widely used text (revised edition) in graduate courses in psychological test usage. Some of his basic ideas are as follows:

> Tests play an important part in making decisions *about* people. . . . (p. 8, italics added)

> Tests provide facts which help *us* to understand people. . . . (p. 9, italics added)

> Tests are useful to many professions, but in the hands of persons with inadequate training they do a great deal of harm. (p. 9)

Cronbach's ideas are not different from those of most well-trained and professionally oriented test users. Anastasi (1960), R. L. Thorndike and Hagen (1955), and other text writers also take these positions.

Effective self-interpretation of test data by students is a relatively new concept in most schools. Students have long been told their percentile scores, quartile standings, or other derivative data about their performances; however, student use of test results based upon an understanding of interpretation processes is less common. This new stress on *student use* of test results is exemplified in several recent publications:

> Therefore, an effort has been made to propose a properly safeguarded, but practical and simple, method of using test scores and marks for *pupils' appraisals of their abilities.* (Katz, 1959b, p. 14, italics added)

> The entire outline of the self-analysis essay has provided an opportunity *for students to draw together* their knowledge of themselves. (Glanz and Walston, 1958, p. 212, italics added)

> . . . knowledge of these four (test) areas should provide you with an adequate basis for self-appraisal. (Martinson, 1959, p. 42)

> The best kind of guidance consists in helping you to learn how to analyze your particular problems and to reach your own decisions. (Mahoney and Engle, 1961, p. V)

Students in these programs are using test results in group situations to increase their understanding of themselves. They are building upon a knowledge of measurement principles and interpreting data for their own use. Individual students, particularly junior high school students, are not deemed experts in test interpretation, but they are recognized as one of the most important consumers of test results.

Student understanding of test data depends upon their personal involvement in the process of interpretation. The achievement of meaning by students results from an understanding of patterns of facts and related data, not upon the listing or codification of isolated bits of information. This type of comprehension by students cannot be obtained in a single test interpretation interview; detailed prior involvement is necessary. Some research results are equivocal (Gustad and Tuma, 1957), but other data arising from programs of this type seem to support this conclusion (Gribbons, 1960; Glanz, Calia, and Smith, 1962). The actual value of tests to students and to counselors (in counseling with students) would seem to be closely related to the methods utilized in helping students to understand the data.

The appropriate utilization of psychological test data in a counseling and guidance program rests upon several basic assumptions: the philosophical premises of a program of psychological testing, training for consumers in principles of measurement, effective application of group principles in aiding students to apply test data to themselves, and an integrated approach to the use of tests and test data in a counseling program. Each of these concepts will be examined in turn in the succeeding pages.

A PHILOSOPHY OF PSYCHOLOGICAL TESTING

The actions of a person, a school system, or a program of counseling and guidance may be partially predicted and understood only as the basic beliefs underlying the actions are examined. A registrar of a small women's college in the East once told the author that she had two jobs: "I have to collect and maintain accurate data, and I have to see that they are properly and creatively used. The first task can be done by an intelligent compulsive . . . the second job is by far the most important and challenging responsibility!"

Apocryphal, perhaps, but the story of the school principal who had his office walls covered with graph paper and recorded every student's "IQ" in an appropriate block, also reveals an attitude too frequently present in some schools.

Professionally trained persons can insure accurate and effective administration and scoring of psychological tests. Persons qualified in such tasks are often not skilled in training faculty members and students to be able to use the same data. Yet, how useful would millions of new automobiles be if there were no drivers who could use them. Tests for any psychological and educational purpose must be looked upon as instruments which demand not only professional administration and scoring, but also professional assistance to students in learning from such data.

Teachers, counselors, and students were often used in the past as clerical workers to score, profile, and record all data. As test use was developed into a professional aid to schools, scoring was relegated to a machine and the recording of data to electronic devices. Enlightened administrators (superintendents or guidance directors) have long since recognized that the cost of outside scoring, profiling and recording should be considered as initial costs of a testing program. Many downtrodden teachers and counselors, still overburdened with such tasks, would plead that such service be listed in all test catalogs as part of the cost per person for the test.

The freedom that has been gained through the use of test-scoring machines has allowed counselors and guidance persons to spend more time with students helping them to understand the results of the tests. However, philosophy and technique in test interpretation have not kept pace with the mechanical genius of the electronic age. Many counselors have been left with the standard technique of interpreting a percentile to students who, in spite of a counselor's admonition, insist upon translating percentiles into percentages, or tend to see test scores as "revealed truth." Newer approaches are demanded, as the time to help students is now available. Group approaches can supply new techniques.

GROUP CONSUMER TRAINING

... and then it looked as if I should plan to become a farmer. You know I have never even seen a farm!

I think I agree with Dad; all of this business is a bunch of junk.

She told me that I should become a lawyer ... she said that I was high in "persuasiveness."

The scores on the "SAT" of the college boards seem to be all they care about.

These words have haunted every experienced guidance worker and counselor. Careful interpretation of test data seems sometimes to fall upon deaf ears and preconceived notions about what tests can do. Students, parents, many teachers, and some counselors are unable to understand the application of test results. Twice the author has had phone calls from a person in the community asking: "Do you give the test?" The first call was disconcerting until the person explained patiently, "the test that tells you what to do." The second phone call was easier to handle.

Happily, many students are now becoming so "test wise" that they are beginning to understand the frailties and distortions of tests. Skilled aid to students can allow them to enter into the interpretation process, to become knowledgeable and co-operative in aiding in the clarification of data meaning in tests. Poorly skilled counselors may find that present-day students, having taken the Otis, the Kuder, or the Strong many times, are better able than the counselor to understand the results as they apply (or do not apply) to life. The change in individual student reaction depends upon personal experiences and pupil aptitude for learning the facts and interpretative skills. Students can become involved in such learnings through groups. The following quotations are drawn directly from student papers, "Self-Analysis Essays" written as part of a required guidance course:

Vocational interests form different patterns for each individual. A vocational pattern will naturally fall into an area where there has been some previous enjoyment or experience. My Kuder profile on the test data sheet reveals that my strongest areas of interest lie in Social Service, Scientific and Persuasive. These are areas that I have found most enjoyable in the past because of their affiliation with people. It was within my ability to help these people, and in return I received a great deal of self-satisfaction. My part-time hobbies have consisted of donating my time to older people at the Boston Dispensary and working with children at the West Newton Community Center. From these experiences and my service time, I have concluded that I must work with people, preferably with those who have physical and psychological problems. A physical therapist must contend with problems similar to these, and must be motivated in every way to help correct them. (Glanz and Walston, 1958, p. 310)

Concerning my intelligence and scholastic aptitudes, I only have two bits of information to submit. This is simply because the results of my tests taken during and prior to Orientation Week were somehow lost in the shuffle. I feel compelled to say that this is not meant as a swing at the administration, it is not intended as such.

The two bits of information mentioned are the results of the California Mental Maturity and Snader General Math examinations. The results are as follows:

CALIFORNIA MENTAL MATURITY

	Raw Score	General Population %ile
N.L.	36	40
L.	36	70
Total	72	60

SNADER GENERAL MATH

R.S.	12th Grade %ile
112	85

In my opinion, without any flattery, my intelligence and scholastic aptitude are about average. The problem lies, if anywhere, in the application of these two. (Glanz and Walston, 1958, pp. 318–319)

Student involvement

Students need to be involved in the interpretation and understanding of the test results which can aid them in planning for their own futures. Group procedures in junior high school as well as at higher levels can help to train students in the interpretation of their own test scores. Many a prospective counselor or guidance worker has been dismayed by the prospect of understanding the principles of measurement in graduate school courses. How then may students in the eighth grade, or even somewhat older students, learn such principles?

Test results need to be viewed as facts: facts which can help in the thinking process; not powerful or mysterious forces which can make decisions for students. The processes of self-evaluation and choice of educational areas are constantly varying and shifting developmental patterns. A decision is not made in an instant of time. The problem of aiding youngsters in the eighth grade to learn principles of measurement and to understand the process of self-planning is a complex issue. Katz (1959b, p. 14) tackles the problem directly:

> The purpose of all this is not to give students a course in statistics. However, even without being exposed to "reliability," "standard error of measurement," "validity," and "norm groups," pupils can learn that a mark or a test score can best be interpreted not as a single, exact point on a scale, but in terms of the area or band in which it occurs; that predictions from marks and tests can more confidently be expressed in terms of broad but meaningful probabilities than in terms of precise certainties; and that comparisons, to be less than odious, must be made with an appropriate or relevant group.

And further, talking about the eighth grade student using such an approach:

> Many of the concepts in this book (*You: Today and Tomorrow*, Katz 1959) are admittedly difficult . . . so are many of the concepts in mathematics, language, art, science, and other courses.

Katz has supplied one area for a meaningful content in a "group guidance" course. He supplies many other concepts to be used by eighth and ninth grade students. He assumes that the teacher or the counselor responsible for conducting the group experience will "find ways to get across the key concepts and will be rewarded in watching the changes that occur as students grow in self-understanding, knowledge, and ability to plan." Perhaps Katz is optimistic, but group techniques do exist for involving students, and with a content such as he offers, the group-oriented teacher, counselor, or guidance worker can be off and running with specific approaches. Such goals are not dreamy or unpractical. Gribbons (1960) specifically evaluates the techniques offered by Katz (1959a), and Katz and Shimberg (1960) offer detailed data on a study of such procedures on a nation-wide scale. Glanz, Hayes, and Penney (1959) describe such a program on a college level and Glanz, Calia, and Smith (1962) evaluate it on a school-wide basis.

Involvement methods

Guidance and counseling procedures designed to involve students in a determination of their own futures can be drawn from the best practices of counseling and group work. Group procedures in a class; group approaches in orientation programs; specifically planned discussion groups preceding the availability of test results; case study discussions (problem-solving type, task groups) working with actual data; group discussions about individual members (tricky and dangerous, but possible); and trained, available, understanding counselors are specific approaches which can involve students in the process of self-planning and demonstrate the respect for students in which counselors and guidance persons believe.

A description from an actual group situation demonstrates the delicate interweaving of counseling, group techniques, and a program of involvement of students:

Don was in a course designed to help him develop plans for his own future. It was a guidance course which met regularly as a class, and during alternate weeks the students were formed into discussion groups. Principles of measurement and techniques of test interpretation had been presented in lecture; specific reading assignments had been completed from readings appropriate for his level of understanding. A specially prepared profile of test results had been distributed to all students. The group discussions were all centered on a case study of a boy facing similar problems to the members of the group.

Don was quiet in the early stages of the discussion of the case. The group assessing the appropriateness of the subject's ability and intelligence for a stated goal of law training. Don interrupted the discussion and entered his opinions in heated fashion:

"I don't think those tests are worth a damn!"

The group was startled by his intense feeling and all discussion ceased.

Don continued, "I don't care what the test results show. If Jim (the subject of the case) has the determination and the drive to get ahead, I think that he can do the job and get to law school."

The counselor-group leader suddenly began to be aware of the problem Don was facing. Don wanted to become a lawyer and perhaps the case was coming too close to home. The counselor wondered about Don's own test scores. He was uncertain of exact scores, but he felt certain that Don's scores were not nearly as low as the subject of the case study.

The group continued its discussion and some members began to disagree with the position Don was defending. They stressed the importance of scholastic aptitude and intelligence in completing the many years of college and law school which lay ahead for the prospective lawyer. Other students supported Don's position.

Don was alternately vehement and morose. He argued with emotion. The counselor-group leader noticed that he was perspiring, was agitated, moved constantly in his seat, and kept looking at a sheet of paper. The paper was Don's own test profile about which he evidently had been stewing. The counselor-group leader was leery of what would happen. Don was so emotionally wrought up that his ability to continue with the discussion was questionable. Suddenly Don spoke very sharply and with definitely hostile implications directed toward the group leader.

"Look at my profile. . . ." Don showed all of the seven members of the group his sheet. He held it longest in front of the leader. "You can't tell me that this stuff means anything. Look at what my score is. I am not that low; even if I am that low, I know that I want to get to law school and that I am going to do it."

The fat was in the fire, and the leader could either stop the group and handle the problem individually with Don later, or allow the group to attempt to handle the problem. The leader decided to permit the discussion to continue. Don quickly withdrew from the discussion and was somewhat chagrined after his outburst.

A few of the group leaped into the fray and began to point out to Don that he would have trouble in getting to law school, just as the subject of the case study would. Other members of the group rose to the defense of Don. They espoused his case. Don became very quiet.

Suddenly one of the members of the group who seldom spoke pointed out: "Your profile shows that you are above average in the 'language' portion of the test and below average in the 'non-language' part." The group picked up this clue and pointed out that 'language' or verbal ability was much more important than 'non-language' or non-verbal ability.

The counselor had not said anything since Don's outburst. The tension level of the group was high throughout the episode; as the stress increased on the members, they became more careful of their manner and of particular discussion points. Courtesy and care were the pattern of discussion. The group members had correctly diagnosed the situation and were reacting in an understanding and accepting fashion.

Don said very little during the remainder of the meeting. He valiantly attempted to participate; however, he was emotionally spent. The group broke up, as the time of the period was over. The members left in a reserved manner, somewhat uneasy. The leader spoke to Don quietly as he was leaving. "Don, would you stop in to talk with me after the last class?"

Don agreed, and the counselor studied the counseling folder on Don. The group had been right. Don's scores on the "language" portion of the California Mental Maturity had placed him in the third quarter, well above average; his score on the "non-language" sections was definitely below average in the second quarter and near the twenty-fifth percentile.

A non-routine counseling session followed the last class. Don explored all of his feelings and expressed the same ones he had displayed in the group meeting. He was alternately hostile, depressed, argumentative, and withdrawn. The counseling session was successful in helping Don to begin to accept various positive and negative aspects of himself. Don continued in the class, the group, and in counseling sessions. He progressed rapidly in all areas and was a leader among the student group. Several weeks after the explosion, Don was able to look back upon his behavior and laugh.

Don's problem and his handling of it, the skill of the group, Don's academic success, and his growing maturity were rewarding. Many situations may not work themselves out so satisfactorily. However, it clearly illustrates the interdependency of the elements of group work, counseling, and the content and process of each. An analysis of the many crisis points reveals the delicate judgment that must be exercised by the person who attempts to work with students in an emotionally loaded situation. The cohesiveness of the group, the ability of the other students to empathize in a communicating fashion with Don, the motivational factors that were driving Don, the particular problem-solving phase in which the group found itself (building upon previous knowledge and interpreting new information), the follow-up of the class situation with a discussion group, the counseling which followed the group—these elements of groups, groupwork, guidance, counseling, and test data demonstrate most of the issues that are important in the involvement of students in the process of learning.

MEASUREMENT PRINCIPLES AS GROUP CONTENT

A knowledge of measurement principles and an appreciation of individual differences are significant elements in the involvement of students in the interpretation of their own test results. A skilled counselor needs considerable time to help students place their test results within a framework of conceptual knowledge which contradicts their previously learned expectations about the exactness of a science of numbers. Many students in test interpretation interviews are so emotionally involved in a defense, or fancied defense, of their own self-concept that such instruction falls upon deaf ears. Instruction in the concepts necessary for test data understanding needs to precede the actual communication of the personalized data to the student.

Group experiences in a regular classroom, or in specially designed task groups, can provide the actual learning experiences which must precede and surround any individual fact of test data. The content for such task groups can be drawn from known areas of measurement and statistics. The degree of detail offered in such a program will need to vary with the educational level of the students and their potential to incorporate such learnings. Regardless of the level of the group or the capacity of individual members, there are basic concepts that must be offered and treated.

Individual differences

Students know well the basic principles of individual differences, but they need to place such factual information into an organized pattern. The following samples of instructional materials are drawn from several levels of group educational practice.

> Some [athletes] are "naturals." There are probably some others who excel in one or two sports, but don't have the same all-around ability. For example, the best runner or jumper on the track team may not be a good baseball or tennis player. (Katz, 1959a, p. 13)

Examples can be drawn from many areas of activity that are common to all students. Abilities in art, music, dancing and various academic subjects are well within the everyday ken of each student. Mixing test concepts and everyday life, Katz (1959a, p. 27) continues:

> There are good artists who are weak in mathematics, good mechanics who may not have strong verbal ability, people with "green thumbs" who might not pass the college preparatory course, and so on.

High school students are more capable of understanding the concept of individual differences and of strengthening their own background of conceptual information. Mahoney and Engle (1961) approach the problem of supplying information in the following fashion as they write for students in the later years of high school in their book, *Points For Decision:*

Thus you can see that intellectual ability is a complex quality. To get a better understanding of it we will go on to the question of how much your ancestry and your environment affect your make-up. (p. 18)

And:

It does mean that your score was higher than the score made by sixty-five per cent of the large group used in standardizing the test. (Standardizing is the procedure described above—giving the test to a large number of individuals to determine what can be considered "standard" or "average" performance.) (p. 27)

Statistical concepts

Many counselors and teachers may begrudgingly agree to treat individual differences as a topic for students; however, such ideas are only a prelude to more sophisticated principles which must be presented to students. Knowledge of statistical concepts must be available to individual students or the test information will become so much flotsam and jetsam drifting within the minds of counselees. Measurement concepts have frightened many prospective counselors, group leaders, and teachers. Robert L. Thorndike clearly reported on a city-wide survey in which simple mathematical questions were asked as a part of the study; he humorously raised the question as to whether or not there existed a national neurotic reaction to quantitative concepts. Test users, counselors, group leaders, and teachers have no choice; test data can only be understood within a framework of ideas which are quantitatively based.

Students often acquire their dislike for mathematical or statistical concepts from their parents' dislike of the same, or their teachers' discomfort in handling such data. A refreshing approach is offered as these concepts are being taught in the eighth or ninth grade. Again Katz is quoted as he writes for a junior high school population:

But suppose you score between the 26th and 45th percentiles on verbal ability (3rd quarter of population sample). And suppose you get passing English marks but not high ones (3rd quarter of your class). What do these facts tell you? Do they mean you can't succeed in the same subjects? No, but they mean your chances may not be so good unless you make up for lower verbal ability in other ways. . . . (Katz, 1959a, p. 21)

Students need not be made into research statisticians. The concepts which need to be treated with students can be offered within an apperceptive framework. Educators are often surprised by the extent of student knowledge of baseball statistics, concepts, and data manipulation. "Batting averages, slugging averages, earned run averages of pitchers, games behind the leader" and similar quantitative concepts in all sports are based upon a sophisticated manipulation of data, and yet these ideas are often bantered about by the failing student in the fourth or fifth grade.

Minimal statistical or measurement principles would include most, if not all, of the following:

1. Frequency distributions
2. Measures of central tendency (mean, median, mode)
3. Population samples
4. Norms and norm groups

5. Derived scores
   a. Percentile
   b. I.Q.
   c. Age scores
   d. Grade scores

The detailed presentation of these concepts would depend upon the particular grade level involved. Student capacity and the curriculum of the group will also be influencing factors. Students in the technical, industrial, or business curricula may need to study concepts that can help them to understand the General Aptitude Test Battery of the United States Employment Service; other curricula may use and interpret the Differential Aptitude Test Battery of the Psychological Corporation, or other test instruments.

Student reactions

Many guidance persons are hesitant to divulge intelligence test data to students as well as parents or teachers. Student reactions to learning about themselves vary according to many factors. However, research has demonstrated the value of involving students in the process of self-evaluation and self-directed planning. Often the view is expressed that a sharing of such information is valuable with average or even superior students, but that the poor student is the one who is dangerously threatened and hurt by such data.

C. C. Ross (1938) paired eighty freshman students at the University of Kentucky on several variables and drew all forty pairs from the lower fifth of the class in terms of intelligence scores. Half of the students (the experimental group) were involved in an interpretation of the test results and also a discussion of the implications, problems of college success on the basis of such results, and similar factors. The control group was told nothing. Ross reports that the experimental group had definitely exceeded the control group in achieving academic success throughout the entire first year of college.

Gribbons reports on the use of guidance and test materials with eighth grade students and on group procedures which included the involvement of students in the interpretation of their own test results within a framework of knowledge of individual differences and measurement principles. Gribbons (1960, p. 745) found that students could "make accurate appraisals of their abilities, values and interests." These students could not integrate all of the data into a specific vocational or educational decision, nor was this a goal of the study. Students were involved in a learning situation which stressed the *process* of self-directed planning and decision making. Vocational and educational planning are not isolated decision points in a sense of time, but are developing processes based upon attitudes and student learnings about self-appraisal and integrated planning.

Other writers have stressed the value of reporting test data to students and the desirability of involving them in the process of self-understanding (Punke, 1951; T. Snyder, 1937). Demands that such procedures be handled in a professional and skillful fashion have been sounded by Shoben (1951) and Pullias (1939). There is no question that a person's view of himself, in the area of intelligence as well as other measurable areas, is vital and at the core of the concept of the self. Group leaders, counselors, and teachers need to be adequately informed about the elements of personality and the dynamics of self-concept as they seek to help students.

Student reaction to the availability of test results is favorable, even without detailed preparation and training in measurement. Rothney, long interested in this issue, reports on large numbers of students in two different studies (Rothney, 1952; 1958). In each study there was a strong reaction on the part of students for an opportunity to learn of their test data through counseling and a positive feeling about the experience. Rothney is disturbed about the failure of tests to live up to their advantages as claimed by publishers; perhaps better methods of imparting the information to students would allow for more successful applications of test data. Research data on the specific comparisons of supplying test data through counseling alone and supplying test data through counseling *after* preparation of the students through group procedures and learnings in measurement are not yet available. The implications of the independent research studies quoted certainly point in this direction.

The case of Don, earlier presented, revealed the use of many group approaches as they were combined with counseling in the area of test interpretation. An examination of the many techniques available to guidance workers can highlight the application of groups in the area of psychological test use and student interpretation. The content for many types of possible groupwork has been offered; concepts of individual differences, measurement principles, statistical techniques of interpretation are all potent subjects with which groups may grapple.

The group process techniques used in the area of imparting information about test results are not significantly at variance with the approaches used in other areas of counseling, guidance, and personnel work. The necessity of utilizing a specific content (measurement principles) tends to stress the importance of task-centered groups. Although the actual emphasis upon the task of learning facts, principles, and concepts is uppermost in the minds of students, group leaders and teachers need to be aware of the over-all growth emphasis that surrounds the particular activities of the group.

Standard teaching techniques are also appropriate in the area of test interpretation. Additional group designs and patterns might include the following: case conferences, case studies, discussion groups, role playing, and certain experimental methods. Each of these applications of groups will be presented in detail with examples of practice and reference to the dynamics of the group operation.

Standard teaching techniques

Problems of measurement and individual differences demand that students learn a series of principles, concepts and facts. The material to be learned is similar to the measurement course which is offered to students at a college or graduate school level. The content of the college or graduate school course is, of necessity, more comprehensive. Similarly, a course in American History is more comprehensive on a college or graduate school level; however, American History is also a portion of every elementary school pupil's curriculum. Junior high school students study our nation's happenings, and in many states American History becomes by law a required course in high school.

Text publications or specially prepared reading materials are a must in the area of measurement. Students cannnot visualize a frequency distribution or a median. A "bell-shaped" curve is easier to conceive, but also better seen on paper.

Large classes are appropriate as specific information is communicated to students. Large classes can provide the time for following group discussions or case-study problem solving. The subject matter needs to be approached in a dynamic and skillful fashion. The employment of actual group techniques in a large lecture class can help provide an understanding of new material. Buzz sessions, informal group discussions in the middle of the hour, and the submitting of questions on cards can help the lecturer or the teacher clarify problem areas for students.

Standard teaching methods can be supplemented with all types of group techniques. The 1960 Yearbook of the National Society for the Study of Education, *The Dynamics of Instructional Groups*, can aid any teacher to do a better job in teaching virtually any subject. However, most guidance personnel can not spend a long time, nor can they expect that measurement principles can be covered in a regular course program and periods of instruction. (Counselors or guidance personnel who have such a program or wish to build toward such a program are referred ahead to Chapter XIV.)

Structured group meetings

Organized groups of students can be developed out of large meetings, lectures and didactic-type sessions with students. After all psychological tests have been administered, but prior to the availability of the results, guidance personnel can schedule large meetings with all members of the class concerned. Large schools can divide the sophomore or senior class into smaller units for the same purpose. Concepts of individual differences, measurement and statistical facts, and specific analysis of the testing instruments used in the program can be presented to large groups. Variable group techniques that were mentioned in regular classes or lectures can help the instructors to insure adequate understanding of the principle concepts.

Small discussion groups, meeting once per week, once per month or on any schedule which is appropriate for the particular school, can then be organized to provide a follow-up on the data presented in the larger meetings. Counselors, teachers, guidance personnel, even upper class students (trained and ready) can serve as group leaders. The student group members can focus on the task of understanding and manipulating the ideas presented in the large lecture type meetings. Group leaders will need to be adequately prepared in the content areas of study and also in the procedures designed to assist individual group members to master the material. The ability of students to direct and participate in a discussion was demonstrated by elementary school pupils of the fifth grade in the Franklin school in Lexington, Massachusetts. These youngsters were on a nationwide television program "The Influential American," produced November 13, 1960, by the General Electric Corporation.

An evaluation of the learnings that are hopefully taking place in these large and small group meetings can be obtained through a subject-matter examination (true-false, multiple choice, fill-in, or essay types). Grades may be offered to students or examinations may simply be corrected and returned to students. Grades for students are appropriate in credit programs; progress reports may be even more valuable in noncredit experiences. Evaluation of the process of learning the content of the meetings may also be postponed until after the actual returning of psychological test results to students in group test meetings and in counseling (Gysbers, 1960). Determination of procedures will relate, of necessity, to the especially designed program in each school unit.

Case conferences and case studies

Faculty members and students can profit from the use of the case method. Faculty members can be helped to understand test interpretation, counseling procedures; in fact, most of the elements of a counseling and guidance program through the use of case conferences. Case study problem-solving discussions within student groups can aid students in a similar fashion to understand a content of measurement and individual differences. Each of these methods—the case conference and the case study discussion—can be spaced and scheduled according to the stress of problems, the time available, and the skills of the teachers, counselors, and group leaders. These case methods are considerably more flexible than standard class procedures and may be adapted to the needs of the individual school program.

STAFF CASE CONFERENCES. The counselors, guidance personnel, health department, and teachers, as well as administrators, need to be informed adequately about tests and test use before students are involved in the use of psychological test data. The case conference as a method is described in detail in several sources (Strang, 1953, pp. 410–452; Allport, 1938; H. B. McDaniel, 1956). Use of the case conference is a standard tool of the guidance person to (1) provide for individual problem solving in student cases; (2) promote in-service growth on the part of guidance, teaching, and other professional as well as nonprofessional personnel; and (3) promote functional understanding of all participants of the responsibilities and contributions which can be made by all persons within a school system.

The leader of the case conference, whether he be the guidance director, counselor, principal or faculty advisor, must be skilled in enabling a group to become a task-oriented, problem-solving group with opportunities for each member to grow in positive attitudes and values towards students.

Case conference groups may develop spontaneously, as serious student problems arise; however, organization and planned structure most frequently precede successful meetings. The assumption of responsibility for planning usually falls to the guidance person. Other members can be invited and encouraged to attend; assignments from an administrator, however well intended, can establish an atmosphere of authoritarianism before the group even begins to function. As successful case conferences are conducted, teachers, faculty advisors, health personnel, and all interested persons will begin to want to be included in the meetings. The group can grow through functional service to the participants.

The problem of communication among persons in a case conference is heightened because of the interdisciplinary nature of the conference. Physicians, nurses, teachers, and guidance personnel may disagree violently about the meaning of "confidentiality of records." Each person often views "the other person" with suspicion and concern. Shared objectives with varying methods promote such issues. The members need to seek a block-and-gap type of consensus in solving problems of students. The areas of disagreement can easily destroy such a group if the members are unaware of the problems of building a climate of co-operation and mutual effort.

The service nature of the case conference is its primary strength and value. Case conferences can help the participants to understand and aid students, and to appreciate other persons' approaches to problem solving. Case conferences can raise the level of co-operation among staff and faculty, and can promote human relations values. If such outcomes are not apparent in meetings called case conferences, such meetings are not case conferences.

STUDENT CASE STUDIES. Students do not normally hold case conferences about other students. (Exceptions to this are treated in later chapters on the use of groups in counseling procedures.) However, the benefits of case conference work in terms of learning and manipulating data can be available to students through case study task groups. Previously organized case study materials, homemade or from published sources, offer students the chance to enter into a case conference.

The study of measurement materials provides the background knowledge for students to enter into case analyses in which psychological test data are involved. Published cases may not have data from the instruments used in the particular school; however, guidance persons can change the data reported so it may conform to local practice. Supplementary measurement data or even the printed test results can be placed on a blackboard. The visual presence of the data can help students to be aware of such facts and incorporate the meanings into their discussions.

Counselors and guidance persons are trained to interpret test data as a part of a total case study. Counselors and guidance persons are therefore natural leaders for such group discussions if they are able to understand and to apply the principles of group operation or group dynamics.

The "Case of Karl" was prepared by the director of guidance in the school system. All senior class counselors were conducting group discussions on the "Case of Karl"; lectures and group discussions on individual differences and measurement principles had been completed in the sophomore year of the program. The students as juniors also had previously completed investigations into occupational information and had prepared occupational and educational research papers. College planning had been incorporated into the educational planning sections of these papers.

Karl had been a student at the high school several years before. The director of guidance had been his counselor and had available all of the pertinent data. "Karl" was not the name of the original boy; however, all of the facts of the case had been drawn from a case conference scheduled for the faculty in Karl's junior year.

The "Case of Karl" included data on: (1) the statement of the problem (Karl had been a classical under-achiever), (2) personal and home information, (3) educational history, (4) work history and experience, (5) psychological test data, (6) counselor's summary and report, (7) teachers' observations and reports, (8) health records, and (9) physical education director's report. The director of guidance had rewritten the material in order to make it appropriate to the level of the high school seniors; essential facts were not changed, and all psychological test data had been included.

A staff meeting of all counselors and guidance personnel had been devoted to the development of plans for the use of the "Case of Karl" with the senior student groups. The following instruction sheet had been drawn up by a subcommittee of the guidance department:

(1) Counselors should introduce the problem to the student groups. Goals and group procedures should be explained at this time. Karl should be identified as a previous student.

(2) Groups should be instructed to develop specific recommendations for Karl, the counselor working with Karl, the school, and Karl's parents.

(3) Copies of the case study should be passed out to students in advance. A minimum of one week should be allowed for students to read and study the material.

(4) Group leaders should be prepared to introduce the topic and allow the group to assume responsibility for the task of writing specific recommendations.

(5) Group leaders need to be aware of problems of excessive identification with Karl, personal knowledge of Karl's real identity, student ability to interpret data and to integrate available data, projection of students' own problems into the case discussion, and the motivations of individual students as they participate in the group discussion.

(6) The recommendations of each group will be discussed and integrated at the next staff meeting, and a summary of group recommendations will be returned to the student groups in a large meeting. A discussion of the outcome of the actual Karl will be offered to the students at that time.

Students may be involved in the writing of a case study as well as in the determination of recommendations for problem solving with case studies. Further use of student discussions with case material is included in subsequent chapters. Advanced groups of students need to incorporate test data along with sophisticated knowledge of the other factors which enter into the analysis of a specific case study.

Role playing

Students enjoy being offered opportunities to defend their opinions in live, nearly real situations. Role-playing programs with psychological test data can provide such meaningful opportunities. The two examples which follow are only beginnings; variations and modifications of the approach will occur to a counselor or guidance person working with students at any age level. The first report is from an eighth grade counselor teaching a "group guidance" course.

> The "Kuder Vocational Interest Inventory" profile offered us a chance to use role-playing techniques in our eighth grade class. The students had taken the inventory as a part of their "group guidance" program. The class as a whole had completed two copies of the profile, after scoring the test themselves. One of the profiles was for their guidance folder and one copy was for them to keep for their own use.
>
> The groups in the class (four groups of nine each) had discussed a sample profile and attempted to relate the results of the inventory to their previous unit on abilities and intelligence. The groups had presented their conclusions to the class, and considerable discussion had centered around the relationship of ability measures, achievement patterns and their measured interests. We were discussing these problems when one of the students raised the question of talking over their results with their parents.
>
> Violent disagreement broke out in the class. Several members of the class insisted that their parents should not see the results; other students were strongly in favor of joint discussion with their parents. I suggested that the class might explore the possible reactions of parents to the test data. The students agreed that this would be an interesting experiment. We selected one boy to play the role of the father, a girl for the role of the mother, and one of the youngsters who had wanted to take his results home volunteered to play the role of the child seeking help from his parents.
>
> Our "student" brought home his profile and began to discuss its meaning with his "parents." The discussion was not long, but the interest of the class was tremendously high. Immediately three other students wished to assume the roles. We played another "scene" which was completely different from the first. The discussion and debate continued until the bell. What a class!

Integrated test usage

Psychological test data can seldom exist independent of a total guidance program. Achievement, aptitude, ability, interests, personality, reading, and speaking are only a few of the many aspects of individual differences that may be measured through varying types of test situations. Guidance workers, counselors, principals, superintendents, teachers, and parents need to utilize co-operatively the facts that are available through psychological tests. Test results are no better than the use and specific applications that are accomplished with the raw data. Tests and test data can never make a single decision for a person; tests and test data can only provide factual information that must be related to all other facts that are available. Group procedures can provide additional means for making test data meaningful and useful for students, teachers, and parents. The complexity of the many functional applications of test data highlights the importance of the "content" of group discussions; creative uses of group procedures can be limited only by the creative ingenuity of the staff and students using test results.

SUMMARY

Psychological test data provide a major content area in any guidance program. Tests can provide useful diagnostic data for counselors and meaningful facts for students to use in self-planning. A philosophy of test-use supporting counselor and student interpretation can provide a basis for effective group techniques for test interpretation.

Students need to be trained in concepts of individual differences, measurement principles, and interpretation techniques. Examples of test materials written for students and student use of test results are offered. The "Case of Don" illustrates the detailed use of test data in student group discussion while it is co-ordinated with individual counseling.

Research results are offered to support the use of test data with students. Case conferences and case study procedures offer newer methods of involving students in psychological test interpretation. Role playing can be employed in many guidance classes to aid students in understanding tests.

SUGGESTED READINGS

American Council on Education, *Helping Teachers Understand Children.* Washington, D. C.: American Council on Education, 1945.

Clark, Margaret, "Role Playing in a Group Guidance Class," *California Journal of Secondary Education,* 26, 1951, 34–36

Cronbach, L. J., *Essentials of Psychological Testing* (2nd ed.). New York: Harper & Bros., 1960.

Greenleaf, W. J., "Sociodrama as a Guidance Technique," *California Journal of Secondary Education*, 26, 1951, 71–75.

Hymes, James L. Jr., *A Child Development Point of View*. Englewood Cliffs, N. J.: Prentice-Hall, Inc., 1955.

Prescott, Daniel A., *The Child in the Educative Process*. New York: McGraw-Hill Book Co., 1957.

Swanson, E. O., "No I. Q.?" *Bulletin and Occupational Newsletter*, Student Counseling Bureau, University of Minnesota, April 15, 1960.

The College Board Today. New York: College Entrance Examination Board, 1960.

Thurstone, T. G., *et al.*, "Your Child's Intelligence," *N. E. A. Journal*, 50, 1961, 33–48.

Williamson, E. G., *Student Personnel Services in Colleges and Universities*. New York: McGraw-Hill Book Co., 1961.

12. EDUCATIONAL PLANNING

An exchange of letters between an eleven-year-old and former President Dwight D. Eisenhower during the early days of the space age reveals an example of educational and vocational planning.

Dear Mr. President:

It has come to my attention that when I graduate out of medical school there will probably be space travel with human beings. It has come to my attention that a doctor (maybe a surgeon like I hope to be) will be needed on these flights, and many men will apply, and this my application to be among those who will make the first flights. I am 11 years old and have done the following:

I have given ants artificial respiration, taken care of a toad that had been run over with a lawn mower, and know some human anatummy. Please consider my request.

Thankfully,
Wayne Trebbin

Dear Wayne:

Of course I shall see that your application to be a space flight surgeon will be carefully filed, but I rather suspect that it would be a good idea for you to renew your suggestion at the appropriate time. None of us can quite visualize the world we will live in when you are a full-fledged doctor—say, fifteen years from now. In the meantime, I am fascinated by your medical knowledge and practice and wish you every success in your chosen career. You are fortunate to know exactly what you want to do with your life.

With my best wishes,

Sincerely,

Dwight D. Eisenhower

Educational opportunities and career development are intertwined throughout each person's life. Vocational decision making has been studied and continuing research in career patterns has been conducted. The selection of a job or career is never the result of a single decision or choice— career growth is a developmental process marked by many individual choices and directional patterns. The characteristic element in such growth is the process of decision making.

The major units of schooling contribute to the patterns of educational and vocational development that are adopted by each person. The points of decision in school years, the occupational models of childhood and adolescence, and the processes of securing and holding jobs are wide areas for the use of groups in guidance and personnel work. Each of the next two chapters will examine one of these topics.

POINTS OF DECISION

Educational planning is an integral part of the entire learning process within elementary schools. The nonspecialized nature of the curriculum involves every child in similar experiences and requires that educational practice equip each child to move ahead within the school scene. Guidance, counseling, and groupwork are intimately related to the class and the out-of-class programs in the early years. Junior high school provides for the needs of children during the transition to adolescence. Major educational decisions are necessary during these years which affect the remaining periods of education. The choices regarding career, college, or training school are made in high school, often the last educational environment of the individual. Technical school and university life require still further decisions that relate to ultimate career patterns.

Elementary school

The bud and twig of the proverbial tree are growing and developing in the early years of school. Unfortunately guidance procedures have been slow to develop in these important years of school. Problem prevention, early redirection of undesirable characteristics within the child, and most of all, the positive foundations for a profitable educational experience are accepted objectives within the early grades. The role of guidance in these experiences of the child has been stressed by Cottingham (1956) and Krugman (1954), among others. The importance of relating classroom experiences to guidance practices has also been highlighted by McCabe (1958), Barr (1958), and Redl and Wattenberg (1959).

The constant thread uniting all of these writers is the need to aid in the development of positive, inner directional talents by individual youngsters. "Controls from within" is the phrase used by Redl and Wineman (1951). The role of groups in the development of mature modes of behavior cannot be overestimated. The self-direction, the respect for peer members of a society, and the self-starting and self-maintenance skills of personality and character cannot be developed within a sterile, authoritarian class in which rote memory feats are prized. Teachers, drawing from the assistance of guidance and other specialized personnel, are the primary force which can effect such growth patterns. The role of groupwork in actual classroom procedures and exclusively by classroom teachers has been presented in many publications indicated earlier. Guidance persons can strengthen such educational practices by effective knowledge of the role of groups in the many environments present within a school system. The classroom teacher, the school psychologist, the school social worker, and the guidance person can form a total team within the elementary school. The presence of the combined efforts, genuine talents, and contributions of all are the hallmarks of outstanding schools (Harrower and Goldstein, 1959).

The educational planning and developmental responsibilities of the elementary school may be strengthened as guidance persons are capable of aiding teachers in several specific areas of operation. Special classes for the retarded, gifted, handicapped, and other homogeneous groups are concrete educational contributions to any school system. Heterogeneous groups within grade levels, occupational field trips, and even team teaching are additional creative elements within an elementary school. Counselors along with teachers need to create an atmosphere for learning rather than a punitive climate in which emotional blackmail is common.

1. GIFTED GROUPS. Homogeneous groups of children are organized in almost every school in the land. Levels of reading proficiency are reflected in even first grade groups. Talented children are not the same as gifted children and the distinction is often difficult to make (Witty, Conant, and Strang, 1959). Yet the patterns of underachievement so characteristic in high school and college are rooted in the study and learning patterns developed in the first few years of school. Shaw and McCuen (1960) report on underachievement evidence rooted in first grade experiences. Scannell (1960) presents data to support this determination and further shows the relationship of early achievement in elementary school to ultimate achievement in college.

Flexibility and creativity are key concepts in the programming of ideas for use with gifted or talented children.

> Our "school adjustment counselor" is also well prepared in the science area. He conducts several groups of "problem children" in a program of psychological aid to the students, but also works with an advanced group of science students. He helps them to construct experimental apparatus and to follow through with their intense interest in the scientific. (Massachusetts)

> Our guidance department has established a series of group therapy units that work with the gifted, but underachieving students in the first three grades. The children are helped to develop emotional control and to channel their abilities into more constructive types of school activities. (New York State)

Guidance personnel must be aware that the gifted and talented children in a school system are ready and capable of earlier stimulation in the areas of self-appraisal and discussions about educational and occupational planning. The truly gifted child may need help in the sixth or seventh grade that is appropriate for the ninth or tenth grade student in normal classes. Rothney and Koopman (1958) stress these facts as they report (p. 348):

> Guidance for the gifted varies from the usual primarily in these respects:
> 1. educational and occupational opportunities for the gifted are usually of greater proportion than for others,

2. gifted pupils become ready for self-appraisal and self-conceptualization at higher levels and at earlier ages,

3. gifted children may be subject to unusual pressures by parents, teachers, peers, and others.

Programs that are outlined in the next section for junior high school students are often particularly appropriate for an advanced or gifted group of sixth graders.

Counselors are (according to Gowan, 1960) prone to identify in positive fashion with gifted children. Certainly, whether this is true or not, it is vital that a counselor be aware of the quality of his or her own feelings in working with youngsters so talented. Counselors can be aware of the problems of these pupils and can organize groups to aid the students in assuming responsibility for themselves. Ruth Strang has written a first effort in this direction that is distinctly useful in such group patterns. *Guideposts for Gifted Children Themselves*, Strang (1958b), can serve as a major resource for counselors and students in such groups. A companion volume, again by Ruth Strang, titled *Helping Your Gifted Child*, (1960) is directed to parents who face significant problems in helping themselves and their children to face the unusual as it occurs.

2. RETARDED CHILDREN. The recent past has revealed that efforts to aid children unable to keep up with normal classes are more common than programs for gifted children. The relatively new national awareness of the need for talent has helped to push the gifted-child program ahead of historical programs for the slow learners. School personnel in the past and present often simply segregated the slow group and attempted to prevent them from handicapping the other children. Group activities can provide a positive basis for such programs.

A classic publication of the U.S. Government that never received widespread attention was the booklet *Group Activities for Mentally Retarded Children* by E. H. Martens (1933). This publication lists hundreds of activities that are profitable to children in becoming independent and stable in their relations with peers, adults, and the world of work. Group organizations of food markets, toy orchestras, nursery parties, toy telephone activities, and similar programs are described in great detail. There is no specific mention or stress of group dynamics and all material is presented as content for such groups. A skilled teacher or counselor can easily adapt such suggestions to meaningful programs in the present.

Pseudo-retardation is not an uncommon problem in the early years of school. Emotional blockings, extreme withdrawal, physical problems of speech and hearing, and many other possible causes can prevent a child from assuming a normal position in learning situations. Group projects with such young children can help to isolate and diagnose many problems; also, group participation can serve as a primary force in helping to return such a child to the regular class. Sarason (1960) has helped to dispel the modern myth of the omnipresent, happy, carefree young child. The anxieties that must be faced in everyday school life are often beyond the wildest dreams of some teachers and unfortunately some counselors and guidance personnel.

3. ABILITY GROUPINGS. Few, if any, school systems have failed to experience the difficulties and dangers of the "homogeneous group" issue. The selection of groups upon ability measures, academic performance, social maturity, and even parental pressures have been the criteria most often used. Guidance personnel have a responsibility to assist the school in making such decisions. Whether such groupings are appropriate in a given school is beyond the scope of this treatment of groups. If a school has decided that their program is to be segregated in some fashion, it is important that a best effort be employed.

The following example shows the participation of guidance personnel as well as supervisors in the selection and revision of ability groupings in a particular school system. The group process also bulks large in the determination of the judgments. The leadership skills of the counselors and the supervisors were an important factor in the process:

> Our elementary school establishes three special fifth and sixth grade units each year. The fourth grade pupils are all rated by their teachers; the achievement test results for the third and fourth grades are examined; and the teachers rank the pupils on a rating scale for social maturity. Last year we established an additional criterion which has helped immeasurably.
>
> The elementary school guidance counselors and the supervisors in the curriculum area visit every fourth grade room in the system every spring. The class may be in a social studies period or even in a math or science period. These outside persons organize small groups within the class and serve as supervisory leaders for the remainder of the day in that subject. The groups review their past work for the leaders, explain and demonstrate their present per-

formance level, and plan a future unit under the leadership of our supervisors or guidance personnel.

After the completion of the day the visitors rate each pupil in the group on the same factors we use to select future special classes.

The children are always happy to have a "special group day" and to work with the outsiders. The guidance and supervisory personnel find that they look forward to their "spring chores" with considerable enthusiasm. We have been well pleased with our procedures and hope to continue them. (Elementary school principal)

4. TEAM TEACHING.   One of the most creative developments on the entire educational scene has been described as team teaching. The concept of the team has varied from school to school. Some schools look upon a "team" as any group of two or three teachers, often from the same discipline or specialty, that work together in order to present a subject in greater depth than was previously possible. Such systems are desirable, but are little more than the departmental concept of high school or college transplanted to the elementary school. "Pupil-teams" may also be organized within elementary or other class groups. Durrell, Scribner, and others (1959), and Durrell (1961), describe such "pupil-teams."

The more creative concept of faculty team teaching has presented a cross-disciplinary and cross-experiential group of teachers. The teachers form a group and use group techniques in their teaching. The following example is a description of a program developed by local initiative and creative planning. Foundation help was only available in a late stage of training for some of the teachers:

Our school was established and built to accommodate a concept of team teaching. Each team unit is made up of four classes designed in a perimeter arrangement around the four sides of a square. The central area, *centrum,* is also available for instructional purposes.

Each team is composed of four professional teachers and a half-time nonprofessional teachers' aide. The team leader is well trained and is usually the most experienced, career minded, and professional teacher available. Two other teachers are average or usual in their backgrounds and training. A fourth member is usually a new teacher. Each teacher is drawn from a different discipline. One is skilled and experienced in the humanities, one in social science, one in science, and one in a fourth area according to the talents available in the faculty to balance the other members' backgrounds. Music, art, dramatics, or similar fields are usually involved through the fourth member. Each team is assigned approximately 125 students.

The team is responsible for planning the units of the year, drawing from a master plan that is available as a guide. Team meetings are held prior to the opening of school and continuing meetings of a planning or evaluative nature are held all year long.

Student groups are formed according to subject-matter plans, number of teachers involved, space requirements, time of year (training of students in self-direction increases throughout the year), and other related variables. There are large, virtual lecture groups in which two or more rooms are opened together to form a large hall; regular class sizes (25–35); small discussion groups of twelve to fifteen; small remedial groups of four to five; and opportunities for one to one student-teacher conferences. Many groups work without immediate supervision of any of the team teachers or the teacher's aide. Student leaders and student groups are utilized in many fashions.

The guidance counselor meets with the team on a scheduled basis and reviews with the teachers the work and problems of the students. Referrals are made to the guidance department and if individual remedial or treatment action is necessary it can be accomplished. Students from the team may also be formed into treatment groups (reading, speech, etc.) along with students from other teams. (Michigan)

Achievement is reported to be above average in many team systems and the morale is particularly high. Unusual remedial services in small groups are possible in these settings. The use of role playing in small groups to provide reading help is described by Heimbach (1959). Team teaching research results on the elementary school level are not yet available, but expectations are high. A visitor reported on the morale and the student-faculty attitudes in a team system: "The students moved with a spirit and zest; the faculty were interested in what they were doing. Everyone seemed to be involved in and to be committed to what they were doing. Contrary to so many schools that I visited where it seemed as if both students and faculty felt they were in 'jail,' it was a pleasure and a privilege to see this system."

5. TECHNIQUES AND PROBLEMS. Problems in elementary school group-work are numerous. Students are young, spirits are high, involvement is intense; where problems occur, successes can also be great. Ruth Cunningham has written many articles and books on understanding the young child.

She writes of the many advantages of the group approach in differing situations, but warns of the need for time and understanding in the development of self-directed skills in the young child (Cunningham, 1951; Cunningham and Roberts, 1948).

Teachers or counselors as burgeoning group workers sometimes are unaware of the large issues that can bother the small persons in groups. Slavson (1951) recommends clearly understood limits of authority, restraint, and discipline with children under twelve years of age. Experimental work with activity groups shows the essential characteristics of individuals in action remain the same in spite of unusual content or social purposes. Sherif, White, and Harvey (1955) report on the status lines which developed among a group even as the group participated in throwing balls at a target used for aggression displacement. As members of the group developed greater skill in throwing the balls, the status factor entered even this apparent singularly therapeutic activity.

Some writers are encouraging as they urge experienced teachers to apply with caution some of the therapeutic methods of groups in counseling. Maas (1951) sees much similarity between classroom procedures of a mental health nature and the actual therapeutic relationship between therapists and students. Research has not supported such efforts although an understanding of the similarities can undoubtedly make a teacher more effective in the classroom.

The effects of co-operation and competition in young children are not always as predictable as is possible in some adult groups. The findings of Deutch (1949), reviewed in Part Two, are not clearly confirmed in experiments with fourth grade pupils by Phillips and D'Amico (1956). These investigators found that competition does not decrease cohesiveness in the groups studied. Newer means of aiding students to develop group problem-solving skills are becoming possible as tools are available to assess the current skill level of student groups in this field. Damrin (1959) describes the development of the *Russell Sage Social Relation Test*. This instrument allows elementary school groups to be measured in their problem-solving skill. Many inherent weaknesses still exist in the reliability and validity of such an instrument; however, experimental means now exist to compare groups as well as individual contributions and attitudes towards the group. Research data should soon be available.

Perhaps the most apt analogy for the counselor, group worker, or teacher is the comparison by Redl and Wattenberg (1959) of the teeming life of children in a group to the millions of organisms in a cup of sea water or in a square inch of backyard soil. The little people of any class or group possess feelings, attitudes, and problems that are always a challenge to the group leader.

Junior high school

Vocational guidance for secondary school pupils was one of the early emphases in guidance. The neglect of junior high school pupils' needs has been relative and constant until the most recent years. The pressing issues that confront the childlike or adolescent boy or girl in junior high school have seemed to baffle many guidance workers. Johnson, Busacker, and Bowman (1961) offer an organized treatment of guidance in the junior high school. Their book is a first in this area.

The seventh, eighth, and ninth grade students are old enough to begin to verbalize their problems, but still too young to profit adequately from purely verbal counseling. Activity therapeutic techniques are frequently received as insulting by the group. A combination of activity and counseling groups, classroom programming, and individual counseling seems to offer a total concept of guidance for students.

The pressure of peers; the security and strength offered by chums, cliques, crowds, and even group networks; the flare of emotional response to a less fortunate classmate; and even individual and group cruelty sometimes marking the junior high school pupils are all daily challenges to teachers, group workers, and counselors. At least two major strategies of group applications have been developed within junior high schools. Other approaches are used and may be desirable according to local conditions. Intergroup programs through classes or core programs and actual guidance classes have been used in widely different schools with marked success. Each of these major group concepts will be examined in detail.

1. INTERGROUP PROGRAMS. Human relation programs may be instituted on any level of educational practice. However, the involvement of pupils at an early age, when attitudes are still reasonably flexible, is usually most desirable. A study of the peer status feelings of sixth and seventh grade pupils in a Texas community showed that students of this age were more interested in the personality and social traits of their peers than in such factors as mental ability or academic achievement (Laughlin, 1954).

A comprehensive program of human relations and group training has been sponsored by the American Council on Education. Taba (1955b) reports on the program as it took place in several eighth grade classes. A course in social science or social relations was used to offer broad useful training in human relations. Youngsters were trained in group procedures and throughout the year they worked in committees to solve various task problems that related to social science. In addition to the content areas of human relations that were studied in this class, particular emphasis was placed upon the psychological (or process) skills of:

1. Acceptance of self and others
2. Effects of individual and group rejection
3. The meanings and implications of isolation
4. Leadership techniques
5. Individual differences (Taba, 1955b).

Training in these operational meanings of human relations and group work allowed the youngsters to free themselves from the tendency to choose working associates purely according to personal qualities and to select partners and group members because of basic skills or talents (Taba, 1955b, p. 61).

The results of this program were rewarding to the teachers who cooperated on the project and to the students. The actions of individual pupils in the program were often inconsistent with home and community based attitudes of rejection of minority groups and negatively based selection of friends and co-workers. The many committees and joint projects completed by the groups in the class helped the students to accept persons from all racial and religious backgrounds. Sociometric programs to select co-workers were repeated at various times throughout the year. The data showed clearly that the values developed in the classes had become stable characteristics of the students' choice patterns.

Students in one class operated upon a set of values that demonstrated the success of the project. Taba (1955b, pp. 86–91) reports seven characteristic values guiding the children:

1. Personal and social attributes
2. Helpfulness
3. Mutual assistance
4. Common tastes, interests, ideas, and activities
5. Feelings of affection
6. Long acquaintance
7. Success in work and in play.

Taba *et al.* (1952) are convinced that intergroup education is an appropriate concern for students on all educational levels. The principles offered in the 1952 publication show the wide applicability of intergroup education. Growth in four major areas is the goal of intergroup education: factual knowledge and ideas, social sensitivity, rational and objective habits of thought, and social skills.

The American Council on Education project has offered materials for use on all levels of education, from elementary school to secondary school and beyond. The suggested readings at the end of this chapter list the publications in the series.

2. GUIDANCE COURSES. The traditional curriculum selection process of the eighth and ninth grades has made the junior high school or the last year of the eight-four system a fertile ground for so-called group guidance courses. Frequently these courses have been conglomerations of dating, health and diet exhortations, and brief examinations of the curriculum of the high school. The courses have often been called "group guidance" simply because the class has been concerned with guidance matters and the class has been considered a group.

Life adjustment courses based on paperback books such as the Life Adjustment Booklets published by Science Research Associates of Chicago, Illinois, have grown and developed in the high school and junior high school level. The flexibility of the source materials—some several dozen titles are available—allowed teachers to develop the course in accord with the local problems of students. Some of the available titles (all published by Science Research Associates) include:

1. *Understanding Yourself,* W. C. Menninger, 1948.
2. *Your Club Handbook,* N. E. McDowell, 1951.
3. *Building Your Philosophy of Life,* T. V. Smith, 1953.
4. *You and Your Mental Abilities,* L. Bouthilet and K. M. Byrne, 1949.
5. *Getting Job Experience,* T. E. Christensen, 1949.
6. *Discovering Your Real Interests,* G. F. Kuder and B. B. Paulson, 1949.
7. *Guide to Good Leadership,* K. A. Wells, 1956.

The booklets in most cases are well written and appropriate to the school reader. The series is uneven and often reflects the individual bias or approach of the author. Kuder and Paulson (1949) mention other interest inventories, but the entire booklet is keyed to the use of the *Kuder Preference Record-Vocational*. A school that did not use this inventory would have a problem in using the book. Similarly the mental abilities booklet is keyed to the *Primary Mental Abilities Test*.

A series such as the Life Adjustment Booklets presents to the teacher or counselor the problem of constructing the curriculum in an integrated fashion. The process of studying these content areas is not stressed in any of the booklets. Only later publications (e.g. Wells, 1956) begin to examine any of the concepts of group process.

The Rockefeller Brothers Fund in 1955 helped to sponsor the development of an improved guidance program for junior high school (upper elementary) pupils. The Educational Testing Service of Princeton, New Jersey, undertook the study of guidance programs around the country. During 1958–59 over 100 public and private schools participated in a program using the experimental publication, *You Today and Tomorrow*, by Martin Katz. The program listed three major objectives: 1. to increase the student's self-understanding; 2. to inform him about educational and vocational opportunities; and 3. to help him to understand how the various factors that enter into career planning are interrelated. The content of the course concentrated on three broad areas:

1. Self-appraisal;
2. Educational and vocational information;
3. Decision-making.

Thirty class sessions were recommended for the course. Many experimental tryouts of the course indicated that this time limit could be extended or shortened according to local needs. Evaluation of the program indicated its value to students (Gribbons, 1960), teachers, school systems, and parents (Shimberg, 1959).

The program offered an integrated approach to student learning in interests, abilities, values, and educational and occupational planning. Teachers used group techniques as well as regular classroom procedures. One teacher (Schuster, 1957) reported a wide variety of classroom techniques she employed in the program:

1. Class discussion
2. Student leaders of discussion
3. "Brainstorming" in groups with leaders chosen to report summaries to rest of class

4. Tape recordings of reports (ties in with oral reports and standards for good speech)
5. Written reports (ties in with written communication, library study)
6. Letter writing
7. Scrapbooks
8. Guest speakers
9. Panel discussions
10. Library periods
11. Reading of pamphlets and college catalogs
12. Field trips
13. Film and filmstrips.

Students were involved in case study discussions and wrote analyses of cases designed to help them to assess an individual's chances for success in a college curriculum or in other educational plans. The training in measurement that preceded such reports made possible the degree of comprehension demonstrated. *Sally Jones* and *Elaine* are case studies that were studied in groups and discussed in class. Selected student comments (in their words) are:

SALLY JONES: Sally is a girl with a lot of will to win. She is a good bet for college even though her ability ranks only in the second quartile. (Eighth grade girl)

SALLY JONES: Sally has a lot of "drive" and has a good chance but not as good a chance as Tom to getting into a four year college. She has an eight out of ten chance. (Eighth grade boy)

ELAINE: Elaine is a student with ambitions and drive who finds her studies difficult. I think she has made a wise choice. She should keep away from office work which entails bookkeeping. (Eighth grade girl)

ELAINE: Elaine has made a good choice and is wise not to go to college, but she is wrong about thinking she does not need to know math. (Eighth grade boy)

Parents were generally pleased and reacted positively to the experiences that were stimulating their children. Two quotations, of unidentified parents, were as follows:

I think the project served a purpose for our child. He now realizes that certain subjects are necessary for each vocation. He has learned that he must succeed in his studies to reach his chosen vocation. I say chosen vocation, only for the one at this time. He may change his mind several times before his school days are over. (Rochester, N. Y., parent)

My son has always known what he wants to be. . . . He has been studying for a week and now he isn't sure of anything. Why disturb him? I don't think this guidance . . . is going to be helpful to him. Let it be done with children who don't know what they want. . . . (Eighth grade father)

Classes and courses in guidance are used earlier than the eighth or ninth grades and, of course, extend beyond. Chapter Fifteen will examine in depth the contents, methods, and group implications of guidance classes.

Secondary school

The three- or four-year public or private secondary school presents the last major educational experience for some students, serves varying proportions of students as a foundation for future college study, and hopefully unites all pupils as an integrating force within the American educational system. It is necessary for students to choose programs of specialization and revise and reaffirm their choices throughout their courses of study.

The search for talent in America has heightened the intensity of the educational program across the country. National Merit Scholarship Testing, the pressure for securing an early acceptance to a name college, and even the intimate presence of the space age—all have quickened the pace of secondary education. An early revealing of the talented or gifted child should not blind teachers to the need for constant awareness of the potentially outstanding student who has slipped by all attempts to identify and aid him. Gideonse (1959) and Bond (1959) are concerned with the identification of and aid to these students. They are fearful that all sources of student talent will not be tapped, as educators attempt to skim the "cream of the cream" from the collective American student body.

Effective guidance program administrators, who are aware of the nature of students, will search beyond test scores and IQ's for individuals who need help to fulfill a total concept of capacity. Educational guidance of the type described in many junior high schools can provide a basis for secondary school programs to build upon and to press beyond.

Individual counseling should be a current service in effective guidance programs to students at all educational levels. Secondary school programs are so varied in their essential nature and prepare students for such diverse futures after graduation, it is necessary to assume at all times that group procedures in guidance are paralleled by individual counselings as well as group and individual testing. Testing and counseling can provide an environment in which it is most profitable to use small group procedures to advance the principles of educational guidance (Failor, 1954).

Aptitudes, interests, values, and abilities form a group content area that must be examined as students progress and plan their education. Homogeneous guidance groups can help counselors and guidance personnel to individualize an educational experience. Problems of democracy courses, sociology courses, and even psychology courses also provide opportunities for group applications in educational planning.

1. SELF-APPRAISAL. Extending or beginning the concept of self-assessment in secondary school is a vital responsibility for any guidance program. A common organization of guidance and counseling in a large urban high school provided a background for an unusual use of psychological test data. A senior-year counselor described a three-year experience as follows:

> My 300 students arrived in school as sophomores. I was to be their counselor for their three-year career in our high school. During the sophomore and junior year I also had to teach a three-quarter load in my subject-matter field, English.
>
> Since I would only have a few of the total group in my English class I organized a series of meetings with the students early in the first year. I met them once in the assembly hall and told them of the program that had been planned for them. I asked for volunteers to help me set up topics and times for all of the students. One member from each of the sections assigned to me was selected and this group made up our planning committee.
>
> My plan book had called for a series of section (class) meetings to explain the guidance testing program that had to be completed. The planning committee suggested that the assembly hall be used for all testing and to present all material that would be common to all students. We established a set of three meetings that covered all of the explanations and allowed us to complete the tests (Kuder, Otis, and the Mooney Problem Check List).
>
> Our guidance class meetings (my one-quarter time for guidance and counseling allowed me to meet five sections each week) were de-

voted to discussions of the tests and their appropriate interpretations. We were several weeks ahead of schedule because of the use of the large assembly hall and we decided to establish discussion groups of fifteen to twenty students to go over the test results in greater detail.

The groups were a huge success. Certain groups didn't work too well, but they were in the minority. We discussed the test scores of some student volunteers in some groups and we used case studies in other groups. I had a difficult time keeping up with the demand for individual counseling requests that came out of the group meetings.

Our groups continued during the junior year after we had taken the Differential Aptitude Test again (they had all taken it in the eighth grade). Many students raised questions about the Scholastic Aptitude Test of the College Entrance Examination Board and we discussed this test before and after the students had taken it.

The senior year didn't come quickly enough for me. The groups had been almost too successful. I welcomed the freedom from teaching for my last year. We restructured our groups and focused much more on the student plans for the year following graduation.

The three-year period had been different from any other similar period during all the years I had served as a counselor in the school. The students had responded tremendously to the discussions of tests results and the applications of their test scores to their courses of study and plans after high school. I am planning to establish the same type of program next fall when I "pick up" my 300 new sophomores. Yet, I suppose they will have me working in a new direction if I let them in on the planning. (High school counselor-teacher)

2. HOMOGENEOUS GROUPS.   The diversity of curricular offerings in many schools provides a basis for dividing students into discussion groups to explore the meanings, applications and the next steps of their curriculum. Counselors (part-time and full-time) often establish groups based on the business course, the general course, the classical college curriculum, and other similar course breakdowns in secondary schools. Many problems may be faced in such groups.

The interests and attitudes of students are often similar even though they are in different courses of study. The opportunity to examine their own progress in a course of study also provides students with the occasion to assess the appropriateness of their educational study. Such self-evaluation can raise student performance through self- and group-evaluation. Duel (1958) showed the experimental value of self-evaluation as tasks are accomplished. The carryover into group situations of a curriculum nature is a reasonable generalization.

A recent study of ninth grade youths showed that students of today's schools do not differ significantly in their attitudes and job interests in comparison with students of the last generation (Jones, 1960). Jones also found that a comparison of the students of twenty years ago and today showed that present-day students were more mature on similar measures. The educational programs of most secondary schools offer more vocational preparation for girls, but Jones reports that girls are less interested in thinking about careers than are boys. The reasons for the difference between boys and girls on this variable is not fully explained by Jones, but is probably due to cultural factors.

The discrepancy between students' interest and aptitudes is not clearly related to personality problems (Nugent, 1961). Certainly a group can help its members to explore such variations in self-assessment. Revised courses and even new goals and curriculum plans are desirable (if administratively distressing) outcomes.

The cultural pressure for social acceptability often drives students into college preparatory courses in order to acquire social prestige even though eventual college attendance may be inappropriate. Similarly, students, under parental guidance, may select business or general programs when college would be completely desirable. Counselors should help students to understand that a high school or preparatory school curriculum is not something written by geniuses to be followed by morons. Counselors, teachers, parents, and administrators need to recognize that a great deal of individualization is necessary to fit a student into the educational system of a school. Hutson (1958, p. 205) advocates the abandonment of the college preparatory curriculum as ill-adapted to its purpose. Whether such strong medicine is necessary is questionable; however, flexibility is not only desirable but a necessity. Conant's (1959) comments and suggested revisions of all high school curricula are pertinent and appropriate in this connection.

Curriculum discussion groups can help to determine course change needs, and individual counseling can support such exploratory exchanges between students and counselors in the group setting.

3. SPECIAL COURSES. Special courses in the area of sociology, psychology, human relations, life adjustment, and even problems of democracy are effective vehicles for educational guidance and group operations. The free-

dom of such courses to meet the individual needs of students can provide an environment within which student study or discussion groups are able to explore a topic and develop a plan of action. Often such courses require students to follow up on the implications of their verbal discussion with actual action.

> Our Problems of Democracy course offered an opportunity for us to experiment with ideas, content, and methodology. We established several work groups and each attempted to study the requirements of colleges and to compare the results with the courses offered in our high school. The guidance department became interested in the project of this group and offered to co-operate.
>
> The resulting paper of our group "shook up" our high school. The students found a tremendous variety of courses acceptable for college entrance and also found that some of the old required courses (so-called) were required by only a very few colleges and universities. The guidance department kept a copy of the group's study and agreed to co-operate each year with a study group from our "PAD" course. (High school counselor)

The willingness, even the "more than fifty percent rule" is vital for counselors and guidance personnel as they co-operate with any project of merit within the classroom or other divisions of the school. Counselors or guidance workers can, according to their own previous subject-matter specializations, serve as teachers of an elective course in occupations, sociology, psychology, or even family living. Taba's (1952, 1955, etc.) approaches to human relations training have been discussed in earlier sections. The local situation will determine the means by which a meaningful contribution by counselors and guidance personnel can be made in group and educational procedures.

The advantages and disadvantages of teachers serving as part-time counselors and vice versa are well known. A well-designed program by professionally competent guidance personnel can often incorporate a joint type of program, strengthening the teaching and counseling functions of persons involved in each responsibility. Loughary (1959) examines some of the pertinent issues of this controversy; Strang's (1953) most recent edition of *The Role of the Teacher in Personnel Work* also can help a guidance administrator to construct a co-operatively based program.

Physical education has long been an area in which teachers are "counselors without portfolio" according to the Dean of Sargent College of Physical Education at Boston University, George McKechnie. The informal and nonacademic atmosphere of the many activities of physical education is often conducive to effective counseling and group relationships. Adamson (1934) speculated upon the possibilities of personal as well as personality development through such a medium; and more recently, Gregory (1953) described a program of "group guidance" through physical education. Other applications are possible in shop work, home economics, and courses within which education can be seen as a greater whole than that represented by any single course.

College and university

A colleague and faculty member in a large liberal arts college recently expressed concern to the author upon learning of a reduction in the number of days of freshman week.... "When will I have a chance to do my educational counseling. . . . I do my counseling during registration." Too frequently such a view of educational counseling is present in institutions of "higher" learning. The mechanical selection of a series of courses is a poor substitute for adequate educational advising, much less educational counseling.

Many investigations have shown that faculty advisors are most effective if they are involved with students on a continuing basis throughout a year. Glanz (1950) found that classroom contact with assigned students was a significant factor in successful programs of faculty counseling with students. Student-faculty similarity in subject-matter interests was not as important. Group meetings with assigned advisees can substitute in larger colleges where classroom contact is impossible.

The training of faculty advisors through group procedures described by I. Gordon (1950) showed the efficiency and effectiveness of groups in involving faculty members in such advising programs. Brunson (1959) views counseling and guidance as integrating and unifying forces in all education on the college and university level. Similar views have been expressed by Fisher and Noble (1960), Hardee (1955, 1960), and Hoffman and Plutchik (1959a). These writers all look upon groups as a primary tool in the total process of education and stress the use of groups by guidance personnel. Hoffman and Plutchik (see Chapter 9) have integrated a concept of groupwork into higher education through orientation units spaced throughout the freshman year of college.

Upper division programs of educational advisement and counseling are most commonly found within small informal groups of students associating with their major professors. The social, academic, and professional interests of students and faculty are merged through coffee hours, professional clubs, home entertainment, and related activities. Again, the responsibility of the guidance person is to build upon local custom, tradition, or even local law! Wary counselors have found that a thorough knowledge of such sociological facts is necessary prior to the institution of personally upheld and defended systems. The key is again to operate within the framework and existing idea of the program. Improvement can be "added to," rather than "substituted for."

SUMMARY

Educational and vocational planning present many varied opportunities for the applications of group techniques. Psychological testing, individual counseling, and groupwork approaches are interdependent and most efficient as they are co-operatively designed for use.

The educational "points of decision" are presented as they exist in the elementary, junior, and senior high schools as well as in colleges and universities. Special provisions must always be made to create opportunities for the advanced or retarded child in facing critical decisions in educational plans and course curricula.

SUGGESTED READINGS

American Educational Research Association, *The Education of Exceptional Children*, Review of Educational Research, Vol. 29, Number 5, December 1959.

Axline, Virginia M., *Play Therapy: The Inner Dynamics of Childhood*. Boston: Houghton Mifflin Co., 1947.

Baker, Harry J., *Introduction to Exceptional Children* (3rd ed.). New York: The Macmillan Co., 1959.

Drews, Elizabeth M., ed., *Guidance for the Academically Talented Student.* Washington, D. C.: National Education Association and the American Personnel and Guidance Association, 1961.

Hefferman, Helen, ed., *Guiding the Young Child from Kindergarten to Grade Three* (2nd ed.). Boston: D. C. Heath & Co., 1959.

Hutt, Max L., and R. G. Gibby, *The Child: Development and Adjustment.* Boston: Allyn and Bacon, Inc., 1959.

Kelley, J. A., *Guidance and Curriculum*. Englewood Cliffs, N. J.: Prentice-Hall, Inc., 1955.

Moostakas, C. E., *Children in Play Therapy*. New York: McGraw-Hill Book Co., 1953.

Rogers, Dorothy, *Mental Hygiene in Elementary Education*. Boston: Houghton Mifflin Co., 1957.

Schiffele, Marian, *The Gifted Child in the Regular Classroom*. New York: Bureau of Publications, Teachers College, Columbia University, 1953.

Super, Donald E., *et al.*, "The Role of Counseling in State and Regional Programs," in American Association for the Advancement of Science, *Identification and Guidance of Able Students*. Conference Report, 1958.

Taba, Hilda, *With Perspective on Human Relations*. Washington, D.C.: American Council on Education, 1955.

————, *School Culture*. Washington, D. C.: American Council on Education, 1955.

Taba, Hilda, and Deborah Elkins, *With Focus on Human Relations*. Washington, D. C.: American Council on Education, 1950.

Taba, Hilda, *et al.*, *Curriculum in Intergroup Relations: Case Studies in Instruction for Secondary Schools*. Washington, D.C.: American Council on Education, 1949.

————, *Elementary Curriculum in Intergroup Relations*. Washington, D. C.: American Council on Education, 1950.

————, *Diagnosing Human Relations Needs*. Washington, D. C.: American Council on Education, 1951.

————, *Intergroup Education in Public Schools*. Washington, D. C.: American Council on Education, 1952.

Trump, J. Lloyd, *et al.*, *Images of the Future*. Washington, D. C.: National Association of Secondary-School Principals, National Education Association (Ford Foundation Commission), 1959.

13. OCCUPATIONAL PLANNING

Educational and occupational planning are closely related throughout school life. The separation of these topics may take place for purposes of emphasis or illustration; reality factors demand that joint consideration be accomplished whenever possible.

The role of occupational information in guidance and education extends throughout the school years. Often, it is direct, open discussion of occupations; at other times, it is possible to extract from almost any discussion the side learnings that take place in the area of occupational orientation. Elementary classes in social studies often study the lives, occupations, and cultures of children and adults in foreign lands. Literature classes in high school read, discuss, and dissect the characteristics of a novel such as *The Forsyte Saga* by Galsworthy showing the occupations and lives of three or more generations. Television exerts a significant influence upon children's expectations about work. Incidental learnings and unplanned experiences are haphazard and need to be supplemented and organized within more orderly learnings. Counselors and guidance personnel may assist in this task at every grade level.

The concept of the round peg for the round hole has simplified a complex process of vocational development that has recently been assessed more carefully in terms of its true dimensions. J. Brewer (1932), Davis (1914), and Kitson (1954) were some of the early names in the (vocational) guidance field. Present-day guidance owes its start to such men. Recent developmental theories by Super in his many studies of careers and career patterns (see suggested readings at the end of the chapter) and Tiedeman (1958, 1961) have shown the dynamic process of occupational development in all persons. Roe (1956), Caplow (1954), and Ginzberg (1951) have all helped to extend the understanding of the world of work, careers, and vocational choice patterns.

The choice of an occupation, viewed as an instant in time, has been replaced by the design of a constantly developing concept of occupational adjustment or maturity. Elements of self-concept, cultural backdrops, personality characteristics, as well as opportunity—all these enter into the actual determination of an occupational pattern. The role of occupational information is only one of the many items that are involved in the *process*. Arbuckle (1960, p. 121) tersely states the case for occupational information in the school program:

> Vocational information, *per se*, will probably be as valueless, as much of the other information which is presented "willy nilly" to the child as he goes through school. We may talk of education, or learning, or guidance, or counseling, but in all cases, it is the *process* which is the basic and crucial factor.

The developing and maturing child may collect as much valuable data concerning an ultimate vocational choice by understanding his own culture or selected facts about his own interests or aptitudes as may be obtained in a long detailed study of an occupation. Previously examined elementary school learnings can provide a beginning attitude towards work and jobs. A vast reservoir of over-all concepts of Western civilization are developed in these years. Following the first five or six years of school a child may begin to focus, more narrowly, on occupational thinking and vocational planning.

ELEMENTARY SCHOOL

The first few grades in school are seldom stressed in recommendations for the acquisition of occupational information. However, the impressions and emotional attitudes internalized by kindergarten and first grade children may bulk more large in later years than any other experiences of equal time and intensity. Bailard (1952) and Duffy (1950) each defend the importance of early learnings in these grades. Dramatic play, field trips, story telling, even "show and tell" periods in kindergarten and the earliest grades are profitable experiences for children.

> Our school adjustment counselor helped to start us on a series of "multi-purpose" field trips. For many years we had always taken the children on trips to see the cows and chickens at a nearby farm, to the woods to see flowers and trees, and other types of trips. He suggested that we always plan to have a worker talk with the children whenever we were on a trip. The local dairy farm is always a high spot in our year. The children are always excited to see all of the animals, to get a drink of milk, and to find out about all of the things a farmer has to do. Most of the time the work of the farmer is the most startling and interesting part of the trip. Other teachers also take similar trips in the later grades. (Kindergarten teacher)

Counselors and guidance personnel can offer to take the lead in sponsoring such field trips and in helping teachers to develop similar activities. Role playing with kindergarten or first grade pupils may be an uncertain task to the newcomer in such classroom techniques. Volunteering one's service can help the teacher begin the use of such techniques. Many teachers then find the children's response so positive that they use the technique in many other classroom activities. Knepler (1959) offers a helpful discussion on uses and problems in role playing in school.

A creative approach to the joint consideration of occupational and educational concerns is illustrated in a plan advanced by Torrance (1949). Elementary school students are trained to play the roles of physicians, lawyers, and other specific occupations. After a role-playing scene the class completes a discussion concerned with the discrepancies between the role as portrayed and the facts as they know them. The educational and personal requirements of such positions are soon brought out in such a discussion.

The curriculum offers many meaningful opportunities for teachers to introduce and treat occupational information as an important element in the course of study. A classical treatment of this approach is described in detail in one of the earliest books on the use of occupational data in elementary school programs. McCracken and Lamb (1923) describe a school curriculum designed to familiarize students in all elementary grades with the major elements of our society. Course units organized around such topics as food, clothing, housing, and related areas provide a vehicle for introducing functional learnings into social studies, science, and other content areas in the curriculum.

Directors of guidance and other resource persons from the guidance area can often serve as leaders and training directors in school conferences designed to help teachers to include such ideas and treatments within their classes. School-wide workshops can profitably adopt occupational information as a topic for consideration on all grade levels.

Eight specific purposes are listed by Hoppock for presenting occupational information in elementary school:

1. To increase the child's feeling of security.
2. To encourage the natural curiosity of young children.
3. To extend the occupational horizons of the child.
4. To encourage wholesome attitudes toward all useful work.
5. To begin developing a desirable approach to the process of occupational choice.
6. To help students who are dropping out of school and going to work.
7. To help students who face a choice between different high schools or high school programs.
8. To show children who really need money how they can get it without stealing. (Hoppock, 1957, pp. 344–346)

Counseling, groupwork, and teaching may provide means for implementing each of the listed objectives. The design and content of the program will depend upon the ingenuity, skill, and initiative of guidance persons within the program.

SIXTH TO TWELFTH GRADE

There are vast differences among students in the upper grades of school whenever occupational adjustment is considered. Some sixth grade pupils are potential skilled workers and wage earners. Other young students are naïve, protected, and uninterested, as well as unskilled. The process of acquiring vocational maturity depends upon a wide assortment of variables. Group procedures can provide for somewhat generalized attacks on occupational orientation and at other times can assist in providing for individual variations from a norm pattern within a class or school.

Group programs need to stress the significance of the process of

decision making involved in the narrowing down in occupational development. Katz (1960) defends this as an overwhelmingly important element
of group experiences directed toward occupational choices. The weighing
and assessing of factors, forces, environments, etc. in making such choices
can aid the student in achieving a decision when the time is appropriate.

The unreality of student thinking is often a primary obstacle in
facing decision making as a process in vocational planning. Dipboye and
Anderson (1959) found that ninth and twelfth graders were alike in expressing a value system of occupational choices based on personal interest
and security. Group discussions on a simple introductory basis can help
students to meet problems such as this unthreatened and secure.

Our seventh graders are all scheduled for a series of three
group conferences on educational and occupational planning. We
select our groups on a random basis to provide a wide variety of backgrounds and occupational plans and hopes. The counselors all participate and stay with the group for the series of three meetings.

The counselor serves as leader and begins the discussions with
a general introduction that covers the forthcoming need to choose
courses in high school and to plan for an occupation after graduation.
Each student is requested to introduce himself and to state his hopes
and plans for the future. After all persons have said their piece we ask
for volunteers to allow others to question them on their reasons for
such choices and for their ideas for carrying out their plans.

Oftentimes the discussions are uneven and spotty. Some students
can present very adequate defenses of their ideas; other students are
sketchy and purely unrealistic. My task as leader is to keep the discussion on a positive basis and to prevent any extreme type of personal comments from galloping in. The other counselors have the
same problems.

The conferences have been successful in most years. Students
who do not participate actively still secure a more adequate picture
of what is involved in the problem. Our eighth grade students take a
guidance class and are able to follow up on the foundations that are
built in the seventh grade. (Junior high counselor)

Conferences such as these described can introduce students to the
concepts of interest, aptitude, ability, the labor market, and the matching
of self and occupation. Field trips with more sophisticated design, individual research papers, career conferences, planned group sessions, and occupations courses can help students to advance in occupational choice.

Interests, aptitudes, and abilities

Group techniques can be combined with individual counseling to assist students to build an understanding of the meanings of such concepts as interest (expressed and basic), specific and generalized aptitudes, intelligence, skill, ability, and related variables. Psychological test programs are dovetailed into systematic plans for using all available data to help students know themselves and assess their own futures. The group techniques for educational planning described in an earlier section are inseparable from the treatment of vocational concerns. Jobs, occupations, or career patterns can make concrete the more abstract considerations of course and curriculum planning.

Counselors, teachers, and students should recognize that personality and cultural variables are also significant in the selection of school courses and, ultimately, occupations. Cass and Tiedeman (1960) found that self-attitudes and over-all cultural (socio-economic) forces were more significant in student choices than were interests and aptitudes. Such investigations serve to confirm the theoretical speculations of Super, Roe, *et al.*, and to influence all concerned to avoid overemphasis on the more traditional factors. Test data, even as norms become available for ninth and tenth grade students on such tests as the General Aptitude Test Battery of the United States Employment Offices (Droege, 1960), must be treated as only individual facts. A distorted view of any single factor is dangerous.

Field trips and research papers

Field trips, and group research papers following them, place students in a planning atmosphere that is second only to the real process of making decisions about jobs. Care again must be taken that students are not encouraged to believe that they are making final choices as they select industries to visit or occupations to study. Role-playing sessions preceding or following such activities can also increase the involvement of students.

Career conferences

Despite discovery each year by certain schools of the career conference plan as a useful program design, this well-known device continues to be alternately discarded and revived. Many so-called current career conference managers could profit from a reading of the ideas expressed in

Wright's (1928) recommended methods of conducting such conferences. Shosteck (1955) reveals similar concerns for proper use of outsiders in aiding students to secure occupational information. The uncritical arrangement of a "big day" for visitors and speeches often leaves the student wondering whether or not the program was planned for him or for the visitors.

"Career Days," and "College Nights (or Days)" have most often been shifted to a series of small conferences scheduled every few weeks and integrated into the over-all educational and vocational development plan of the guidance department within the school. The emphasis is on learning and the students rather than a circus type extravaganza.

Homogeneous groups

Guidance counselors can serve the needs of groups of pupils by scheduling discussions of occupational patterns and maturity in self-planning. Prospective apprentices in all of the skilled trades can be aided through an examination of the total process of training as a journeyman. Students in a business program may be aided in anticipating problems of placement, working conditions, advancement, etc. that must be faced in work adjustment. The United States employment service offices throughout the country are prepared to aid school guidance programs by administering the General Aptitude Test Battery to prospective student workers.

The career pattern study by Super and others (1957), and related publications arising out of the study (Super and Overstreet, 1960), show that even ninth grade students are aware of the requirements of various occupations, although their specific goals have not been determined. Group involvement can help students to explore the meaning of the choices which lie ahead. The interrelationships of personality, job requirement, self-concept, and home culture are issues that are not easily sorted out in the minds of potential employees.

Gifted pupils may similarly be aided to explore the meaning of their greater talents and skills. Frequently, the gifted children are caught in the dilemma, opposed to that of the retarded or below average group, of being qualified and appropriately placed in a number of widely different career patterns. Gifted children in high school may profit from programs designed for college students. Adaptation is necessary, but the content may be more appropriate for their level of comprehension.

Retarded groups may also be aided in facing the demands of employment through special courses. Lurie, Goldfein, and Baxt (1960) describe a program of this type in which aptitudes, interests, personality characteristics, and job requirements are intensively studied. Again, it is often possible to delay such a planning stress within a program for retarded or slow learners just as it is possible to offer early programming for advanced groups.

COLLEGE AND UNIVERSITY PLANNING

It is often assumed that if students have entered college therefore they have solved their occupational and educational planning problems. The experience of college counselors and counseling bureaus can testify to the incorrectness of such an assumption.

Students selecting a professional training program such as art, music, architecture, or other highly specialized programs must commit themselves to goals at the beginning of their college careers. Changes after a first or second year often lead to a completely new beginning and a loss of credits. General education programs and liberal arts courses allow students to postpone the selection of an area of specialization; curriculum choice may be deferred until the junior year in some cases. Psychological testing, group techniques, and individual counseling are all appropriate with such college students facing educational and occupational decisions. Success in college courses, as in high school courses, is often used as a guide in the selection of future career development. Bonser (1916) advocated the use of curricular evidence long before the advent of reliable and valid test instruments or even presently known methods of counseling or personality assessment.

Many colleges offer orientation courses that stress vocational choice issues. Borow and Lindsey (1959) and Martinson (1959) are typical of sourcebooks used in many courses. First-year psychology courses are also often designed to help students to know themselves more effectively and to select educational and occupational goals in accord with their own self-knowledge as well as the elements of culture, socio-economic factors, and personality characteristics. Glanz and Walston (1958) tackle this task directly. Many other psychology texts are designed to touch upon such issues in accord with the wishes and talents of the instructors. Richardson and Borow (1952), Borow (1958, 1959b, 1960), Glanz and Penney (1961), and Ivey (1959) report on the varied effectiveness of such programs. Considerable evidence is available that such courses can be very helpful to college students.

College courses in occupations, orientation, or even psychology draw heavily upon group procedures in the actual teaching methods. Most of the group techniques usable in the upper grades of secondary schools are also usable with variations in college and university settings.

New and different combinations of techniques are possible in college (and also in some private secondary schools). A dormitory counselor used group procedures to aid the students in his dormitory to explore their own future occupational and educational plans.

> There were over 150 freshmen and sophomore men in our dormitory. Most of them had talked with me in semi-social or counseling sessions throughout the fall term. A majority, in fact a vast majority, had expressed many doubts about their future plans.
>
> The governing council of the dormitory was very interested and willing to sponsor a series of faculty dinners in the small dining room. We established a committee and selected a list of faculty members to invite. The men posted sign-up sheets for other dormitory residents to select tables for the dinners. Most of the men selected faculty members from areas in which they hoped to major.
>
> The dinners were very successful and we plan to continue them. In fact, one of the other dormitories with upperclass men has asked to join with us. We hope to provide a plan for each table that will include a few upperclass majors from the department of the faculty member who is the guest. (Dormitory counselor)

Variations on this approach are possible in all schools. Inter-fraternity and pan-hellenic groups may also be able to assist guidance personnel in securing the joint social and learning benefits from such programs.

The use of student leaders and a specific organization on an entirely group basis was established at Pennsylvania State University to aid students in preparing to enter a vocation and to improve their learning in a particular subject matter, psychology. The report below is taken from the "Pyramid Plan" by Davage and Carpenter (1958, p. 1):

> The Pyramid Plan, as originally conceptualized, is a system of supplementary learning opportunities offered in small working groups in which students of various academic levels, without the actual presence of a faculty member, interact with each other and receive social reinforcement for scholarly motivation and work.

It is hypothesized that active participation in the intellectual climate of skillfully guided discussion groups supplied with selected materials will enable students: (1) to sharpen their definition of themselves as students majoring in an academic field, (2) to gain the skills and work habits that will help them to pursue scholarly work more independently than normally, and (3) to accept greater responsibility for their own learning. In general, the Pyramid Plan seeks to promote in students strong personal involvement in scholarly work.

The term "Pyramid" is derived from the schematic arrangement of the participants in the program. This schematic arrangement is a function of the *number of participants at each level* of academic maturity from freshmen to faculty members and is observed at each of the steps in the planning and application of a Pyramid program. A diagram of the schematic arrangement is presented below. In this diagram the levels of academic maturity constitute the vertical axis, and the sequence of planning and application of a pyramid program, the horizontal axis.

	Planning Groups	Developmental Group(s)	Work-Study Groups
Faculty Member	X (1)		
Graduate Assistants	XX (2)	X (1)	
Seniors	XXXX (4)	XX (2)	X (1)
Juniors		XXXXX (5)	XX (2)
Sophomores			XXXX (4)
Freshmen			XXXXXX (6)

The diagram shows the basic unit of one pyramid; hundreds of students with similar proportions of organizational balance can and have been used in the work at Pennsylvania State University.

Several experiments have been performed comparing "Pyramid Groups" with control students. Results seem to be very favorable and to promise much in instruction techniques and student learnings. Reports of results have been made by Davage (1958, 1959) and Carpenter (1959a, 1959b). Future reports are planned by the experimenters. There would seem to be little question that such creative designs could be used in high school and junior high school as well as elementary school.

PLACEMENT EXPERIENCES

Part-time, summer, and full-time placement is a problem in secondary school and college. Placement counselors have often been disillusioned by the scope of the task of working with large portions of the graduating class. Group techniques have begun to be used with profit and efficiency in solving such problems.

The problems of placement can be outlined in large lecture groups to all students interested in securing positions after graduation. Printed materials often are used to supplement the verbal presentations of the placement director. The next step is to gather together the students interested in similar types of job placement—education, insurance, or other major occupations in a comunity. Camping, secretarial, and similar breakdowns may be used in high school and college, and in accord with local curricula and opportunities within the community or regional area for temporary or "permanent" placement.

The activities of small, student action groups present the opportunity to observe actual interviews with employers, to role-play interviews and to evaluate student strengths and weaknesses displayed. The problems of adjusting to the position, once secured, are also often involved in such group meetings. Socio-drama techniques, illustrating human relation's problems, promotion, job initiative, and responsibility to an assigned task are useful and stimulating group projects.

The involvement of the town through school-community co-operation in placement projects is illustrated by Williams (1954). Williams describes how a town and school project prepared and published a booklet about the town and its jobs to aid students in appreciating the advantages and opportunities in their local community. Siegel (1960) describes the use of groups in orientation and placement procedures in an educational setting. Harlow (1956) applies the same methods to the summer problems of placement faced by a community counseling agency. He reports that over 500 students were involved in the project and that over 200 found work "on their own" or through the help of the agency. The actual contributions of the program are not isolated in his report (Harlow, 1956, p. 442).

The issues of job placement at any educational level are capable of being solved in many fashions. Placement is the culmination of the processes of educational and vocational counseling, guidance, and groupwork. The co-operation, sharing of records, and joint participation of the guidance departments involved can help a harassed placement counselor to face the major tasks of aiding a large number of students within a very short period of time.

SUMMARY

Occupational or vocational planning is the reverse side of the coin that has educational decision-making on the other side. Early experiences in the first few grades of school help to establish attitudes and emotional feelings about occupations and work. The junior and senior high school years are times that allow for actual discussion of jobs and educational patterns that can lead to jobs. Cautions concerning the developmental process of occupational choice are offered. Examples of actual uses of groups in all areas of educational and vocational planning illustrate the issues presented.

Placement in a job or career is the advanced step in the educational and vocational planning process. Large and small group procedures along with specific techniques are effective and efficiently related to the problems of placement.

SUGGESTED READINGS

Baer, M. F., and E. C. Roeber, *Occupational Information: Its Nature and Use.* Chicago: Science Research Associates, 1958.

Caplow, Theodore, *The Sociology of Work.* Minneapolis, Minn.: University of Minnesota Press, 1954.

Forrester, Gertrude, *Occupational Literature: An Annotated Bibliography.* New York: H. W. Wilson Co., 1954.

Ginsberg, Eli, *et al.*, *Occupational Choice: An Approach to a A General Theory.* New York: Columbia University Press, 1951.

Mahoney, Harold J., *Occupational Information for Counselors: The Essential Content for Training Courses.* Tarrytown, N.Y.: World Book Co., 1952.

Roe, Anne, *The Psychology of Occupations.* New York: John Wiley & Sons, Inc., 1956.

Shartle, Carroll, *Occupational Information* (2nd ed.). New York: Prentice-Hall, Inc., 1952.

Super, Donald E., *The Psychology of Careers.* New York: Harper & Bros., 1957.

Super, Donald E., and P. Overstreet, *The Vocational Maturity of Ninth Grade Boys.* New York: Bureau of Publications, Teachers College, Columbia University, 1960.

Super, Donald E., *et al., Vocational Development: A Framework for Research.* New York: Bureau of Publications, Teachers College, Columbia University, 1957.

————, *Scientific Careers and Vocational Development Theory.* New York: Bureau of Publications, Teachers College, Columbia University, 1957.

14. GROUP COUNSELING

Individual counseling and therapy have a long and detailed history; group approaches to counseling and therapy are more recent discoveries and have developed in erratic, fitful fashion. The vitality and magnitude of the applications of group efforts promise an eventual professional stature for groups in counseling and therapy that may provide equal acceptance with any individual, one-to-one, concept.

The early beginnings of the group treatment process were only occasionally recognized in the literature of counseling, guidance, and therapy. Perhaps the first systematic use of a group concept in therapy seems to be traceable to the organization of several patients into a group for the treatment of consumption (Pratt, 1906). Moreno established a children's theater in Vienna in 1911 (Moreno, 1946, 1955), where he created "spontaneity plays" for children to "play out" problems. The first group therapy, using a lecture method, for mental disorders was described in the work of Lazell (1921). Actual medical use of group approaches (cf. Schilder, 1938) was sporadic until after World War II. Slavson's early books (1943, 1947), along with the work of Klapman (1946) and Foulkes (1948), signalled that a new and useful tool could be available in helping persons in groups. A very complete bibliography presented by Kotkov in 1950 helped to establish a summary of practice to that date. A spurt in writing, practice, and newer applications followed in succeeding years.

The early nonmedical applications of group therapy and counseling were recognized in special situations, particularly in helping young delinquents. Rathbun (1945) listed many school applications of group counseling. Strang (1948) told of varied uses of groups in aiding potential delinquents in a Cincinnati school system. Froehlich (1958a) and Driver (1954) began to isolate specific applications of group counseling with students and adults of all ages. The descriptions and research data concerning groups in counseling and therapy settings have multiplied by almost geometric proportions since these early beginnings.

The presentation of the many concepts of group counseling and therapy must involve a clarification of terms and ideas that have contributed to the present shotgun-type effect of the use of groups in counseling and therapy. An analysis of specific group activities indicates that a firm line of demarcation cannot always be drawn between group counseling and group activities of a similar, but not identical, nature. Some of the additionally important issues that need to be clarified in a study of groups include: the similarity between the learning process (as indicated by movement or problem solving) in group and individual counseling; the results of concurrent group and individual counseling; and the complex role of the counselor and group leader that must be fulfilled as group counseling is undertaken. These concerns will comprise the major units of this chapter on groups in counseling.

GROUPS, COUNSELING, AND THERAPY

Group counseling and group therapy are almost contradictory concepts to the individual not familiar with the detailed practices present in groups, counseling, and therapy. Multiple counseling, group guidance, and the almost interchangeable use of counseling and psychotherapy have added to the uncertainty of the dimensions and true nature of these new concepts.

Terms and definitions

The issues concerning the use of the terms *counseling* and *therapy* have been thrashed out in several decades of counseling history. Group workers have often reopened an almost closed issue. Therapy has been a term commonly accepted for use in treating physically ill individuals. Nonmedical treatment of mentally disturbed patients has also been termed therapy, and this is usually conducted by psychologists and psychiatrists outside the hospital. The word therapy usually connotes sickness of a severe type, either functional or organic. Counseling is a process different in degree rather than in kind from therapy. Counselors use similar, even overlapping, techniques with less seriously disturbed persons. School guidance programs are most often engaged in counseling rather than therapy.

Group counseling is related to group therapy in the same fashion that individual counseling is related to individual therapy. Psychotherapy is used in individual or group practices as a synonym for therapy. Confusion of terms often arises when practitioners try to impress the consumer by overtone and connotation, in order to establish a climate for treatment. Such was the purpose of the physician who stroked his imaginary beard and said, "I guess I'll give your sprained ankle a little hydrotherapy," but the climate quickly changed when the patient, an experienced athlete, replied, "You mean you're going to put my foot in the whirlpool bath?"

Multiple counseling is another term that has been claimed by several guidance writers. Its essential nature is expressed by a somewhat simpler and more commonly understood term, *group counseling*. Again the potential guidance person may choose the term or the words that best serve his particular purpose. The new guidance director may describe his ideas for elementary pupils more clearly to the principal by talking of "counseling with a group," than by grandiosely alluding to "multiple psychotherapy." Again, the purposes of the person using the words are more important than his adherence to a technical definition.

Group counseling involves an understanding of the principles of counseling and of groupwork. A counselor well trained in the techniques of individual, one-to-one counseling may find himself badly confused if he attempts to begin group counseling with no understanding of the dynamics of group operation. Furthermore, it is ethically questionable for a group worker to attempt group counseling with no knowledge of counseling theory and practice. Counseling is the more basic knowledge that must be possessed and understood if group approaches are to be used. The treatment of group counseling that follows presupposes previous or concurrent training and study in counseling philosophies and practice.

An operational definition of group counseling stresses the establishment of a group possessing a warm, accepting climate. In the group the person can evaluate himself and his choice of action, while accepting a controlled degree of responsibility for his evaluations and choices. Relationships can be developed between the counselor-leader and group members, or between members themselves, that can help them to function better outside the group. Group counseling may overlap with the use of other group activities in a guidance program and may also overlap with group therapy. Group counseling emphasizes intra-individual change through learning, whereas group structures in guidance are primarily fact-imparting and educationally oriented. Group therapy treats seriously disturbed or sick patients.

Group guidance and group counseling

There are many uses of groups in a guidance program, and each of the preceding chapters has isolated particular applications and formulations of these. A common confusion in many guidance programs is the misnaming of group activities in guidance as group counseling. The line dividing such related patterns of guidance and counseling is difficult to describe. The similarities outweigh the differences in a quantitative sense, but the significant qualitative differences between group counseling and the use of groups in guidance need to be stated.

Group counseling, as is true in individual counseling when compared with guidance, is concerned with assisting the individual members of the group to face and resolve personal and emotional problems. Many group procedures in guidance approach this goal but are more directly concerned with acquiring information, gaining orientation to new problems, planning and implementing student activities, collecting data for occupational and educational decisions, or similar guidance rather than counseling activities. Group therapy sessions, as is true when therapy is compared with counseling, are concerned with remedying serious problems of mental or emotional sickness.

Counseling and guidance, in groups or on an individual basis, are directed mainly toward a positive, preventive view of future mental health problems. Therapy connotes a concern with the correction or removal of a present handicap or illness. The nature of the problem of the pupil, client, or patient will determine the particular type of technique that is used. All of these approaches are related and differ more in degree than in kind.

PRE-COUNSELING GROUPS

The use of many group approaches in guidance can help to establish a broadly based service to all of the students in a school or system. Guidance must be concerned with all students rather than with simply the problem-child and the troubled individual. Groups provide a technique designed to affect and aid the school careers of all students. At the same time such guidance groups can utilize the data collected in the psychological testing program and individual inventory service.

Students who participate in the school group program can be screened for individual or group counseling opportunities necessary in a well-constructed guidance program. Teachers, counselors, and teacher-counselors in group situations can discover students who need to be invited or encouraged to participate in group counseling sessions. Students who move from guidance groups into counseling groups may similarly be helped to obtain individual counseling along with or instead of group counseling.

The referral and service process in such a brief analysis may appear similar to the treatment accorded a product in moving from manufacturer or farmer to consumer, such as a clock or a can of pumpkin; however, a skilled guidance administrator can help pupils, counselors, and teachers to co-ordinate a referral program smoothly. The pupil, contrary to the feeling (?) that may be postulated within a clock or a can of pumpkin, is not mechanically manipulated but will be served by a system designed to help and assist when and where problems and issues demand in a comprehensive approach. The student will be better able to attain and to achieve up to his inherent capacity. Guidance can live up to its promised individualization within an educational structure and system.

Certain group structures that may be used in a guidance program are closely related to possible group counseling sessions. Discussion groups centering upon the interpretation of psychological test data, assessing the nature of the group members' aptitudes, interests, values, and occupational plans—even case study groups may easily slip into group counseling. The counselor or group leader must be aware of the underlying factors in various aspects of group counseling. Often the inherent dangers in the framework are only apparent after a specific issue has taken place. The case of Don in Chapter 2 illustrated the level of feeling that can occur in group discussion meetings. Some students may not wish to become involved in the more personal and emotional dredging that other students often begin.

Ethical concern on the part of counselors and guidance workers would seem to dictate that it is undesirable to involve students in a group counseling session until they have entered voluntarily. Some institutional (hospital or prison) practices may violate such a code of practice, but this is done very rarely, even in extreme circumstances.

An invitational attitude appears to be more successful when students are encouraged to become members of group counseling sessions. Two examples of such an attitude arising out of pre-counseling group activity are present in the reports of two different counselors:

> Our eighth grade students are all enrolled in a guidance class. Discussion groups are organized when we come to the unit on the interpretation of all of the psychological test data available on the students. The discussions often become very personal and I need to guard carefully against overinvolvement on the part of many students.
>
> After our three scheduled meetings I offer the opportunity to any member of the class to join a counseling group. The test discussion groups are always held in class periods with student leadership under my supervision. The group counseling sessions are held in study periods or after school. I serve as counselor-group leader in all of these sessions and we center upon the specific problems of the individual members of the group. (Junior high school counselor)

> Our college requires all freshmen to complete a course in psychology. We conduct many group discussions as a part of the content of the course. The counseling staff in the college teaches the course and serves as assigned counselor to all of the students in several sections.
>
> Individual and group counseling parallel the course, but are really not a part of the course. Attendance is required in the course, but any individual or group counseling is voluntary. We have found that the groupwork in the course, the content of the course, and experience in individual counseling are all predisposing factors in scheduling group sessions for the students with similar problems. (College counselor and psychology teacher)

Variations on these practices exist in schools of all levels in which required and voluntary group practices are found. The step between group activity in a guidance atmosphere and the needed personal involvement in a group counseling session is a step that needs to be consciously and deliberately taken by the participating student.

Ostland (1953) describes a project that stressed the sociometric structuring of groups, rotation of group membership, and a climate of problem solving within a case discussion course. Such activity is a desirable pretraining atmosphere for students who may engage in group counseling; however, such activities would not normally be classified as group counseling. Many applications of the use of case studies, often of former students in a school, can precede counseling experiences in a group. The case study approach brings students face to face with problems, but with problems of other persons, not members of the group. The next step of facing personal and/or personality problems present within the group is a large step.

GROUP COUNSELING PROCESS

The adolescentlike forcing of practicioners into "camps," rigid systems, or schools has plagued both theorists and practicing counselors. Interpretative or directed group experiences exist as well as nondirective techniques, but all counseling is essentially client centered. Group writers have continued to stress these differences in approach or technique; however, most theorists in group and individual counseling have begun to compile the areas of agreement among all counselors and to attempt to sort out the differences through research.

Axline (1947) describes the improvement of reading, although no reading instruction was given, through nondirective play therapy groups. Fleming and Snyder (1947), Peres (1947), and Sheldon and Landsman (1950) describe play therapy programs and group therapy sessions in a nondirective atmosphere. These research programs showed evidence that such group programs of help to individuals did make a difference. The methodological battle lines have become more blurred in recent years and even Carl Rogers is less militant in his narrow interpretations of process and methodology. More recent reports are demonstrating that a large common agreement exists in counseling technique. Disagreements and research are centered more upon specific applications of counseling and its varying effects (in groups and in individual fashion) in the solution of persons' problems.

Practical problems

Aside from the importance of involving students on a voluntary basis in group counseling, many counselors feel irritated by the many seemingly small, but important issues that must be resolved as group counseling sessions are planned and inaugurated.

How many, what kinds of problems, how long, how frequently, and similar issues are concerns that must be solved prior to an initial effort in any group counseling. Sometimes it is even possible to state that such items may be ignored and to make a start on the basis of the problem at hand and the facilities available. Lerner (1953) even reports on an exploratory effort in group counseling with alcoholic inmates within a city jail!

Warters (1960) summarizes the research on group size, the selection and grouping of members, and the length, interval and duration of group counseling sessions. Warters reports that the size of a group counseling unit is small rather than large, but that exact size or even a range of sizes has not been established through research. Six, six to eight, six to ten, ten to fifteen—some authorities even recommend groups larger than twenty as appropriate for group counseling and therapy (Warters, 1960, pp. 174–175).

Group composition is similarly unclear. Warters reports on authorities recommending voluntary and involuntary groups; sex segregation in clinical groups; nonsegregated, in fact equally balanced in school groups; and homogeneous as well as heterogeneous groups in particular problem areas (Warters, 1960, pp. 176–178). Reasonably compatible groups are essential in all recommendations.

Decisions about size, sex composition, and even characteristics possessed by the participants need to be established in accord with local issues and the talents of the counselors attempting to use group counseling procedures. Bach (1954) defends this concept in recommending that a selection of participants must be made on the basis of the issue that is facing the group. Exclusion rather than inclusion policies seem easier to formulate. Hobbs lists three types of persons that are detrimental to group counseling activity (1951, pp. 312–315).

1. Psychologically sophisticated persons who use knowledge of psychodynamics cruelly on others;
2. Extremely aggressive or hostile people who destroy the atmosphere of acceptance and freedom essential to the success of the group; and,
3. People who are continuously in close contact with each other outside of the group.

Bach (1954, pp. 18–22) offers four criteria for excluding persons from membership in a counseling group:
1. Insufficient reality contact;
2. Extremes of culturally taboo or illegal behavior;

3. Chronically dominant persons who monopolize the group's time; and,

4. Persons with psychopathic defenses or attributes.

The issues of physical location of a group, duration of single meetings, and the over-all length of treatment must be handled with intelligence and discretion by the counselors and guidance persons. Research has not differentiated a desirable pattern in general or specific cases.

Closed or open groups (closed to new members or open for the entry of new members) are also issues that are still unresolved. Obviously, the many interrelationships of these practical matters must be faced by counselors. Small closed groups may destroy themselves as members drop out. The open or closed nature of the group is thus related to the beginning size. Sex restrictions may hamper or help a group in the discussion of a particular type of problem. The counseling background of the new group counselor is vital in attempting to establish proper effective working conditions for any group.

Bach (1954) offers a mimeographed instruction sheet that is distributed to each potential group counseling member. He covers six major topics which help to summarize the "housekeeping details" and to illustrate some of the ethical concerns that must be faced in group counseling or therapy.*

GROUP THERAPY PROCEDURES

Preparation Sheet for New Patients

1. *Size of group.* The group's size is limited to a minimum number of six and a maximum number of ten patients.

2. *Admission of new members.* When an old member leaves the group his or her place in the group will be filled by a new patient. The selection is made by group decision, from several candidates considered suitable for group therapy by the therapist.

3. *Extraoffice meetings.* The regular office meetings of the group with the therapist, while of central therapeutic importance, are only part of the total program. Experiences during the postsession and during any other out-of-the-office contacts between members of the group, provide important material for self-observation and analysis.

4. *Sharing of mutual experiences.* Group members usually adhere to the principle that everything anybody says, thinks or does,

* Reproduced with permission from George R. Bach, *Intensive Group Psychotherapy* (New York: The Ronald Press Company), pp. 29–30.

which involves another member of the group, is subject to open discussion in the group. In other words, the emotionally important experiences of any member are shared by all members. There are no secrets inside the group.

5. *Ethical confidence.* In contrast to Principle No. 4, everything that goes on within the group—everything (!)—must remain an absolute secret as far as any outsider (nonmember) is concerned. The only exceptions are professional visitors, scientific observers, and/or psychiatric consultants and assistants who may help the therapist's professional work with groups. Anyone participating in group therapy automatically assumes the same professional ethics of absolute discretion which bind professional therapists.

6. *The group's goal.* The group goal is free communication on a nondefensive personal and emotional level. This goal can be reached only by the group effort. Experience shows that the official conductor cannot "push" the group; the group has to progress by its own efforts. Each member will get out of the group what he puts into it. As every member communicates to the group his feelings and perceptions and associations of the moment as openly as he can and as often as he can, the group will become a therapeutically effective medium.

Many variations have been developed on this form and may be used according to local demands and needs. Brammer and Shostrom (1960) have all participants sign a copy of a statement based upon the reproduced form of Bach.

Phases in group counseling

Any attempt to isolate and to describe in detail the chronological phases or stages in group counseling sessions is as impossible as a similar task in individual counseling. However, it is productive to examine the total process of group counseling and present time periods that are found in most, if not all, types of sessions. The order, the intensity, and most of all an estimate of a length of time spent in any single period, are impossible to offer.

Ohlsen and DeWitt (1950) in an early recognition of group counseling attempted to isolate some of the ways and means of the process. They listed several variables that affected the possible success of group counseling efforts. Size, climate, type of problem attacked, the skill of the leader, and the composition of the group were offered as significant variables. Most of these items have since been removed from the heart of the counseling process and seem to be related environmental variables.

Carl Rogers (1948), as he has done so frequently in the whole field of counseling, has offered a comprehensive and discerning analysis of the process of learning and growth in groups. He writes of groups in general rather than of specific group counseling, but his expressions are as fresh today as when they were offered in 1948:

> The phases of the group process, as well as of the individual process, would seem to be:
> 1. emotional release;
> 2. gradual exploration of attitudes;
> 3. growing conscious awareness of denied elements;
> 4. a changed perception of the problem in an altered frame of reference;
> 5. a changed concept of the group and the self;
> 6. a new course of consciously controlled action better adapted to the underlying reality of the situation; and,
> 7. a resulting improvement in social and inter-personal relationships. (Rogers, 1948, p. 28)

These processes or stages in individual change presented by Carl Rogers are similar to those he used in later writings and in his article "The Characteristics of a Helping Relationship" (1958), in which he identified significant attitude issues which must be faced by any counselor working with individuals, alone or in groups. He has also reaffirmed this analysis of the group process in later writings (Rogers, 1959).

A view of the process or phases involved in group counseling can be presented that is more in accord with the issues of group dynamics presented in this volume. These phases are not offered as differing from Rogers or any major theorist in counseling. There is no longer a wide divergence of views in this area. Rather, different emphases or elements may be selected out of the process of counseling for examination at any given moment. A thorough knowledge of counseling theory and practice is again assumed in the analysis of a group in a counseling climate. These phases are presented in order to emphasize the group nature of the process:

1. rapport
2. acceptance
3. listening and observing
4. promoting group and individual understandings
5. problem-solving skill development
6. closing evaluations and procedures

1. RAPPORT. Voluntary groups will have differing problems of rapport from institutional requirements forcing attendance by individuals. Even forced groups may be offered a choice of beginning "now or later," or even a choice of topics for discussion. Gersten (1951, 1952) describes a broad gauge experiment with institutionalized juvenile delinquents in which he attempted to use democratic procedures in accord with the research reports of Lewin, Lippitt, and White (1939). He attempted to establish rapport with many varying techniques. Much of his effort with the members of the group involved "activity therapy" and the use of play-handicraft materials.

The choice of the content for the group counseling sessions can have much to do with the rapidity and degree of rapport that is established. Driver (1954) advocates a simple beginning through the use of voting techniques. Eiserer (1956) suggests that students can bring up anything that enters their mind. Such simplicity may be only superficial and actually dangerous. Knowledge of the divisive nature of voting in a group can demonstrate the necessity of group dynamic skills on the part of a counselor. Talland and Clark (1954) point out that "not every topic is as useful as any other." They recommend that a thorough period of time be alloted for the selection of topics. The counselor-leader will need to be thoroughly aware of the defensiveness of groups in early sessions and provide for the adoption of beginning objectives of a simple (psychological) nature. Revised goals and plans can be developed through a flexible climate in the group. Talland and Clark (1954) evaluate the content of group therapy choices on the basis of a psychoanalytic frame of reference. Experienced counselors will need to translate early opening problems as, "I don't know what college to go to." and "What job should I plan for?", in the light of their knowledge of expressed problems as they vary from actual problems.

Rapport cannot be established by any simple device or short-term "gimmick." The relationship among the members of the group as well as with the counselor can develop only slowly and fitfully. Rogers (1951, 1958) defends the deepest meaning of rapport (a relationship) and feels that it can be the single most important element in counseling.

The role of anxiety as it affects rapport in individual persons and in groups is only partially understood. Sarason (1960) speaks of the importance of viewing children from their inside view of the world. Their anxieties are often related only distantly to the objective, observable, and outsider's concept of the world. Banghart (1959) believes that anxiety is related to the ability of a group ultimately to solve problems and to relate to one another. He attempted to isolate these variables in an experimental situation but was unsuccessful. His conclusions raise many questions about anxiety that must be considered as important. The counselor in establishing rapport with and among the members of a group is dealing with one of the most poorly understood concepts in all of groupwork. Caution and care are necessary attitudes as groups begin.

2. ACCEPTANCE.   Acceptance is closely related to rapport and often the degree of rapport that may be established in a group can be dependent upon the degree of acceptance that is present within the climate of the group. The acceptance by the leader of all members and their problems is assumed. However, the group needs also to create its own atmosphere. Often, individual members may express rejection by word or deed to other members and yet the person may feel accepted in the group as a whole. The reverse situation may depress a member. Such are the varying situations that can develop within groups, contrary to expected patterns that may be transferred from individual counseling.

Some early hospital experiments helped to explore the dimensions of acceptance within groups. Curran (1939) organized a group of adolescents in a hospital ward for treatment purposes. His belief in activities and play as a basis for members' acceptance of other members was basic to the hopes for growth treatment. McCann and Almada (1951) used an actual wooden "round table" in the ward of a hospital to help to establish a degree of acceptance and rapport among the members of the group therapy unit. A superficial analysis of these activities may raise the question of whether they provide a sound basis for generalization in group acceptance. Hospital settings are not schools and the simplest beginning of acceptance in these hospital therapy groups is a large first-step in treatment of the subjects.

The therapeutic use of silence can be important in a group just as in an individual counseling session. A group with many minds and ideas is different from a single person. Silence in early sessions may be threatening and hostile to new members. Hughes (1958) attempts to defend silence since in a group everyone is silent most of the time because only one person can talk at once. Hughes presumes "everyone is thinking." Such an assumption depends upon all of the dynamic interactions that have preceded the period of silence. Again, the skill of the counselor as a perceptive, sensitive person, and an observant and trained group leader must be the determining factor in arriving at a decision about talking, reflecting, interpreting, or remaining silent.

Acceptance in groups is dependent upon startlingly different variables than are apparent to many observers. Sacks (1960) demonstrated that the perceived distance between members was related to the perceived distance of the group members with their parents (attitudes outside of a group). Sacks measured the acceptance of group members toward each other and toward important figures outside of the group. He found that such perceptions were related in mutually interdependent fashion. Such research results are in accord with the over-all research findings presented in an earlier chapter on perception and communication in groups.

The growing development of acceptance in a group is intimately related to the attitudes of each individual towards himself and the persons around him. Group experiences tend to expand such tendencies within members whereas such factors are often diminished within individual counseling and therapy. Lundy (1956) shows that the process of judging others is intimately related to one's attitudes toward self and one's own needs to distort or project feelings.

3. LISTENING AND OBSERVING.   The lay observer is often deceived by the nonactivity of a counselor. Experience has taught most counselors the value of active, intense listening and observing. Groups place an even greater responsibility on the counselor-leader because of the complexity of the situation.

Group members, as they become caught up in the counseling process, must also become effective listeners and observers. Crawford (1953) describes a year-long therapy program for seven junior high school boys. The boys attempted to test the limits of the situation very early and ended up in a "rubber band war." The counselor watched and waited with the group. The boys soon found that the activity was not forbidden and that they were not arousing the expected feelings of anger and hostility in the counselor. They cleaned up the mess themselves after observing that they were responsible for their actions and that they were establishing their own climate and atmosphere for activity.

Resistance is a common phenomenon in group counseling sessions. Often the subtle forms of resistance may escape the notice of the individual members. The counselor often must wait and help the members to recognize and deal with such forms of defensiveness. Redl (1948) indicates that unless such recognition is present, little chance exists for the success of the group. The counselor is helping others to learn and cope with problems that, for him, may be clearly seen; however, the group is involved in the growth and learnings of every member and must be aided in a similar type of recognition.

The functions of listening and observing are related to later developments within group counseling sessions. The ability to empathize or to "feel with" other members of the group is one of the key signs in the development of insight and learning about one's self. Ackerman (1955) reports that a group of mixed adolescents began to feel better understood by others as they themselves were able to increase their acceptance of the differences present in others and to observe and accept individual peculiarities. The dynamics in this process are somewhat the reverse of the standard process of projection. The individual, as he can see, understand, and accept other persons, begins to become more comfortable with himself and to comprehend his own actions and attitudes. The significant psychological growth factor is within the person and the nature of one's own attitudes towards one's self.

4. PROMOTING GROUP AND INDIVIDUAL UNDERSTANDING.   Understanding becomes a primary goal after the initial meetings of a group counseling unit have been completed. The climate or atmosphere of the group is directly related to the development of individual and group understanding. Fiedler, Hutchins, and Dodge (1959) found that startling results could take place even in so-called nontherapy-oriented groups. These research workers placed students and soldiers into living groups that were, by measurement, accepting, warm, and permissive. The changes in personality, again through actual pre- and post-measurement with standard devices, occurred in a relatively short period of time. These results took place in spite of the fact that there had been no direct attempt to help the student or soldiers, or to provide a therapeutic effort. These experimental findings were not duplicated in small college and military groups that did not provide such a climate. The implications of these data are clear for group counseling and therapy groups, and also clear for guidance and personnel workers in all areas of education.

Various techniques are available for aiding group members, as individuals and as group members, to achieve a beginning degree of understanding of their own and others' actions. The frustrations and resulting aggressive acts that are present in many groups have been studied in several situations. The turning of aggressive actions into material for understanding is a useful and productive group technique. Trapp (1959) attempted to assess the nature and direction of aggressive acts in groups. He found that as frustrations increased in a group situation that some threatened members became extrapunitive (aggressions directed outwards) while others developed intrapunitive outlets (aggression directed inwards). Meals and Summerskill (1951) in an earlier experience attempted to use such aggression to develop understandings. These investigators (similar to the "rubber band wards" group) were dealing with young boys from nine to twelve years of age and were faced with considerable hostility and aggression in the group. The five boys were given freedom and encouragement to throw objects at a board upon which various pictures were placed. The opportunity to direct their aggressions outwards towards inanimate pictures provided for a type of cathartic release and made possible more constructive group action following the "throwing."

Role playing is a process that can provide for the "working through" or the expiation of aggressive needs whether they are essentially intra- or extrapunitive. The opportunity to act out a distressing situation and to play the role "to the hilt" provides a more sophisticated version of the throwing board or the rubber band war.

The age of the members of a group is no barrier to the use of role playing. However, skill in role playing and the value of the outcome are always dependent upon the environment of the group and the actual insight that can be achieved by members. Mead (1934) first offered an explanation of the need for an individual to be able to understand the actions of others (to be capable of taking the role of another) in social situations. Sarbin (1954) supports this view and presents evidence that such skill and capacity are later developments in the personality. The perceptual and social skills that are inherent in such tasks are acquired at differing rates and maturity levels. Role playing in group counseling sessions can provide the vehicle for stimulating growth and maturity in insight and understanding.

Clear evidence of the value of group counseling in aiding individuals to obtain a more meaningful self-understanding is presented by Caplan (1957). He established experimental and control groups of twelve- to fifteen-year-old junior high school pupils. These young persons were drawn from a reservoir of "unruly, inconsiderate, and antisocial" persons in the school. Ten fifty-minute periods of group counseling were provided for the experimental groups. He reports that there was significant shift in self-concept understandings, as measured by Q-sort techniques within the experimental groups; and that there was no comparable or even significant change in the control groups. The growth in grade achievement was slight but related to the experimental groups. Changes in achievement are normally secondary change patterns that depend upon previously accomplished attitude changes.

5. PROBLEM-SOLVING PHASES. The inability to characterize the developmental or chronological stages present in any group counseling program does not make it impossible to isolate a problem-solving phase in most groups. Too early concern with this problem can lead to superficial or even distorted individual answers for participants. Rapport, acceptance, understanding, and insight can provide a basis for the development of problem-solving activities.

To plan activities or even to conduct a discussion of attitudes toward action, as a prelude to problem solving, can create healthy feelings in any group. The counseling climate can provide a supportive yet evaluative atmosphere for individual members engaged in this process. "Suppose I do . . ." is a phrase that is common in a group session. Other members are free to evaluate and to presuppose or even to role-play the probable results of any particular plan of action.

A. L. Brewer (1958) lists as one of the values and objectives of group counseling the collective judgment of a group that can be focused upon a common or even individual problem of the group. As Assistant Principal of Pettingill Junior High School in Lansing Michigan, she lists six major objectives present in a series of three group counseling sessions planned for seventh grade pupils in her school. The entire seventh grade population was involved in group counseling for a period of twenty-two weeks. Four seventh grade counselors served as counselor-leaders. The list of objectives for the program was:

1. to develop desirable pupil-counselor relationships by giving the pupils an opportunity to see their counselors;
2. to open an avenue whereby the pupils may feel free to discuss any problems that may arise by asking for individual conferences;
3. to guide the pupils by giving information;
4. to service more pupils on certain general topics in a given length of time;
5. to focus collective judgment on common problems;
6. to develop desirable ideals and habits of citizenship. (Brewer, 1958, p. 152)

The establishment of plans is often a gross and nonspecific process. Pepinsky (1947) in an early approach to the values of classroom types of "therapy" attempted to help students set goals with reference to the culture and their own particular behavior within that culture. Values were stressed and each student encouraged to examine his own adopted values and to establish means for achieving newly adopted values. The outcomes in such a comprehensive program are, of necessity, nonspecific and developmental.

6. EVALUATIVE AND CLOSING PROCEDURES.   To close or to obtain closure with a group counseling unit is more difficult than to achieve a similar goal in a one-to-one individual counseling session. Adjustment is a constant ongoing and developmental process; any instant of time can only be a cross section of successful adjustment. Each participant begins at a different developmental level in a counseling group and similarly will end at a personally and privately determined stage. Progress is subject to individual differences and to widely varying forces within a functioning personality.

Group counseling and therapy may uncover more problems than are actually solved in the process of treatment. Such a conclusion (even on a tentative, nonconfirmed research basis) may appear to be depressing to guidance workers and counselors. Yet, an understanding of the nature of personal growth and development may help counselors to recognize that such conclusions are in accord with an understanding of human personality and developmental growth. Many persons needing help are unable to face, and hope to solve, many of the issues and problems that are inherent within their personalities. Counseling reveals and releases such issues and presents the person with the opportunity to solve the problem. Change within the self, changes in attitudinal structure within personality, and change within coping patterns of adjustment are all necessary predisposing elements to the solution of external or people-centered problems.

Peres (1947) found that problems were on the increase as the plan of group therapy was brought to a close. The participants had worked together for six sessions and the more successful (in terms of external measures) persons in the group had developed more positive attitudes about themselves and their problems; however, these persons were faced with more problems to solve than had existed (consciously) at the beginning of the sessions.

Powdermaker and Frank (1953, pp. 141–161) describe the rising and falling level of anxiety as a barometer of the process within a group therapy unit. The discomfort (anxiety level) of patients is high in beginning sessions, begins to recede as rapport and a working relationship are established, rises again as major issues, themes, and problems are tackled, and falls again as insight occurs and as learning takes place. The cyclical nature of such anxiety patterns has been noted in previously described patterns of acceptance, understanding, and problem-solving phases.

No inflexible rule can be offered or obtained from research about the proper timing and specific procedures in evaluating progress and terminating the sessions of group counseling. The experience of the counselor-leader, the nature of the group involved in the process, and the progress obtained in previous sessions must all be intervening variables in the final decision for group or individual termination.

Types of group counseling

The various phases or stages in group counseling can take place in differing surroundings and in varying patterns (Gill, 1960). The examples that follow in this section are drawn from high school, college, and a hospital setting.

EXAMPLE 1—COLLEGE GROUP COUNSELING. The first example is a portion of actual dialogue and interaction among the members of a college group and their counselor. The college students had been invited to join a group counseling session by the psychology teacher-counselor. All of the instructors assigned to this counselor's student group were questioned to determine the students who were the most withdrawn, retiring, and unwilling to speak in class. The ten poorest students on these criteria out of over 100 were invited to join the group counseling unit. All accepted and were involved in eight group sessions. The following excerpt is drawn from the counselor's notes and a tape recording of the seventh session (Golburgh, 1961).

> KARL: I guess we have gained something from the group. I feel that it's a little easier for me to talk now.
>
> JOSH: Why?
>
> KARL: I don't really know.
>
> JOSH: Are you less afraid to say what comes to mind?
>
> KARL: A little bit, but still afraid.
>
> CONNIE: Of what?
>
> COUNSELOR: Always a good question.
>
> KARL: What people will think of what I say.

JON: What will they think? (pause) I say that so casually, but I feel the same thing.

COUNSELOR: Fearing criticism is pretty common, but that doesn't make it less painful.

KARL: That's right.

CASS: You know . . . (pause)

COUNSELOR: Cass?

CASS: Nothing

COUNSELOR: Hard to say what comes to mind. You decided not to?

CASS: (laughs) I guess so.

COUNSELOR: Give it a try.

CASS: I was going to say that when I was a kid my father always criticized everything I said or did. Maybe that's why I'm so afraid to say what I think.

COUNSELOR: Could you talk more about it Cass?

CASS: Everything I used to say was wrong.

PEGGY: I had the same thing . . . (pause)

COUNSELOR: How so?

PEGGY: My father still criticizes everything I say . . . (pause)

COUNSELOR: Teachers and fellow students aren't your fathers. I guess in some ways we tend to see them this way.

CASS: You know, that really is true (firmly)

COUNSELOR: Cass, why was it hard for you to tell us about your father?

CASS: I don't know . . . I guess I was afraid you would criticize me.

COUNSELOR: Me?

CASS: Ya . . .

COUNSELOR: I feel your comments are very useful to the group. Why should you expect me to criticize you? I'm not your father.

CASS: It's hard to realize that everything you say isn't wrong.

COUNSELOR: Or bad. It sure is. But, even so, does being criticized by others make someone a bad person anyway?

PEGGY: It does when you're a child.

COUNSELOR: Right. But why hold onto these attitudes?

PEGGY: You know, there is a great deal similar about us in this group.

CASS: Dr. Golburgh, do you always feel relaxed in the group?

COUNSELOR: Usually, now,—I didn't at first.

CASS: Nervous at first?

COUNSELOR: Sure

PEGGY: Really?

COUNSELOR: Um hmmmmm. (long pause)

COUNSELOR: I guess you're thinking, why was I nervous.

JON: That's what I was thinking.

CONNIE: Me too.

COUNSELOR: To answer the question, I was nervous at first because it was a new group to me. But more important, how is it that no one asked what you were thinking?

KARL: Maybe it is safer to be more free in what you say. It's very hard though. It didn't seem right to ask you.

KEVIN: Why not? (pause)

CASS: I was always afraid to ask my father the things I wanted to ask him. He never really seemed to care or be interested. He usually found something to be mad about. I decided to keep quiet most of the time. It was safer.

COUNSELOR: Both you and Karl have used the word "safer". (pause) Fear of fathers . . . teachers . . . criticism . . . safer . . . But that was then . . . a while back . . .

MAT: My father was a lot like this. But I don't fear teachers. I usually hate them. I don't expect to get criticized by them.

KEVIN: Why do you hate them?

MAT: I don't know. They are hard to get along with.

CASS: He's afraid of them. Like Dr. G. said. You sort of think that they are your father or like him.

MAT: (to Cass) God—how come you're so talkative today. (angry)

COUNSELOR: You seem angry, Mat.

EXAMPLE 2—MULTIPLE COUNSELING, HIGH SCHOOL. Helen Driver (1953; 1958) was one of the first persons to present a comprehensive plan for using many group dynamic techniques in order to help persons of all ages to learn more effectively through small group discussion. A summary account of fifteen "multiple counseling" sessions shows the wide variety of specific group procedures that can be used with high school students (Driver, 1958, pp. 230–233).

GROUP: Ten high school seniors: 7 girls, 3 boys (non-counselees)

This project was organized as an activity club for a limited number of senior students who were interested in learning about personality, human relations, and "getting along with people." There were 16 weekly sessions held during the regular school activity period: 15 were discussion sessions, 1 (the last) was used for writing evaluations of the group project. Adjunctive counseling consisted of an average of 2.5 interviews per student.

Chronological list of discussion topics in 15 sessions

1. Getting acquainted: self descriptions.

2. What is an attractive personality? Difference of opinion among boys and girls as to desirable traits.

3. Analysis and criticism of a high school poll listing eight characteristics of "a smooth person." Group worked in couples to draw up lists of desirable traits (boy and girl) in rank order.

4. Why do you like or dislike a person? (At end of session the group members rated themselves on nine behavior traits).

5. How do we differ, one from another? Nine behavior trait ratings, feeling toward parents, brothers and sisters.

6. Discussion of various work experience and vocational choices of the group members. They guessed at A and C ratings for themselves on the Strong Interests Inventory (recently taken, but not yet scored).

7. What personal traits are characteristic of emotional maturity? A well-balanced life. (Autobiographical outlines distributed, explained.)

8. What is a well-adjusted person? A ninth grader, a twelfth grader, an adult. Changes in behavior, likes and dislikes, as one grows up. What about honesty, drinking?

9. Sociograms: Negro and Jew on train. Discussion of racial prejudice and the Negro problem. Should a white girl date a Negro if she is not willing to marry one? Difficulties of interracial marriages.

10. Sociodramas: (1) Jewish nurse applies for job in Catholic hospital, (2) Scout master argues with Lutheran clergyman. Discussion: What can we do about prejudices? How can one learn to be more understanding and tolerant?

11. Discussion on "being outstanding": What would you be in life if you could have your wish?

12. Sociodramas: (1) the wrong way to apply for a job, (2) the right way. Discussion: analysis of errors of behavior in applicant; unrealistic behavior of employer in second scene.

13. Why do people act the way they do: be-boppers, alcoholics, the under-dog. Influence of four basic drives in causing behavior. Second discussion: What would you do if a bomb dropped today, wiping out your family and home?

14. Defense mechanisms (typed sheets with simple definitions and examples of identification, projection, sublimation, rationalization, compensation). Discussion: examples of defensive behavior in everyday life of group members.

15. Can defense mechanisms be used in a good way? Huddles discussed this and reported back to group with examples. Discussion: Is rationalizing really lying?

Sociometry of group

A closely knit group of four girls; two other girls who were friends; one girl isolated; two boys who were acquaintances but not friends; one boy isolated.

Group structure, dynamics, leadership

Structure 4 (leaderless free discussion) was used as often as possible, and the assistant leader (a male graduate student) participated in group discussions in support of the three male members. The leader started sessions with a short talk, a springboard question, or typed material. Most frequently the free discussion was allowed to go in any direction and the leader exerted controls only when violent arguments or "ganging up on one member" became disruptive.

The chief characteristics of the discussions were the out-going behavior, frank self-revelations, strong feeling-expressions used by the dominant members (four girls and one boy). Boy-girl competition and antagonisms decreased after six sessions.

Auxiliary activities

Self-appraisal devices consisted of autobiographies, self-ratings on nine behavior traits, the MMPI, Strong, and MAPS. Role playing was used as the main activity in three sessions. Written evaluations of the project took up one session.

Adjunctive counseling

There was no briefing interview. The summary interview was held immediately following the conclusion of the group project; the follow-up interview two to three months later. Before or after the administration of the projective test (MAPS), a short conference with each participant revealed reactions to the project, personal problems, etc. Several of the group members were counseled during the year following the end of the project.

Outcomes

The general results for the majority of the group were:

1. Improvement of discussion and social skills.

2. Reduction of tensions; satisfaction from bringing them into the open

3. Support and reassurance regarding worthiness as a person.

4. Motivation toward improvement of personal weaknesses.

Results of the questions asked in the written evaluation were as follows:

	Yes	No	?
1. Do you think you understand yourself better because of participation in Personology Club .... (affirmative answers require explanation)	8	1	1
2. Do you think the discussion, role playing, test, etc., helped you understand and accept others better ...... (affirmative answer requires explanation)	8	0	2

3. Do you think there may be any carry-over in the future to make you more

understanding and tolerant of others (affirmative answer requires explanation)	4	1	5
4. Did you find the role playing helpful	7	3	0
5. Were you helped in vocational guidance areas	9	1	0

Results of the summary interview and the follow-up conference usually substantiated answers given in the written evaluation, especially in regard to the influence which implemented the learning. For example, one participant repeated his appreciation of test results and comments of fellow members. Another gave evidence that changes in attitude and behavior were influenced by her discovering others had similar problems of rebellion against parental control. While the majority of the group had been upset, confused, and unhappy at the beginning of the project (beginning of the senior year), many of their "growing up" problems were fading by the end of the year. The frank discussions, mutual problem sharing, and influence of adult leader-counselors, helped them through a difficult growth period.

EXAMPLE 3—HOSPITAL GROUP THERAPY. Powdermaker and Frank (1953, pp. 200–203) present the dynamics of a therapy group in meeting number 65.

SITUATION ANALYSIS 14: Dr. N's Group 1, Meeting 65

Present: Coombs, Eubank, Gugis, Milton, and Trippitt

Setting

The attitude of the patients toward the doctor and one another was largely negative, although there had been little verbalization of this. Milton had been very resistive to therapy for the last two months, constantly reverting to the fact that Dr. N had made him angry by misinterpreting what he had said on one occasion. Eubank was usually silent in the group, and his attitudes toward it had not appeared. In a recent individual interview he had said that he was angry at the group. Trippitt's attitude was primarily positive, but in the meeting preceding this one he had indicated disappointment with his progress. Coomb's attitude toward Dr. N was compliant, but he had shown hostility to the group, especially to Trippitt. Gugis had indirectly expressed negative feelings toward Dr. N.

The patients were accustomed to expressing hostility toward one another by asking probing questions. The habit of self-examination was well established. This meeting began with Milton's expressing his sensitivity to the sign "Mental Hygiene Clinic." When the group failed to support him in this feeling, he withdrew. Trippitt broke the silence which ensued on Milton's withdrawal to ask whether anyone had had heart pains since the death of Weber, who had suffered a heart attack two months earlier, soon after being discharged from psychiatric treatment. (There had been only a brief discussion of feelings about it in meetings 59 and 60, while the regular psychiatrist was on vacation.) Dr. N ended the discussion which followed by questioning whether it would be profitable to continue. (He stated to the observer after the meeting that he might have been unknowingly sensitive to Weber's death.) This was followed by a tense and awkward silence.

Dr. N tried to deal with the situation by asking if anyone wanted to discuss anything from individual interviews. There was another long silence, all the patients seeming self-absorbed. Trippitt tried to shift the focus to Coombs by commenting on his appearing engrossed. Coombs said that he was "just sitting."

Precipitating events:

Gugis, with a malicious smile, said that he had been waiting to see whether Trippitt or Milton would speak first. He said that it was characteristic of Trippitt that he couldn't bear an awkward situation, whereas he, Gugis, did not mind it. Gugis then asked if this actually was an awkward situation, saying that he and others didn't feel it as such.

Events:

There followed a discussion of how various patients reacted to a silence in the group. Trippitt stated defensively that in breaking the silence he took his cue from the doctor. Dr. N asked what was awkward about silences, and Trippitt said that he talked in order to "maintain himself." Milton spoke to Dr. N about his inability to stand a silence, and Dr. N interpreted this in terms of Milton's anxiety about what people might be thinking of him. Milton said that he had also found the silence awkward. Gugis tried repeatedly and unsuccessfully to shift the discussion to Trippitt's not "giving anything to the group" when he talked. Trippitt suggested that others had problems too. There followed an acrimonious discussion punctuated by silences, in one of which Gugis commented that everyone was so "damned silent" and Milton remarked again that he was uneasy. Coombs brought the discussion back to patients' feelings in the group, saying that Trippitt always thought that he did all the talking and Coombs thought that he (Coombs) did the talking.

Effects:

There was tension-relieving laughter as Gugis remarked that whenever he talked he felt as if he had been tricked into it. Eubank said he felt "caught all the time" and was afraid that, because he smiled while talking, others would think his problems were not important. This led to a fairly extended discussion of his feelings.

Trippitt talked about his problem of loving his girl, and in a friendly way he and Gugis together analyzed how their attitudes toward girls were related to their sense of inferiority. The meeting concluded with Trippitt asking Gugis how he knew his relative didn't like him and Gugis saying that he gave them "no incentive." Trippitt asked why Gugis had to give them an incentive, and Gugis responded, "That sounds like Trippitt's problem." Trippitt: "It is!" Gugis: "Mine too!" Laughter over this ended the meeting.

Discussion:

An uncomfortable silence arose when the doctor terminated the discussion of patients' feeling about the death of a former patient. This topic had been introduced in an atmosphere of negative feelings carried over from previous meetings and may have been an indirect expression of hostility toward the doctor. Gugis took the lead in trying to break the silence by calling attention to it. He was the patient whose negative feelings about Dr. N seemed closest to direct expression. In calling attention to the silence he seemed to be pointing out the hostility of others to the doctor.

It appears that in rallying around examination of their feelings about silences, the patients displaced resistance from the doctor to the group. That is, they talked as though their feelings about breaking a silence were related to their feelings about one another, rather than, as seemed to be true in this case, to their feelings about the doctor. The tension was released, as signalized by laughter, when they shifted from feelings about silences (i.e., resistance to therapy) to feelings about talking (i.e., acceptance of therapy). The active intervention of the doctor was slight and did not affect the course of the discussion. Only after everyone had participated in this release of tension could the patients participate in collaborative discussion of personal problems—indicating that their resistance had been worked through.

Tentative deduction:

From this situation it appears that when the patients of an experienced group are blocked by hostility toward one another and the doctor, the patient most easily able to express hostility may lead the others to rally around a discussion of their present behavior, with resulting relaxation of tension and return to consideration of personal problems.

4. ADDITIONAL CLASSIFICATIONS. Particular approaches to group counseling and therapy have led to many categories and methods. Hadley (1958, pp. 234–244) lists six classifications which vary from "technique oriented" to age differentiations. His list includes:

1. Lecture-discussion technique
2. Activity group procedures
3. Client-centered group counseling
4. Analytical oriented group procedures
5. Psychodrama
6. Groupwork with children

A lecture-discussion technique, as group therapy, is an intellectual, didactic and "class type" experience (Klapman, 1941, 1944, and 1946). Activity group procedures are permissive, action centered, and depend upon an intense use of conditioned reinforcement (reward and praise rather than punishment); individual counseling parallels group activities. Slavson (1943, 1947, 1950) is a primary theorist and practitioner in activity group approaches. The work of Carl R. Rogers and his co-writers is very familiar to counseling and guidance workers. Analytically oriented (psychoanalytic) group treatment has been patterned after the individual practices of Freud and his followers. Free association, dream analysis, interpretation, and similar classical analytical concepts are used. Schilder (1938), Schilder and Bender (1951), and Wolfe (1949) are representative of writers in this area. Psychodrama is best represented by Moreno's writings (1946, 1955), and draws heavily on role playing, sociodramas (socially centered), and psychodramas (self-involvement). Children's techniques are of many types.

Special applications

The essential nature of group counseling as a process provides a flexibility and a capacity for widespread application. Research reports from all levels of education and from all types of community and child guidance sources show the scope and depth of the process as a helping device for persons of all ages.

Group counseling (perhaps more correctly, an application of a group structure in a guidance program) was used to provide upper class students in a junior high school with an orientation about guidance and counseling services. These students in turn were to convey the information to lower class students (Richards, 1958).

A detailed study of the effects of group or multiple counseling on gifted under-achieving adolescents (high school) was a doctoral project of Broedel (1958; also reported in *Journal of Counseling Psychology,* Broedel, Ohlsen, Proff, and Southard, 1960). Sixteen multiple counseling sessions were provided for two experimental groups (six pupils in one and eight in another); two control groups of approximately the same size received no counseling. The results showed that the experimental groups, when compared to the control groups, showed a significant increase in acceptance of self, higher scores on achievement tests, and an improved ability to relate to others. Academic achievement was not increased in the experimental subjects. Long-range studies are needed in order to clarify such failures to affect academic achievement. Again the probable explanation factor is the length of the experiment. Glanz and Penney (1961), and Glanz, Calia, and Smith (1962), showed definite student achievement changes in experiments designed on a longer time pattern and on more broadly conceived experimental techniques. Wrightstone (1960) reports on significant student changes resulting from more gross-type educational experimentation including groups.

A variation of group play therapy, as play therapy is a variation on counseling, was attempted (D. C. Davis, 1958) with kindergarten children. Puppet-play techniques, actually a type of role playing for young children, were used with experimental groups. The children that participated in the program showed significant behavior changes when compared with the control groups. Applications with more abnormal children of younger age levels have also been encouraging. J. McDaniel (1960) has explored, with encouraging signs, the use of group techniques with the mentally retarded. Yonge and O'Connor (1954) report on generally favorable results with defective delinquents after the use of group psychotherapy. An incisive article by these same authors (O'Connor and Yonge, 1955) explores the need for effective criteria whenever group therapy techniques are used by experimenters.

The weight of evidence is clearly in favor of the use of group techniques in counseling. Negative results or even minor effects have been reported by many observers (such as Biersdorf, 1958; Kobliner, 1959); however, the widespread reports of such varying but effective utilizations of a technique that is not yet standardized and may never be thoroughly uniform is impressive.

PARALLEL GROUP AND INDIVIDUAL COUNSELING

The use of group counseling procedures is not designed to replace, but, rather, to supplement individual counseling. Very few writers and workers in the area of group counseling object to the parallel use of individual and group contacts. Kotkov (1955) fears that one process will interfere with the other. Caplan (1957, p. 124) seems to cry out against individual counseling by saying that his results of successful group counseling are "a challenge to widely held one-to-one counseling methods." His challenge is more to the belief that only individual methods can be effective rather than a view that group counseling must replace individual techniques. Most writers and counselors openly stress the importance of both processes (A. L. Brewer, 1958; Driver, 1958; and Sheldon and Landsman, 1950). The parallel availability of group and individual methods offers a dual resource that can be used as circumstances dictate.

Several studies designed to compare the effectiveness of group and individual counseling approaches seem to conclude that no significance can be attached to the fact that the process is group or individual (Hewer, 1959; Froehlich, 1958; E. W. Wright, 1959). The challenge may be present as Caplan (1957, see above) states. The need is to determine differentially the problems or issues that may be handled by individual methods and those to be served through group procedures. Hoyt and Moore (1960) in reviewing the literature of the field come to this conclusion.

Group counseling and groupwork procedures in all areas of guidance have come of age. Group trained counselors and guidance workers must now begin to isolate those specific areas or problems that can be handled *best* by groups.

THE COUNSELOR AS GROUP LEADER

The counselor who attempts to serve the needs of a group in *interpersonal* and *intrapersonal* fashion is tackling two major tasks. The use of discussion, action, formal or informal groups in the many aspects of a guidance program demands that these joint needs of the group members as individuals and as group members be ever-served. However, group counseling places intrapersonal growth ahead of, in fact an objective of, the interpersonal aspects of the group.

The leader of the group must be aware, within the group, of factors relating to organization and structure, leadership and member roles, perceptual and communicative processes, individual and common motivations and learnings that affect the group, and, of course, the movement and progress of the group and individuals toward stated goals. These tasks are staggering to even the skilled person. Yet, is there a choice? Redl in most of his writings has stressed the need for teachers and counselors to be aware of the dynamic elements that affect classes, groups, and individuals. Two specific articles (Redl, 1942; 1943), written many years ago, clearly spell out the answer for the counselor-leader. The leader must be aware of all of these forces; to the degree that he fails, a contagion of negative feelings, hostility, and other group enervating forces are released.

Positive evidence is present in all literature regarding the importance of leadership in the dynamics of groups. Leadership is a vital key to the group structure and the movement of the group. The quality of thinking of the group is related to the leader's effectiveness. Meier and Solem (1952) showed that a leader's use of minority opinions helped the group to raise its level of operation. Can a counselor be less responsible for helping the group and the individual members? Many writers have attempted to isolate the factors and forces that can help the leader or counselor to effectively aid the group (see Chapter 4). Glatzer and Durkin (1945) stress the importance of relationships to the individuals within the group and to the group as a whole. Medical sources, such as Schilder and Bender (1951), often stress the intellectual obligation that the leader-counselor must assume. Most guidance workers and counselors will reject the heavily interpretative role that is often assumed by medical personnel (Rinn, 1961). Where will answers be found?

A recommendation advanced in 1950 by Joel and Shapiro has not been widely accepted or perhaps noticed. These investigators suggest that two therapists, of opposite sex, be employed in group therapy situations. Brammer and Shostrum (1960, p. 299) also improve upon such an idea by allowing one to function as counselor or therapist and one to function as observer-interpreter-summarizer. These authors speculate upon the possibility that these male and female group therapists (counselors) may be able to fulfill the classical Freudian concept of father and mother images.

The conceptual design of joint counselors may have merit in many of the counseling problems that may be undertaken in school systems. The coresponsibility of such persons may allow for a more complete understanding of the dynamics of the group and of the individuals within the group. The process and the content of the group counseling sessions may be isolated and proper focus placed upon each. Research designs of the future may report upon the results of these and other experiments that can point the directions for the counselor-leader in a group counseling session. However, if and until such results are available, it becomes mandatory for the guidance person to be skilled, sensitive, and alert to all of the responsibilities of the job.

SUMMARY

Group counseling presents the counselor and guidance worker with the special opportunity to engage in group activities that are both interpersonal and intrapersonal. The dynamics of operation in group counseling are related to the functioning of any group; at the same time the group is organized to aid and assist individuals in solving personal and emotional problems.

Counseling, therapy, and psychotherapy may be titled individual, group, or multiple. The variations and nuances of word choice are shown to be related to historical and personal preference.

The use of pre-counseling groups is explained and related to the screening process that can help to establish group counseling units within a school system. Group counseling as a process is presented. Six major phases or stages are presented with illustrations from research to delineate the joint importance of individual and group forces within a counseling group. Rapport, acceptance, listening and observing, the promotion of group understanding, problem-solving phases, and closing and evaluative procedures are presented in order. Examples are drawn from high school, college, and hospital settings. Special applications of the group counseling process are also offered.

The issue of parallel or joint individual and group counseling services to the same students is examined and conclusions from research outlined. The counselor-leader role is seen to be a combination of group process responsibilities and of individual growth (student) responsibilities. Possible trends for the future characteristics of group counseling close the chapter.

SUGGESTED READINGS

Bach, George R., *Intensive Group Psychotherapy*. New York: The Ronald Press Co., 1954.

Brammer, L. M., and E. V. Shostrom, *Therapeutic Psychology*. Englewood Cliffs, N. J.: Prentice-Hall, Inc., 1960.

Corsini, Raymond J., *Methods of Group Psychotherapy*. New York: McGraw-Hill Book Co., 1957.

Driver, Helen, *et al.*, *Counseling and Learning Through Small-Group Discussion*. Madison, Wis.: Monona Publications, 1958.

Foulkes, S. H., *Introduction to Group Analytic Psychotherapy*. London: Wm. Heinemann Medical Books, 1948.

Hinckley, R. G., and L. Hermann, *Group Treatment in Psychotherapy*. Minneapolis, Minn.: University of Minnesota Press, 1951.

Hobbs, Nicholas, "Group-Centered Psychotherapy," in C. R. Rogers, *Client Centered Therapy*. Boston: Houghton Mifflin Co., 1951.

Klapman, J. W., *Group Psychotherapy: Theory and Practice*. New York: Grune and Stratton, Inc., 1946.

Moustakas, C. E., *Children in Play Therapy*. New York: McGraw-Hill Book Co., 1953.

Rogers, C. R., and R. F. Dymond, *Psychotherapy and Personality Change*. Chicago: University of Chicago Press, 1954.

Slavson, S. R., *An Introduction to Group Therapy*. New York: The Commonwealth Fund, 1943.

———, *The Practice of Group Therapy*. New York: International Universities Press, 1947.

———, *Analytic Group Psychotherapy with Children, Adolescents, and Adults*. New York: Columbia University Press, 1950.

———, ed., *The Fields of Group Psychotherapy*. New York: International Universities Press, 1958.

15. ORGANIZED GUIDANCE COURSES

Work in personnel and guidance depends upon a varied, flexible approach to program building. Local needs, determined by persons thoroughly familiar with the school, the staff, and the pupils, must guide decisions about the nature of a guidance program. Patterns and constructs of personnel and guidance work are becoming available for use in widely varying circumstances. The tools and techniques for implementing any adopted program are similarly available and flexible. There are no narrow paths to truth, glory, or a successful guidance program. Too many counselors and guidance personnel presume to know that a certain technique or type of program is best. The dogmatic guidance person who presumes to know the single way to help students or to organize a guidance program reveals his own hidden needs for expression or manipulation (cf. Wrenn, 1959, p. 43).

Individual and group procedures are all useful and desirable within a guidance program. Other variations upon basic or newly developed ideas may help to attain the stated objectives of any program. Wrenn

summarizes the nature of guidance and states the objectives of any program as he writes (1959, p. 43):

> The task is to assist the pupils to self-understanding, more mature
> purpose, improved skills in interpersonal relations, acceptance of the
> realities of societal limitations as well as opportunities. It is also
> to provide facilities for optimum development in the areas of financial
> planning, living arrangements, part-time employment with eventual
> job placement, and health facilities.

Lloyd-Jones and Smith (1954) similarly warn against guidance and personnel persons becoming "technicians," and recommend that to be "educators in a somewhat unconventional and new sense" is a more desirable
goal.

The many arrangements that may be present in a specific guidance
program are difficult to circumscribe and assess. Four conceptual designs
appear to be present on the current guidance scene and are models for
future revisions and reinterpretation. Numerous variations on major models
allow each school system to build a meaningful local pattern.

One of the newer types of guidance programs, organized guidance
courses, offers a useful vehicle for the guidance worker to integrate individual and group approaches while providing for variations of staff competencies and pupil differences. Several program patterns will be examined to
offer a wide range of choices for the prospective guidance person. Practical
problems within each type of guidance course will be presented with an
examination of the issues involved.

PATTERNS OF GUIDANCE [1]

The patterns of Topsy-like growth in guidance services and programs have
resulted from varying interpretations of student needs. The particular approach adopted in a community has often reflected individual or multiple
causes such as: the availability of special guidance workers, a particular
administrative understanding of guidance, parental pressures, or certifica-
tion requirements and financial resources. The National Defense Education
Act of 1958 helped to focus the attention of all communities upon guidance.
Thousands of guidance workers and counselors have been trained through

[1] Many of the concepts expressed in this section have appeared in an article, "Patterns and
Concepts of Guidance," by the author in the *Personnel and Guidance Journal,* 40. This
restatement is by permission of the American Personnel and Guidance Association.

summer, and yearly, institutes and are seeking to establish meaningful programs of guidance in the school system in which they work.

The practices of the past are becoming channeled into trends, and it appears that at least four basic organizational patterns are emerging. Other emphases are present in the field, but are below the surface of widespread notice. Four models of counseling and guidance appear to be:

1. Centralized Specialism,
2. Decentralized Generalism,
3. Curricular Counseling and Guidance ("Group Guidance"),
4. Human Relations and Group Work (Mental Health).

These four trends may be labelled differently, or recognizable in other ways. They seem to be basic to the many present approaches to the functioning of guidance in schools and colleges.

Centralized specialism

The skills of clinical counselors, reading consultants, test administrators, and other highly qualified specialists offer aid to students of all ages and in all types of school programs. In the beginning, the classroom teacher or faculty counselor was usually encouraged to "leave it to the specialists." But the significant contribution that can be made by faculty members has recently been recognized, and nonspecialists have been urged to become co-operating partners in the total program.

Many strengths are inherent in this view of guidance, personnel services, and counseling. These strengths include the use of highly qualified personnel in specific positions to solve difficult problems, co-ordinated services through centralized control and administration, and interrelated referral resources. Weaknesses are also inherent in this approach. These include the high cost and uncertain supply of qualified specialists, and the centrifugal tendencies of bureaus, clinics and even individual specialists. The whole student is frequently forgotten as each unit treats compartmentalized needs of students.

The chief administrator is a key person in a specialized program; the *services* (an important word in this approach) must be co-ordinated and controlled. The central office becomes a directing and authoritative voice while individual services often attempt to enlarge or develop new emphases. Discipline is usually handled by administrative deans. Large city systems, many elementary schools, state universities, and urban universities are frequent examples of this pattern of guidance in operation.

Chronologically, this method of offering guidance may be recognized by an examination of how services have been added or "tacked on." The characteristic elements of this type of program are separate units or services and the presence of, or need for, a purely administrative control center.

Decentralized generalism

The importance of a guidance or personnel point of view in all areas of education has led to a movement designed to involve all educative personnel in the guidance or counseling process. All levels of education have been affected by this view of counseling and guidance. Specialists were avoided at one time, but have been sought in recent years to serve in a supportive role. "Every teacher a better counselor," has often been a watchword for adherents to this concept of guidance and counseling.

A concern for the total learning atmosphere, and an appreciation of the contribution of every person within an educational program have been rubrics in this approach. Other strengths include an active support for the value of the classroom teacher, a concern for the process and climate for growth, and an identification with the classroom learning experiences. The essential comprehensiveness of this view of guidance has bred inherent weaknesses that must be faced as programs are established. Among these problems are the sometime employment of poorly trained practitioners in specialized areas of guidance such as testing or clinical services, vitiated efforts of all personnel through the attempt to be all things for all persons, and a depreciation of the value of guidance through the belief that anyone can be a counselor or guidance worker. Sometimes it is possible to uncover unethical practices (however unintentional) in areas where standards need to be tenaciously upheld.

Single units of school systems, and small institutions, are frequent examples of generalized concepts of guidance. Financial necessity has sometimes created this view of service to students. Other programs have employed skilled and sensitive leaders to implement a freely selected concept of guidance. Recent innovations in "generalist" programs have included specialized or clinical services within the total approach. The essential feature, recognizable within any variation of this pattern of guidance, is a stress upon philosophy, integration of effort, and a denial of the "services" concept.

Curricular counseling and guidance

The integration of guidance into the academic curriculum of schools and colleges has been a flirtatious affair for many years. Many persons have attempted to evolve a pattern of this type, but successful implementation has been uncertain. Experimentation in "group guidance," vocations courses, life-adjustment courses, as well as social planning and orientation units, have been forerunners of this third major construct of guidance. The general education movement (NSSE, 1952; Morse and Dressel, 1959) with its curriculum roots in the past and its forward view of the educational process, has provided a sensitive and nurturing environment for the growth of such programs on the college level (Hardee, 1955). Foundation support for experimental programs has made it possible for improved programs to be constructed on various school levels.

Curricular approaches have been characterized by the offering of guidance and counseling preparation within a classroom setting through a course in vocations, psychology, or life adjustment. The early lack of meaningful subject matter for such courses was a deterring factor in its growth. "Group guidance" became an almost equivalent term for unimportant learnings. Self-concept study, self-analysis, vocational and educational planning, an examination of values, and the increasingly varied aspects of individual psychology have overcome this problem for classroom activity.

Strengths:
1. parallel structure with other academic courses
2. use of psychological content to aid in individual counseling and guidance
3. placement of counselors and guidance workers within the framework of academic teaching rather than in the role of administrators and co-ordinators
4. realistic emphasis on guidance as a continuing process rather than as a "one shot cure"

Weaknesses:
1. "group guidance" offered as a shallow, superficial, and meaningless timefiller
2. pressure for dual qualifications as effective classroom teacher *and* counselor

3. inflexibility demanded by classroom contact and scheduling
4. need for a larger number of well-qualified personnel to implement the goals of a program
5. high cost (compared to 1–300 counselor-student ratio)

EXAMPLES. College and high school programs have predominated thus far in the implementation of this approach. Occupation courses (Hoppock, 1957) and adjustment approaches to curricular guidance (Borow, 1958, 1959b, 1960) have often provided the subject-matter foundation for these courses. Junior high schools have also experimented in this area. Recent developments in the program of text materials have spurred this pattern of guidance (Katz, 1959; Glanz and Walston, 1958; Mahoney and Engle, 1961).

VARIATIONS. Curricular patterns are a recent end product of earlier experimentation in the previously cited areas of "group guidance," occupations, orientation and life adjustment courses. Chronologically, these types of programs pre-date the curricular pattern but are still technically variations on a theme.

The significant factor in this guidance concept is the *classroom contact with meaningful subject-matter content*. Elements of the first two major patterns (centralized specialism and decentralized generalism) can be seen in variations of the curricular pattern; but the broad concept of guidance and counseling necessary for successful teaching and counseling activities has tended to bring the generalist view, rather than the specialist view, into the curriculum and the classroom.

Human relations and groupwork

A fourth pattern of guidance has recently emerged as a method of providing guidance for youth. This model includes human relations centers and mental health programs designed to promote student growth. Such programs have not been narrowly focused on such topics as vocational and educational counseling or psychological testing but have tended to strive for the broad general outcomes of adjustment, mature thinking, effective interpersonal skills, and mental health.

Guidance workers have often viewed with suspicion the emergence of a human relations effort within a school or college. Somewhat belatedly, many persons have realized that the goals of this human relations-groupwork design were almost identical to those of guidance.

Specialized programs for maladjusted children, school-wide programs of mental health, and developmental programs on skill training have all demonstrated the techniques of this varied approach and its applications.

Strengths:
1. a broad concept of guidance and education which stresses adjustment and maturity
2. a special tool of group work—highly developed and utilizable by all workers in guidance
3. a desire to co-operate (and to effect better total programs) with any existing program of guidance
4. a cross-disciplinary approach with strong roots in all social sciences
5. a stress on the importance of all personnel working for common goals

Weaknesses:
1. the lack of specificity in the major tools of guidance, viz., counseling, testing, occupational techniques
2. the need for recognition as a guidance pattern, since many guidance personnel are provincial and often chauvinistic in their own techniques and tools
3. the tendency for some workers trained in human relations and groupwork to lack thorough or even minimal training in all of the major techniques upon which guidance rests—(counseling, testing, teaching)

EXAMPLES. Human relations and groupwork specialists have entered high school and college programs as catalysts in aiding others. Such personnel aid in the development of a focus on helping students and faculty alike in identifying common goals in education, guidance, and personal growth. Such programs may ally themselves with other approaches. As catalysts, these personnel tend to lose their own identity occasionally and to serve as strengthening units in existing programs. As such, this pattern may be denied as a pure model, and yet it has been an increasingly effective and practical method of reaching guidance goals. Samler and others (1959) have described several variations on this basic theme.

Many strengths can accrue to a co-ordinated and clear concept of guidance programming on any educational level. Inconsistent organizational patterns can vitiate the inherent strengths of any single approach.

Educational standards of policy and practice demand excellence in any guidance pattern. Future research designs will need to test the relative effectiveness of each approach. Beginning research design (Ivey, 1959; Glanz and Penney, 1961) show only indications rather than clearly demonstrable results.

CURRICULAR PATTERNS OF GUIDANCE

Course approaches to guidance in all levels of school have developed through several different methods. Some of the particular patterns have been restricted to special school units. Homeroom programs in junior and senior high school are seldom duplicated on a college or elementary school level. Team approaches are found on college and elementary levels and are growing in secondary schools. The overlap is evidence of the widespread applicability of flexible conceptual design.

Five methods of curricular guidance programs will be examined in this treatment of organized guidance courses:

1. occupations courses,
2. homeroom programs,
3. guidance classes or courses,
4. core guidance programs,
5. psychology and other related courses

Varied uses of groups are major strategies in each of these course methods of providing guidance aid to students. The applications of group techniques will be offered as illustrations of practice as each concept of guidance courses is outlined.

Occupations courses

Robert Hoppock has become the primary spokesman for the use of occupations courses in all levels of education. Hoppock's book *Group Guidance* (1949) was almost wholly concerned with the organization of occupational courses, a revision of this book was titled *Occupational Information* (1957).

The study of occupations in a regular class provides students with the opportunity to examine themselves and many possible careers. The integration of these two processes can help students to develop meaningful educational and occupational plans for the future. The stress in an occupations course is upon the learning that takes place about the world of work and the place of the individual within that world.

Investigations of the effectiveness of such courses have been almost uniformly favorable. The reports of Hoppock and his students and co-workers have outlined such evaluations on every level of education. Sinick and Hoppock (1959) summarize recent research in occupations courses; Carter and Hoppock (1961) report on college courses in careers.

Recent as well as earlier descriptions of occupations courses have shown the applicability of the approach in a total guidance and counseling program. Hewer's (1959) research project, examined in the previous chapter, showed the usefulness of group counseling in such courses. Wright (1956) describes the importance of self-appraisal and self-analysis in such courses. He reports that such activities are even more prevalent than the study of occupations. Stone (1948) and Richardson and Borow (1952) report on related research in the effectiveness of occupations courses and the use of group procedures. These persons support group techniques as a major strategy.

The comprehensiveness of most recent occupations courses belies the narrow title that has been historically employed. The need to help students in the process of self-analysis, educational planning, value determinations, and even personal problem solving has stretched the meaning of the word occupations to the breaking point. Similar concerns have led to the use of more broadly conceived titles and concepts.

Homeroom programs

Probably no other educational idea has been subject to more attack and abuse than the homeroom. There is little question that a homeroom period can be a complete waste of time or a contributing factor in a total educational program. The variables of teacher, pupils, methods, curriculum design, and school program are all significant in the ultimate success of this approach. Cupp (1958) takes a look at the many arguments on both sides of the issue and concludes that the homeroom is here to stay. She summarizes surveys that seem to reflect consistently the hostility of teachers to the homeroom and the interest of the pupils in a satisfactory and useful period.

The homeroom can provide an environment for guidance activities if there is time for more than "coat hanging and attendance taking." Wey (1948) and Strang (1948) each describe the homeroom as an agent for remarkable individual change through group activities. Wey shows how an individual teacher through group programs can counter a hostile guidance atmosphere within the school. Strang reports on the very marked changes which took place within a group with the worst truancy and tardiness record in the school. She believes that real prevention of delinquency took place within the group.

Many reasons can be advanced (and probably proved) for failures in a homeroom program. A positive view of the problem would offer group techniques, test procedures, and the use of individual and group counseling as methods that can help a homeroom program to fulfill its promise in a school. Most reports on successful practice (Long, 1954; Novak, 1951; and McFarland, 1953) clearly demonstrate the importance of adequate involvement of students in the process through group procedures.

Many authors have attempted to give direction and aid to the homeroom teachers and to the guidance personnel coordinating the total school effort. Dunsmoor (1941, 1942) was one of the early proponents of the use of the homeroom in a guidance program. McKown (1946), Fedder (1949), V. Ross (1954) and Flanders (1954) all offer detailed data about implementing and coordinating a successful homeroom period into the whole guidance program. A specific weakness in all of these approaches is the little space and concern accorded to a scientific understanding of human behavior within groups. Guidance in a group situation depends upon more than willing and devoted teachers and counselors. The needs of pupils demand that all appropriate techniques be employed with proper regard for the strengths and weaknesses inherent within each.

Many homeroom programs use pamphlets designed for the particular needs of students in either junior or senior high school. Neugarten et al. (1946) offer a series of books appropriate to grades seven through twelve. Other typical sources include Menninger et al. (1954), *How to be a Successful Teen Ager;* Duvall (1950), *Facts of Life and Love for Teen-agers;* Dickerson (1954), *Into Manhood;* and the Science Research Associates, *Life Adjustment Series.* Such source material can fit into a carefully designed effort in any school. The pamphlets or other printed materials cannot serve as substitutes for an appropriate balance between content and process.

Core course approaches

Guidance units are sometimes included as a part of a single required course such as English, history, or social studies. When a very broad concept of subject matter is established, such as a combination of history, social studies, and guidance, the course is often referred to as a core course. Problems courses are also closely related to a core concept of education. Other schools construct a core course with the stated objective of helping students in developing personal and social responsibility and include a wide variety of subject-matter areas (Riccio, 1958).

A core course or class may meet in continuous session covering two or three regular time periods of the school. Group attention to guidance problems becomes an integral portion of the curriculum in many such classes. There may be a single teacher in charge of the class or there may be a group of teachers assigned to serve co-operatively. The guidance counselor is often a part of this teaching group. G. Wright (1950, 1952, 1956) has surveyed the varied nature and prevalence of core courses in all levels of education.

The core course may be used in junior high school as a transitional course from the one-teacher classroom for all subjects to the specialized section system of the upper grades. Later placement of a core program most frequently follows local needs and curriculum design.

The rationale for a core program is based upon a knowledge of adolescent needs and the educational responsibility for a common body of knowledge for all students. Small (1957) examines the core program as it fulfills student needs. The entire movement in general education has supported the curriculum stress upon core courses.

The counselor or guidance worker has almost flitted in and out of the core programs in many schools. The task of accepting a curriculum responsibility is alternately frightening and appealing to many counselors. Wrenn (1957) examines the role and status of the school counselor and concludes that although patterns are still evolving, flexibility is needed for counselors to make professional contributions to the school system in accord with local needs and practice. The emergence of the team concept in teaching (Davis and Wicks, 1956; Anthony, *et al.*, 1956) is related to core course concepts and provides a specific role for the counselor to fulfill in cooperation with teachers.

Research in core programs has revealed equally effective learning whenever these approaches are compared with regular class programs

(Capehart, *et al.*, 1952; Mennes, 1955; Jurjevich, 1957). The research of Fiedler and his co-workers (1959), carefully examined in the counseling chapter, is also appropriate in connection with core courses. Whenever accepting and permissive groups can be established within core programs, the student can benefit in many fashions.

Guidance classes

The organization of guidance classes is deeply rooted in American education. Over three decades ago, Richard D. Allen established the pattern whereby class counselors met with students on a regular classroom basis in addition to usual counseling contacts (Reavis, 1932, Ch. 6). Allen's approach to organizational design, case study problems, and class conduct were described in his books originally published in the thirties and combined in a single volume in 1952. Rothney (1936) also foreshadowed such guidance practices. The availability of the *Life Adjustment Booklets* from the Science Research Associates have also provided materials for variations on Allen's design. Froehlich (1954) has provided a review of similar programs. The variations possible with guidance classes have allowed each school system to develop its own particular pattern. Koile (1955) and Roche (1958) each make a case for continued and expanded programs of classroom guidance.

The term "group guidance" has covered many different types of classes and has occasionally served as a focal point for discontented students, teachers, and administrators. The upgrading of the content and methodology of guidance classes is providing a legitimate class structure in which a meaningful subject matter is studied and acceptable academic credit is available. The "Guidance Survey," conducted by the Educational Testing Service with help from the Ford Foundation (Shimberg and Katz, 1960) established the value of a guidance course offered in the regular school curriculum. The major result of this survey was the publication, after several experimental editions, of the textbook, *You Today and Tomorrow,* by Martin Katz (1959). Applications of this approach have been used as illustrations in the earlier chapters. Mahoney and Engle (1961) in *Points for Decision* present a related guidance course for secondary school levels.

College courses in guidance (known by various titles) have been surveyed by Burow (1959, 1960) and Glanz (1961). These courses are sometimes centered on occupations and vocational planning and may also be broader in their scope and content as in Glanz and Walston (1958).

Research on the effectiveness of guidance courses has been uneven and sometimes contradictory. Gribbons (1960) found that students had profited from the guidance class and related group counseling activities. Borow (1959, 1960) reports on mixed results of college level courses. A broadly conceived research program revealing startling student growth on achievement and aptitude is described by Glanz and Penney (1961) and by Glanz, Calia, and Smith (1962). Sachs (1945) conducted a study of the comparative effectiveness of the guidance class concept and the home-room. Sachs found that on most measures the homeroom pattern was more effective. More recent research is needed since the traditional guidance class has changed markedly in the late fifties and early sixties.

Psychology courses

Guidance goals and objectives are often fulfilled through psychology, sociology, and other content courses in high school and college. Some courses in psychology make no attempt to relate the subject matter to the guidance program. Engle (1955, p. 305) reports that unless the high school director of guidance is also the instructor in psychology, there is usually little correlation attempted. Again, the question of the training and experience of the guidance personnel is vital as such a task is undertaken. The widespread use of the high school course in psychology (Engle and Bunch, 1956) deserves the attention and co-operative staffing of guidance workers and counselors. The special commission of guidance (Wrenn, *et al.* 1961) points out the psychological basis for all of guidance and counseling. The high school version of a psychology course (cf. Engle, 1957) is well within the competency of a well-trained guidance person.

College-level courses in guidance and psychology have flourished in institutions offering general education programs (Hardee, 1955). Combined guidance and psychology courses have been offered for over a decade at Boston University in two undergraduate divisions (Glanz, *et al.*, 1959; Glanz and Walston, 1958). The introductory psychology course has often been the vehicle for personal and emotional learnings that are a part of any guidance objective in a college (Castor and Berrien, 1950; Faw, 1949; Berrien, 1947). More recent efforts in this direction are also promising for guidance persons (Eglash, 1954; Lyle, 1958). The need for co-operative efforts by guidance personnel and psychology teachers is often

disputed by the more subject matter oriented psychology teachers; however, the concerns of both groups are beginning to reveal similar and related objectives.

INTEGRATED GUIDANCE COURSES

An integrated course in guidance can provide a vehicle for a meaningful
content and for comprehensive guidance and counseling methods to help
individual students. The course or class may be offered on any educational
level and must be locally designed to meet the particular needs of students
and the community. The specific pattern of the course may be constructed
to follow any of the several models currently available. The content of the
course includes most of the basic concerns that have been identified as
appropriate for the age level of the enrolled students. Course methods are
varied, flexible and drawn from the major strategies of counseling, testing,
group procedures, and creative teaching methods. The practical issues of
staff selection, credit or noncredit status, grading, and text resources are
resolved according to local conditions.

Organizational patterns

It is important to note that as all of the major patterns of curricular guidance were examined, greater agreement and common practice were found
than disagreement about content and method. Whether a course is called
Occupations, Personal and Social Adjustment, Group Guidance, or even
Psychology, no single title covers the common elements in each of these
ventures. Local practice (or pressure) may well determine the name and
the design selected as best suited for the individual school or college.

A significant administrative problem that must be faced by a curriculum committee or a director of guidance is the need to build progres-
sively upon the experiences of students in the educational system. Warters
(1960) points out that duplication of content, assignments, methods, and
even field trips, can effectively destroy the value of such courses to students. Developmental designs with increasing levels of sophistication and
meaningfulness to students are marks of carefully constructed guidance
programs.

An elementary school occupations course may be followed in eighth
or ninth grade with a guidance course stressing self evaluation and plan-

ning. The high school course in such a program might well offer psychology or sociology as a useful vehicle for further learnings. Co-ordinated orientation or articulation programs along with appropriate psychological testing as well as individual and group counseling can integrate such a school-wide guidance program. Reversals of these progressions, or variations in accord with local practice or traditions, are easily integrated within a skillfully constructed design (Dressel, 1959; Bennett, 1959). Colleges or junior colleges may well need to vary their own programs as it becomes apparent that incoming students have already completed the learnings and experiences that are offered in advanced secondary schools or public school systems (Morse and Dressel, 1959).

Content units

The content of any guidance course may be constructed according to local programming and previous classes or experiences completed by students. However, in any grade, and at appropriate complexity levels, most of the following topics will constitute the major guidance course content areas.

1. The Self	5. Decision Making
2. Human Behavior	6. Human Relations
3. Educational Planning	7. Mental Health
4. Occupational Planning	8. The Community

These indicated areas of study are similar to, but significantly different from, earlier "group guidance" courses. A program for the city of Boston schools in group guidance (Taylor, *et al.*, 1948) listed many of these topics, but with no emphasis upon the group process of learning. The use of groups, psychological testing, individual and group counseling can make a guidance course a strangely different creature from the sterile, "classroom" treatment of guidance problems.

The introduction of the study of the self into such a course is an immediately challenging concept. Teachers, counselors, and particularly teachers and counselors of guidance courses need to be alert to the means by which a student can become aware of his own self-concept, and his status and attitudes towards others. Calvin and Holtsman (1953), Phillips (1951), and Justman and Wrightstone (1951) all stress the significance of these factors in the climate of the classroom and the learnings that may be attained by students. Simple and sophisticated methods of helping students to come to grips with these problems are included in all major source materials available for student use. Bugenthal and Zelen (1950) describe a beginning device in which students are helped to study themselves through a "W. A. Y." technique (Who Are You?). Glanz and Walston (1958) offer a detailed approach to self-appraisal and self-analysis.

Typical of the means through which self study (as typical of any major unit in the course) can demand the best efforts of guidance personnel and yet provide the rewards of significant study by students is revealed by Jersild (1952):

> . . . human beings from an early age have more capacity for learning to face, to understand, and to deal constructively with the realities of their lives than we have assumed in our psychological theories or in our educational practices. (p. 3)

and,

> . . . that pupils participate eagerly in a discussion does not necessarily mean that they are digging into their problems. One way to by-pass anxiety is to take flight into a logical and intellectual group discussion. Discussion of a topic may be a symptom rather than a solution . . .

>> But, a group discussion can provide a good learning situation when the participants actually communicate and commune with one another. Where there is such sharing there will be periods when all would like to shout, and there will be periods when all are silent . . . A gesture, a sigh, a smile, a note of anxiety, or a grunt of approval may communicate more feeling and more mutual understanding than a long spoken contribution.

Jersild's words drive deeply into the resources and competencies of the counselor and guidance worker who would attempt to help students in meaningful fashion. Jersild's words are echoed and reaffirmed in the Wrenn *et al.* (1961) report to guidance workers. This Commission was established to assess the role of guidance in the long range future. Guidance persons must understand, utilize, and help students to understand and utilize their own psychological selves and the operation of the self in a society.

The integrated guidance course demands that guidance persons individually, or in team groups, possess the techniques and skills to function as professional counselors, testers, and group workers. The illustrative nature of the complex study of the self can be duplicated in any of the major units that must be expected practice in a guidance course that attempts to establish itself as a legitimate curricular offering for students. The "group guidance" course that treats dating, dress styles, table manners, or personal habits of cleanliness (with texts and movies supplied by soap or paper product manufacturers) must be relegated to the past. These topics are items for student study and learning; however, they must assume a minimal and secondary role as they are treated as elements of larger learnings.

Course methods

Proper balance must be maintained within the methodological approaches utilized in guidance courses. The omnibus talents of the potential guidance counselor and worker may be distressing. Yet, as guidance comes of age professionally there are newer and stronger demands for high level operation by all persons. Borow (1959) reviews the emerging and dominant emphases in guidance research and lists "the social psychology of student groups, group mediated personnel work, process analysis in counseling, and mental health in the school setting," as areas of concern for all.

The road for the guidance counselor is not easily uncovered. Pierson and Grant (1959) exhort the guidance person to become a "counselor" and to eschew all the rest of the "guidance work." Presumedly the counselor will become the high status person and the guidance worker will become the lackey! Maas (1951) and Scheidlinger (1955) struggle with the seemingly impossible problems of making teachers into skilled group therapists while in the classroom. There is no question that attitudes, learnings, emotions, and other classroom activities have their "therapeutic overtones"; however, even guidance counselors and guidance workers need to assess carefully their own talents as therapists prior to launching into "therapy" relations with students, in classes, individually, or in groups.

Effective teaching procedures (Cantor, 1950; 1953) can be combined with the traditional counseling and newer groupwork skills of the counselor or guidance worker to provide for integrated designs of class methodology. Specific courses may serve student assessed needs through individual inventories of problems (Mooney, 1941, 1942; Singer and Stefflre, 1957). More structured courses, still designed to meet the general needs of students, may be patterned after broadly representative surveys of students' needs in curriculum planning (Doane, 1942; Passow et al., 1957).

The combined techniques of teaching, groupwork, and counseling can be so taxing that no single counselor can attempt to cope singly with such problems (Calia, 1956). The total resources of a guidance staff may be necessary to provide adequate staff provisions for required or optional guidance courses. Placement counselors, activities directors, test specialists, and even administrators can help through assuming responsibility for one or more sections of teaching while also serving as counselor for the same group of students (Glanz *et al.*, 1959; Calia, 1957).

The methodological shift involved in using a wide variety of guidance and counseling techniques in a guidance course is primarily a matter of an assumed attitude or philosophy on the part of the guidance person. Group skills and techniques can dovetail into the standard counseling and testing procedures. The acceptance of the usefulness and related nature of these skills requires an accepting attitude on the part of the guidance worker or counselor. H. M. Taylor in describing the use of problem-solving groups in teaching (geography) summarizes the issues well. Counseling needs to be added as these words are read, and guidance substituted for geography. His words indicate an acceptance of problems needed in all classes of geography, guidance, or other subjects (H. M. Taylor, 1960, p. 187):

1. The class should be analyzed first so that meaningful, congenial groups can be established.

2. The teacher must teach the skills necessary for working in groups. The teacher cannot assume that students have these skills.

3. The problems to be solved first should be of a rather simple nature to assure the child success in his initial work.

4. The groups should be highly structured until the students become very skilled in the use of the procedures.

5. It should be remembered that, although the development of group skills is important, the method is designed to teach subject matter, in this case, geographical (guidance) content and skills.

Nothing new, yes, but it all involves adequate planning, problem solving, evaluation, critical and integrated thinking, perfecting of research and communicative skills and the utilization of the various forces generated in a group to more effectively teach geographical concepts and skills.

Hopefully the guidance counselors and administrators in Mr. Taylor's school are also planning to utilize him in helping to establish or maintain a group program in guidance.

The questions surrounding the use of a guidance class concept in a particular school may often relate to the specific issues of staff selection and training, credit or no credit status of the course, grading procedures, and the availability of text sources.

Staff selections and training

Guidance counselors attempting to serve as instructors in a guidance class program need to be prepared or experienced to fulfill the functions of teacher, counselor, and group worker. The demands of the course will often involve the administration of group and individual tests. Most guidance and counselor training programs on a Masters degree level, are now graduating persons prepared to assume such responsibilities, under supervision. The co-ordinator and specially trained persons within such a program are usually individuals educated and experienced broadly. Many co-ordinators or directors completed doctoral programs that have included counseling internships, group practice, and individual testing competencies. The Association of Counselor Educators and Supervisors of the American Personnel and Guidance Association has recommended standards of education and training for guidance counselors that would fulfill the requirements for staffing such guidance courses.

The sensitivities, human relations skills, and standard requirements for any successful guidance counselor would of course be added to any of the specialized training experiences recommended above.

Credit or noncredit status

Historical practice has most frequently dictated that guidance courses be conducted on a noncredit basis. Failure to offer educational credit often has been interpreted (perhaps correctly) by students that nothing of value is involved. Sometimes it may be likened to the situation where child care, family living and driving instruction are noncredit courses. Citizens of our country have many things in common; yet, are there functions of citizenship more in need of study than child rearing, family life, and the lethal weapon aimed by careless drivers?

More positively it is clearly best educational practice to offer credit for the study of individual differences, measurement and statistics, human motivation, learning, decision making, and similar topics. Well designed courses in guidance cannot be offered without credit if the educational contract between a school and a student is not to be broached by the school. The points, hours of credit, or even units under a Carnegie system (for college recommendation) can be arranged with administrators and/or school boards. Money and banking, accounting, modern foreign language, and even literature were at one time (and still in some places) deemed vulgar and noneducational!

Grading problems

Counselors and guidance personnel have long struggled with their consciences and emotions about teaching the same students who are also their counselees. Guidance courses with a meaningful content offer a middle ground for grading and evaluation. The students' learnings in the content area can be evaluated and graded. Students have adjusted well to the grading systems of other courses and do not hate all teachers who give them low grades or love all faculty members that give A grades; similarly, students can understand that teachers or counselors do not extend their emotions (hopefully), with their grades.

Personal documents such as autobiographies, self-analysis essays, and personal planning for an occupation can be treated with S (satisfactory) or U (unsatisfactory) methods. Problems of nonfulfillment of assignments can be resolved through counseling. Research papers on tests, occupations, or other content areas can be graded in usual fashion. Final examinations and intraterm tests at the end of units can also be graded.

The issue that must be clearly understood by students and teachers alike is the stricture that growth, insight, or even adjustment is *not* a legitimate subject for grading.

Needless to say in such courses it is necessary for the counselor-teacher to handle all discipline problems as adjustment problems and that counseling and guidance procedures must be directed to the solution of such problems. Punishment must be replaced by the use of educative and learning techniques (Williamson, 1955; Williamson and Foley, 1949).

Text materials

Local conditions must dictate the selection of text material. A flexible course may be organized around adjustment pamphlets available from standard publishing houses or even *Public Affairs* pamphlets.

Rochester, New York, is typical of many communities that have developed their own course outlines and unit programs out of selected materials. The director of guidance and representatives of each of nine high school co-operatively developed a prospectus of recommended programs for their schools (A. A. Hollander *et al.*, 1958). Similar committees, made up of representatives of all involved schools, developed resource units for their grade levels; eighth grade (Chipp *et al.*, 1960), ninth grade (Steese *et al.*, 1960), and eleventh grade (Gates *et al.*, 1960). A twelfth-grade course in self-appraisal and career planning is described in Christensen and Burns (1954).

Specifically designed text sources have been developed for the upper grades of elementary school, junior high school, secondary schools, and colleges. Early elementary grade material is not yet commercially available. These sources, arranged according to grade level, are recommended:

Grades 1–6

No single text sources recommended; locally written units only.

Grades 7–12

Katz, Martin (1959), *You Today and Tomorrow*. Princeton, N.J.: Educational Testing Service.

Mahoney, H. J., and T. L. Engle (1961), *Points for Decision*, rev. ed., Tarrytown, N. Y.: World Book Company.

Allen, Richard D. (1952), *The Inor Group Guidance Series*, Volumes I-III. New York: Inor Publishing Company.

Engle, T. L. (1957), *Psychology*, 3rd ed., Tarrytown, New York: World Book Company.

Grade 13

Glanz, E. C., and E. B. Walston (1958), *An Introduction to Personal Adjustment*, Boston: Allyn and Bacon, Inc.

Bernard, H. W. (1957), *Toward Better Personal Adjustment*, 2nd ed. New York: McGraw-Hill Book Company, Inc.

Borow, Henry, and R. V. Lindsey (1959), *Vocational Planning for College Students*. Englewood Cliffs, N. J.: Prentice-Hall, Inc.

Martinson, W. D. (1959), *Educational and Vocational Planning*. Chicago: Scott, Foresman and Company.

Hoffman, R. W., and R. Plutchik, eds. (1959), *Controversy*. New York: G. P. Putnam's Sons.

Many of these texts are available with teachers' manuals and guides. The appropriateness of the suggested levels will need to be determined by local examination. Many texts may be used in lower grades with advanced groups; some may be used in higher than recommended levels with below average groups.

SUMMARY

Organized guidance courses are an integrating focus for the use of counseling, testing, and group procedures in guidance. Four patterns of guidance are (1) Centralized specialism, (2) Decentralized generalism, (3) Curricular guidance, and (4) Human relations and groups.

Five specific patterns of curricular guidance approaches are: (1) Occupations courses, (2) Homeroom programs, (3) Core courses, (4) Guidance classes, and (5) Psychology courses.

An integrated guidance course for use in all levels of education is possible. Organizational patterns, content units, and course methods are offered in concrete terms. Practical issues listed and discussed are: staff selection and training, credit versus noncredit status for such courses, grading and evaluation policies. Recommended text materials are offered in bibliographic form.

SUGGESTED READINGS

Association for Supervision and Curriculum Development, *Preparation of Core Teachers for Secondary Schools*. Washington, D. C.: National Education Association, 1953.

Becker, S. L., J. N. Murray, and H. P. Bechtoldt, *Teaching by the Discussion Method*. Iowa City: State University of Iowa, 1958.

Berrien, F. K., *Comments and Cases in Human Relations*. New York: Harper & Bros., 1951.

Conant, James B., *The American High School Today*. New York: McGraw-Hill Book Co., 1959.

Dressel, Paul L., "The Interrelations of Personnel Services and Instruction," in National Association for the Study of Education, *Personnel Services*

Murphy, Gardner (1947), *Personality, A Bio-Social Approach to Origins and Structure*. New York: Harper & Bros.

Murray, E. (1960), "Semantics and Group Processes," *Education*, 80, 286–291.

McCabe, George E. (1958), "Guidance in the Classroom: A Series of Hypotheses," *Educational Administration and Supervision*, 44, 213–218.

McCann, W. H., and A. A. Almada (1951), "Round-Table Psycho-Therapy: A Technique in Group Psychotherapy," *Journal of Consulting Psychology*, 14, 421–435.

McCorkle, David B., and David J. O'Dea (1953), "Some Problems of Home-room Teachers," *Personnel and Guidance Journal*, 32, 206–208.

McCracken, T. C., and H. E. Lamb (1923), *Occupational Information in the Elementary School*. Boston: Houghton Mifflin Co.

McCurdy, H. G., and W. E. Lambert (1952), "The Efficiency of Small Human Groups in the Solution of Problems Requiring Genuine Cooperation," *Journal of Personnel*, 20, 478–494.

McDaniel, H. B. (1956), *Guidance in the Modern School*. New York: The Dryden Press.

McDaniel, James (1960), "Group Action in the Rehabilitation of the Mentally Retarded," *Group Psychotherapy*, 13, 5–13.

McFarland, J. W. (1953), "Developing Effective Home Rooms," *School Review*, 61, 400–405.

McKeachie, W. J. (1951), "Anxiety in the College Classroom," *Journal of Educational Research*, 45, 153–160.

————— (1956), "Group Dynamics: Implications from Research Instruction and for Institutional Programs," in G. K. Smith, ed., *Current Issues in Higher Education*. Washington, D. C.: Association for Higher Education, 175–181.

————— (1958), "Students, Groups, and Teaching Methods," *American Psychologist*, 13, 580–584.

————— (1961), "The Work of the Teacher," in Nevitt Sanford, *The American College*. New York: John Wiley & Sons, Inc.

McKown, Harry C. (1946), *Home Room Guidance* (2nd ed.). New York: McGraw-Hill Book Co.

————— (1952), *Extra-Curricular Activities* (3rd ed.). New York: The Mac-Millan Co.

McLaughlin, K. E., ed. (1960), *Understanding Testing*. Washington, D. C.: U. S. Department of Health, Education and Welfare; Office of Education.

National Association of Student Councils, *Student Council Yearbook*. Washington, D. C.: National Education Association (Annual Publication).

National Society for the Study of Education (1952), *General Education*, Fifty-first Yearbook. Chicago: University of Chicago Press.

————— (1959), *Personnel Services in Education*, Fifty-eighth Yearbook, Part II. Chicago: University of Chicago Press.

————— (1960), *The Dynamics of Instructional Groups*, Fifty-ninth Yearbook. Chicago: University of Chicago Press.

National Training Laboratory in Group Development (since 1947), *Reports of Summer Laboratory Sessions*. Washington, D. C.: National Training Laboratory, National Education Association.

—— (1954), *Explorations in Human Relations Training: An Assessment of Experience*, (1947–1953). Washington, D. C.: National Training Laboratory, National Education Association.

National Training Laboratories (1959), *Report of the First National Training Laboratory for Educational Leaders*, Bulletin No. 12. Washington, D. C.: Division of Adult Education Service, National Education Association.

—— (1960), *Report of the First College Student Leadership Training Laboratory*. Washington, D. C.: Division of Adult Education Service, National Education Association.

Nelson, E. (1942), "The Effectiveness of Freshman Orientation at Fourteen Colleges," *School and Society*, 55, 138–139.

Neugarten, Bernice, *et al.* (1946), *National Forum Guidance Series*. Chicago: National Forum, Inc. (six books for grades 7–12).

Newman, William H. (1956), "A Full-Time Counselor in an Elementary School," *Elementary School Journal*, 56, 354–357.

Norfleet, Bobbie (1948), "Interpersonal Relations and Group Productivity," *Journal of Social Issues*, 4, No. 2, 66–69.

Novak, Benjamin J. (1951), "Don't Sell the Homeroom Short," *Nations Schools*, XLVIII, 49–51.

Nugent, F. A. (1961), "The Relationship of Discrepancies Between Interest and Aptitude Scores to Other Selected Personality Variables," *Personnel and Guidance Journal*, 39, 388–395.

O'Brien, J. P. (1956), "The Use and Abuse of Parliamentary Procedure," *Adult Leadership*, 5, 179–182.

O'Connor, N., and K. A. Yonge (1955), "Methods of Evaluating the Group Psycho-Therapy of Unstable Defective Delinquents," *Journal of Genetic Psychology*, 87, 89–101.

Ohlsen, M. M., and A. F. Dewitt (1950), "Group Counseling: A Report on Ways and Means," *Clearing House*, 24, 335–339.

Ojemann, Ralph H. (1955), "We Can Teach Human Relations," *Journal of Health, Physical Education, Recreation*, 26, 20–21.

Olmsted, Michael S. (1954), "Orientation and Role in the Small Group," *American Sociological Review*, 19, 741–750.

Osborn, A. F. (1957), *Applied Imagination: Creative Thinking* (rev. ed.). New York: Charles Scribner's Sons.

Ostland, Leonard A. (1953), "Group Integration in a Case Discussion Course," *Journal of Educational Psychology*, 44, 463–474.

Passow, A. H., *et al.* (1957), "Adapting the Curriculum to the Needs, Capacities, and Talents of Individual Students," *Review of Educational Research*, 27, 250–261.

Passow, A. H., M. B. Miles, S. M. Corey, and D. C. Draper (1955), *Training*

Curriculum Leaders for Cooperative Research. New York: Bureau of Publications, Teachers College, Columbia University.

Pepinsky, Harold B. (1947), "Measuring Outcomes of Classroom Therapy," *Educational and Psychological Measurement,* 7, 713–721.

Pepinsky, Harold B., and Pauline N. Pepinsky (1954), *Counseling: Theory and Practice.* New York: The Ronald Press Co.

Pepinsky, Harold B., L. Siegel, and E. L. Vanetta (1952), "The Criterion in Counseling: A Group Participation Scale," *Journal of Abnormal and Social Psychology,* 47, 415–419.

Peres, Hadassah (1947), "An Investigation of Nondirective Group Therapy," *Journal of Consulting Psychology,* 11, 159–172.

Peterson, B. H. (1949), "Student Government in Collegiate Institutions," *Journal of Higher Education,* 14, 205–213.

Phillips, B. N., and L. A. D'Amico (1956), "Effects of Cooperation and Competition on the Cohesiveness of Small Face-to-Face Groups," *Journal of Educational Psychology,* 47, 65–70.

Phillips, E. Lakin (1951), "Attitudes Toward Self and Others: A Brief Questionnaire Report," *Journal of Consulting Psychology,* 15, 79–81.

Piaget, Jean (1926), *The Language and Thought of the Child.* New York: Harcourt, Brace & Co.

Pierson, George A., and C. W. Grant (1959), "The Road Ahead for the School Counselor," *Personnel and Guidance Journal,* 38, 207–210.

Pigors, P., and C. A. Meyers (1947), *Personnel Administration.* New York: McGraw-Hill Book Co.

Powdermaker, F. B., and J. D. Frank (1953), *Group Psychotherapy.* Cambridge, Mass.: Harvard University Press.

Pratt, J. H. (1906), "The Home Sanitarium Treatment of Consumption," *Johns Hopkins Hospital Bulletin,* 17, 140–144.

Preston, Malcolm G., and Roy K. Heintz (1949), "Effects of Participatory vs. Supervisory Leadership on Group Judgments," *Journal of Abnormal and Social Psychology,* 44, 345–355.

Pruitt, Wilton (1960), "Group Size and Organizational Planning," *Personnel and Guidance Journal,* 38, 626–632.

Puffer, J. A. (1912), *The Boy and His Gang.* Boston: Houghton Mifflin Co.

Pullias, E. V. (1939), "Should an Individual Know His Own I.Q.? A Mental Health Problem," *Elementary School Journal,* 40, 277–283.

Punke, H. (1951), "Tell Students Their Intelligence Rating," *School and Society,* 73, 407–409.

Raines, Max R. (1956), "Helping College Freshmen Identify Problems Through a Case Conference," *Personnel and Guidance Journal,* 34, 417–419.

Rathbun, Jesse E. (1945), "The Functions of Group Counseling," *California Journal of Secondary Education,* 20, 447–452.

Raven, B. H. (1959), "The Dynamics of Groups," *Review of Educational Research,* 29, No. 4, 332–343.

Raven, B. H., and J. Rietsema (1957), "The Effects of Varied Clarity of Group

Goal and Group Path Upon the Individual and His Relation to His Group," *Human Relations,* 10, 29–47.

Reaves, John T. (1956), "Why Have a Student Council Class?" *School Activities,* 27, 287–288.

Reavis, W. C. (1932), *Programs of Guidance,* National Survey of Secondary Education, Monograph No. 14. Washington, D. C.: U. S. Office of Education, Bulletin No. 17.

Redl, Fritz (1942), "Group Emotion and Leadership," *Psychiatry,* 5, 573–596.

——— (1943), "Group Psychological Elements in Discipline Problems," *American Journal of Orthopsychiatry,* 13, 77–82.

——— (1948), "Resistance in Therapy Groups," *Human Relations,* 1, 307–313.

Redl, Fritz, and W. W. Wattenberg (1959), *Mental Hygiene in Teaching.* New York: Harcourt, Brace & Co.

Redl, Fritz, and D. Wineman (1951), *Children Who Hate.* Glencoe, Ill.: Free Press.

——— (1952), *Controls from Within.* Glencoe, Ill.: Free Press.

Rezler, Agnes G. (1960), "Personal Values and Achievement in College," *Personnel and Guidance Journal,* 39, 137–143.

Riccio, Anthony C. (1958), "Group Guidance: A Step Toward the Core," *Educational Administration and Supervision,* 44, 1–9.

Richards, C. (1958), "Group Counseling at the Junior High School Level," *School Counselor,* 5, 47, 58–60.

Richardson, H., and H. Borow (1952), "Evaluation of a Technique of Group Orientation for Vocational Counseling," *Educational and Psychological Measurement,* 12, 587–597.

Riddle, Ethel M. (1925), "Aggressive Behavior in a Small Social Group," *Arch. Psychology,* 12, No. 78.

Riesman, David, Nathan Glazer, and Revel Denney (1953), *The Lonely Crowd.* New Haven: Yale University Press. (Abridged: Doubleday Anchor Books).

Rinn, John L. (1961), "Group Guidance: Two Processes," *Personnel and Guidance Journal,* 39, 591–594.

Robinson, Jane (1953), "Venture in Group Therapy on Senior High School Level," *Journal of the National Association of Deans of Women,* 17, 25–27.

Roche, W. D. (1948), "What About Guidance Classes?" *Clearing House,* 32, 547–549.

Roe, Anne (1956), *The Psychology of Occupations.* New York: John Wiley & Sons, Inc.

Roethlisberger, F. J. (1941), *Management and Morale.* Cambridge, Mass.: Harvard University Press.

Roethlisberger, F. J., and W. J. Dickson (1939), *Management and the Worker.* Cambridge, Mass.: Harvard University Press.

Rogers, Carl R. (1942), *Counseling and Psychotherapy.* Boston: Houghton Mifflin Co.

———— (1948) *Dealing With Social Tensions*. Danville, Ill.: The Interstate Printers and Publishers, Inc.

———— (1951) *Client-Centered Therapy*. Boston: Houghton Mifflin Co.

———— (1958) "The Characteristics of a Helping Relationship," *Personnel and Guidance Journal*, 37, 6–16.

———— (1959) "A Theory of Therapy, Personality, and Interpersonal Relationships, as Developed in the Client-Centered Framework," in Sigmond Koch, ed., *Psychology: A Study of Science*, Vol. 3, Study I. New York: McGraw-Hill Book Co., 184–256.

———— (1961) "The Place of the Person in the New World of the Behavioral Sciences," *Personnel and Guidance Journal*, 39, 442–451.

Rogers, C. R., and F. J. Roethlisberger (1952), "Barriers and Gateways to Communication," *The Harvard Business Review*, 30, 45–48.

Rogers, C. R., and R. F. Dymond (1954), *Psychotherapy and Personality Change*. Chicago: University of Chicago Press.

Rogers, C. R., and B. F. Skinner (1956), "Some Issues Concerning the Control of Behavior," *Science*, 30, 1057–1066.

Rosecrance, Francis C., and Velma Hayden (1960), *School Guidance and Personnel Services*. Boston: Allyn and Bacon, Inc.

Roskens, Ronald W. (1960), "Relationship Between Leadership Participation in College and After College," *Personnel and Guidance Journal*, 39, 110–114.

Ross, C. C. (1938), "Should Low Ranking College Freshmen be Told Their Scores on Intelligence Tests," *School and Society*, 47, 678–680.

Ross, M. G., and C. E. Hendry (1957), *New Understandings of Leadership*. New York: Association Press.

Ross, Vivian (1954), *Handbook for Home Room Guidance*. New York: The MacMillan Co.

Rothney, John W. M. (1952), "Interpretation of Test Scores to Counselors," *Occupations*, 31, 320–322.

———— (1958), *Guidance Practices and Results*. New York: Harper & Bros.

Rothney, John W. M., and N. E. Koopman (1958), "Guidance of the Gifted," National Society for the Study of Education, *Education for the Gifted*, Fifty-seventh Yearbook. Chicago: University of Chicago Press.

Rush, C. H. Jr. (1957), "Leader Behavior and Group Characteristics," in R. M. Stogdill and A. E. Coons, *Leader Behavior: Its Description and Measurement*. Columbus, Ohio: Bureau of Business Research, Ohio State University.

Sachs, Georgia M. (1945), *Evaluation of Group Guidance Work in Secondary Schools*. Southern California Education Monographs, No. 14. Los Angeles: University of Southern California Press.

Sacks, Joseph M., *et al.* (1960), "Changes in Perception and Interaction in Group Therapy," *Group Psychotherapy*, 13, 101–109.

Salinger, M. D., *et al.* (1960), "The Catalytic Function of the Counselor," *Personnel and Guidance Journal*, 38, 648–652.

Samler, Joseph, *et al.* (1959), *Basic Approaches to Mental Health in the*

Schools. Washington, D. C.: American Personnel and Guidance Association. (Reprint series of seven articles from the *Personnel and Guidance Journal*, 1958–59.)

Sanford, F. H. (1952), "Research on Military Leadership," in J. C. Flanagan, ed., *Psychology in the World Emergency*. Pittsburgh: University of Pittsburgh Press, 17–74.

Sarason, Seymour B., *et al.* (1960), *Anxiety in Elementary School Children*. New York: John Wiley & Sons, Inc.

Sarbin, Theodore R. (1954), "Role Theory," in G. Lindzey, ed., *Handbook of Social Psychology*. Cambridge, Mass.: Addison-Wesley Pub. Co., Vol. I, 223–258.

Scannell, Dale P. (1960), "Prediction of College Success from Elementary and Secondary School Performance," *Journal of Educational Psychology*, 51, 130–134.

Schachter, S. (1951), "Deviation, Rejection, and Communication," *Journal of Abnormal and Social Psychology*, 46, 190–207.

Schachter, S., N. Ellertson, D. McBride, and D. Gregory (1951), "An Experimental Study of Cohesiveness and Productivity," *Human Relations*, 4, 229–238.

Scheidlinger, S. (1955), "Should Teachers Be Group Therapists?" *Progressive Education*, 32, 70–74.

Schilder, Paul (1938), *Psychotherapy*. New York: W. W. Norton & Co., Inc.

Schilder, Paul, and L. Bender (1951), *Psychotherapy* (rev. ed.). New York: W. W. Norton & Co., Inc.

Schuster, Jane (1957), *Report To Educational Testing Service. Research Report on "You: Today and Tomorrow"* (unpublished).

Scott, T. B., and R. Hoppock (1961), "College Courses in Careers," *Personnel and Guidance Journal*, 39, 373–375.

Shaffer, L. F., and E. J. Shoben (1956), *The Psychology of Adjustment* (2nd ed.). Boston: Houghton Mifflin Co.

Shaw, M. E. (1932), "A Comparison of Individuals and Small Groups in the Rational Solution of Complex Problems," *American Journal of Psychology*, 44, 491–504.

——— (1954), "Some Effects of Unequal Distribution of Information upon Group Performance in Various Communication Nets," *The Journal of Abnormal and Social Psychology*, 49, 547–553.

——— (1955), "A Comparison of Two Types of Leadership in Various Communication Nets," *Journal of Abnormal and Social Psychology*, 50, 127–134.

——— (1959), "Acceptance of Authority, Group Structure, and the Effectiveness of Small Groups," *Journal of Personality*, 27, 196–210.

Shaw, M. E., and J. T. McCuen (1960), "The Onset of Academic Underachievement in Bright Children," *Journal of Educational Psychology*, 51, 103–108.

Sheldon, W. D., and T. Landsman (1950), "Investigation of Non-Directive

Group Therapy with Students in Academic Difficulty," *Journal of Consulting Psychology*, 14, 210–215.

Shepard, A. Herbert, and W. G. Bennis (1956), "A Theory of Training by Group Methods," *Human Relations*, 9, 403–414.

Sherif, Muzafer, and Carolyn W. Sherif (1953), *Groups in Harmony and Tension: An Integration of Studies on Intergroup Relations.* New York: Harper & Bros.

Sherif, Muzafer, J. B. White, and O. J. Harvey (1955), "Status in Experimentally Produced Groups," *American Journal of Sociology*, 60, 370–379.

Shimberg, B. (1957), "Progress Report to the Advisory Board, E. T. S. Guidance Inquiry." Princeton, N. J.: Educational Testing Service (unpublished).

———— (1959), "Summary of Questionnaire Results: E. T. S. Guidance Inquiry." Princeton, N. J.: Educational Testing Service (unpublished).

Shimberg, B., and M. Katz (1960), "The Evaluation of *You: Today and Tomorrow*—Student Learnings and Teacher Reactions," American Psychological Association Convention paper (mimeographed).

Shoben, E. J. Jr. (1951), "Tell Students Their Intelligence Rating?" *School and Society*, 74, 169–170.

Shosteck, Robert (1955), "How Well Are We Putting Across Occupational Information?" *Personnel and Guidance Journal*, 33, 265–269.

Siegel, L., J. F. Adams, and F. G. Macomber (1960), "Retention of Subject Matter as a Function of Large Group Instructional Procedures," *Journal of Educational Psychology*, 51, 9–13.

Siegel, Max (1960), "Group Orientation and Placement Counseling, *Personnel and Guidance Journal*, 38, 659–660.

Siegel, S., and L. E. Fauraker (1960), *Bargaining and Group Decision Making.* New York: McGraw-Hill Book Co.

Simmel, Georg (1951), "The Stranger," in R. Dubin, *Human Relations in Administration.* New York: Prentice-Hall, Inc., 124–127.

Singer, S. L., and B. Stefflre (1957), "Concurrent Validity of the Mooney Problem Check List," *Personnel and Guidance Journal*, 35, 298–301.

Sinick, D., and R. Hoppock (1959), "Research on the Teaching of Occupations 1956–1958," *Personnel and Guidance Journal*, 38, 150–155.

Skinner, B. F. (1956), "Freedom and the Control of Men," *The American Scholar*, 25, 47–65.

Slavson, S. R. (1937), *Creative Group Education.* New York: Association Press.

———— (1943), *An Introduction to Group Therapy.* New York: The Commonwealth Fund.

———— (1947), *The Practice of Group Therapy.* New York: International Universities Press.

———— (1950), *Analytic Group Psychotherapy with Children, Adolescents, and Adults.* New York: Columbia University Press.

———— (1951), "Authority, Restraint and Discipline in Group Therapy with Children," *Nervous Child*, 9, No. 2, 187–195.

———— (1952) *Child Psychotherapy*. New York: Columbia University Press.

Small, J. L. (1957), "Why a Core Based on Adolescent Needs?" *Educational Administration and Supervision*, 43, 108–114.

Smith, Ewart E. (1957), "The Effects of Clear and Unclear Role Expectations on Group Productivity and Defensiveness," *Journal of Abnormal and Social Psychology*, 55, 213–217.

Snyder, T. (1937), "Reporting Intelligence-Test Scores to High School Pupils," *School Review*, 45, 105–111.

Snyder, W. U., ed., (1947), *Casebook of Non-Directive Counseling*. Boston: Houghton Mifflin Co.

Snygg, D., and A. W. Combs (1949), *Individual Behavior*. New York: Harper & Bros.

Stagner, R. (1951), "Homeostasis as a Unifying Concept in Personality Theory," *Psychological Review*, 58, 5–17.

Steese, P. A., *et al.* (1960), *Group Guidance Resource Units, Ninth Grade* (rev. ed.). Rochester, N. Y.: Board of Education (mimeographed).

Stock, D., and H. A. Thelan (1958), *Emotional Dynamics and Group Culture*. Washington, D. C.: National Training Laboratory, National Educational Association.

Stogdill, Ralph M. (1948), "Personal Factors Associated with Leadership: A Survey of the Literature," *Journal of Psychology*, 25, 35–71.

———— (1950), "Leadership, Membership and Organization," *Psychological Bulletin*, 47, 1–14.

———— (1959), *Individual Behavior and Group Achievement*. New York: Oxford University Press.

Stogdill, Ralph M., and Carroll L. Shartle (1948), "Methods for Determining Patterns of Leadership Behavior in Relationship to Organization Structure and Objectives," *Journal of Applied Psychology*, 32, 286–291.

Stone, C. (1948), "Are Vocational Orientation Courses Worth Their Salt?" *Educational and Psychological Measurement*, 8, 161–181.

Stout, Minard W. (1948), "The Sources of Revenue for Extra-Class Activities," *School Review*, 56, 410–414.

Strang, Ruth (1945), "Guidance Through Groups," in "Counseling, Guidance and Personnel Work," *Review of Educational Research*, 15, 164–172.

———— (1948), "Prevention of Delinquency Through Guided Group Experience," in National Society for the Study of Education, *Juvenile Delinquency and the Schools*, 47th Yearbook, Part 1. Chicago: University of Chicago Press, 88–90.

———— (1953), *The Role of the Teacher in Personnel Work* (4th ed.). New York: Bureau of Publications, Teachers College, Columbia University.

———— (1958a), *Group Work in Education*. New York: Harper & Bros.

———— (1958b), *Guideposts for Gifted Children Themselves*. New York: Bureau of Publications, Teachers College, Columbia University.

———— (1960), *Helping Your Gifted Child*. New York: E. P. Dutton & Co.

Stroup, Herbert (1956), "The Intentions of Student Activities Systems," *Higher Education*, 27, 256–263, 290.

Sullivan, Harry Stack (1947), *Conceptions of Modern Psychiatry*. Washington, D. C.: The William Alanson White Psychiatric Foundation.

Super, Donald E. (1957), *The Psychology of Careers*. New York: Harper & Bros.

Super, Donald E., and P. L. Overstreet (1960), *The Vocational Maturity of Ninth Grade Boys*. New York: Bureau of Publications, Teachers College, Columbia University.

Super, Donald E., *et al.* (1957), *Vocational Development: A Framework for Research*. New York: Bureau of Publications, Teachers College, Columbia University.

—— (1957), *Scientific Careers and Vocational Development Theory*. New York: Bureau of Publications, Teachers College, Columbia University.

—— (1958), "The Role of Counseling in State and Regional Programs," in American Association for the Advancement of Science, *Identification and Guidance of Able Students*, Conference Report.

Swanson, E. O. (1960), "No I. Q.?" *Bulletin and Occupational Newsletter*, Student Counseling Bureau, University of Minnesota, April 15.

Symonds, P. M. (1936), "The Principal Areas of Personal Problems," *Teachers College Record*, 38, 144–145.

Taba, Hilda (1955a) *School Culture*. Washington, D. C.: American Council on Education.

—— (1955b), *With Perspective on Human Relations*. Washington, D. C.: American Council on Education.

Taba, Hilda, and D. Elkins (1950), *With Focus on Human Relations*. Washington, D. C.: American Council on Education.

Taba, Hilda, *et al.* (1952), *Intergroup Education in Public Schools*. Washington, D. C.: American Council on Education.

Taft, Ronald (1960), "Judgment and Judging in Person Cognition," in H. P. David and J. C. Brengelmann, eds., *Perspectives in Personality Research*. New York: Springer Pub. Co., Inc., 196–209.

Tagiuri, R. (1960), "Movement as a Cue in Person Perception," in H. P. David and J. C. Brengelmann, eds., *Perspectives in Personality Research*. New York: Springer Pub. Co., Inc., 175–195.

Tagiuri, R., and L. Petrullo, eds., (1958), *Person Perception and Interpersonal Behavior*. Stanford, Calif.: Stanford University Press.

Tagiuri, R., R. R. Blake, and J. S. Bruner (1953), "Some Determinants of the Perception of Positive and Negative Feelings to Others," *Journal of Abnormal and Social Psychology*, 48, 133–151.

Talland, G. A., and D. H. Clark (1954), "Evaluation of Topics in Therapy Group Discussion," *Journal of Clinical Psychology*, 10, 131–137.

Tannenbaum, R., and F. Massarik (1951), "Sharing Decision Making with Subordinates," in R. Dubin, *Human Relations and Administration*. New York: Prentice-Hall, Inc., 223–228.

———— (1957), "Leadership: A Frame of Reference." *Management Science,* 4, 1–19.

Tannenbaum, R., I. Weschler, and F. Massarik (1961), *Leadership and Organization.* New York: McGraw-Hill Book Co.

Taylor, A., *et al.* (1948), *Group Guidance Activities: A Program for the High School,* School Document No. 9–1947. Boston: City of Boston Printing Department.

Taylor, F. K. (1950), "The Therapeutic Factors in Group-Analytical Treatment," *Journal of Mental Science,* 96, 967–997.

Taylor, H. M. (1960), "Use of Problem Solving Groups in Teaching Geography," *Journal of Geography,* 59, 187–189.

Terman, Lewis M. (1904–1955), "A Preliminary Study of the Psychology and Pedagogy of Leadership," in A. P. Hare, E. F. Borgatta, and R. F. Bales, *Small Groups.* New York: Alfred A. Knopf, 24–30 (originally published in Psychological Seminary, 2, 1904, 413–451.)

Thelen, Herbert A. (1949), "Group Dynamics in Instruction: The Principle of Least Group Size," *School Review,* 57, 139–148.

———— (1954) *Dynamics of Groups at Work.* Chicago: University of Chicago Press.

Thibaut, John W., and H. H. Kelley (1959), *The Social Psychology of Groups.* New York: John Wiley & Sons, Inc.

Thistlethwaite, D. L. (1960), *College Press and Changes in Study Plans of Talented Students.* Evanston, Ill.: National Merit Scholarship Corp.

Thompson, A. S. (1960), "Developmental Stage and Developmental Needs at the Junior High School Level," *Personnel and Guidance Journal,* 39, 116–118.

Thompson, Laura (1956), "The Societal System, Culture and the Community," in R. R. Grinker, ed., *Toward a Unified Theory of Human Behavior.* New York: Basic Books, Inc.

Thorndike, E. L. (1911), *Animal Intelligence.* New York: The Macmillan Co.

Thorndike, R. L. (1938), "On What Type of Task Will a Group Do Well?" *Journal of Abnormal and Social Psychology,* 33, 409–413.

Thorndike, R. L., and E. Hagen (1955), *Measurement and Evaluation in Psychology and Education.* New York: John Wiley & Sons, Inc.

Thorpe, L. P., *et al.* (1959), *Studying Social Relationships in the Classroom: Sociometric Methods for the Teacher.* Chicago: Science Research Associates.

Thrasher, Frederic M. (1927), *The Gang.* Chicago: University of Chicago.

Tiedeman, David V. (1961), "A Paradigm of Decision in Career Development and Its Implications," *Personnel and Guidance Journal,* 40 (in press).

Tiedeman, David V., and R. P. O'Hara (1958), *Position Choices and Careers: Elements of a Theory,* Harvard Studies in Career Development, No. 8. Cambridge, Mass.: Harvard Graduate School of Education.

Torrance, P. (1949), "The Role Concept in a Vocational Guidance Program," *Childhood Education,* 25, 413–416.

———— (1955), "Perception of Group Functioning as a Predictor of Group Performance," *Journal of Social Psychology*, 42, 271–282.

Trapp, E. P. (1959), "Threat and Direction of Aggression," *Journal of Clinical Psychology*, 15, 308–310.

Triplett, N. (1898), "The Dynamogenic Factors in Pace-making and Competition," American Journal of Psychology, 9, 507–533.

Trueblood, Dennis L. (1951), "Participation of Student Government in the Student Personnel Program," *Educational and Psychological Measurement*, 799–802.

———— (1960), "The Counseling Role in a Group Activities Advisory Context," *Journal of College Student Personnel*, 1, 13–17.

Turner, C. E. (1933), "Test Room Studies in Employee Effectiveness," *American Journal of Public Health*, 23, 577–584.

Vinache, W. Edgar (1957), "Some Variables in Buzz Sessions," *Journal of Social Psychology*, 45, 25–33.

Wagner, J. A. (1959), *Successful Leadership in Groups and Organizations*. San Francisco: Howard Chandler.

Walters, George F. (1952), "Evaluating Student Council Procedures," *School Activities*, 24, 59–63.

Warters, Jane (1956), *High School Personnel Work Today* (2nd ed.). New York: McGraw-Hill Book Co.

———— (1960), *Group Guidance*. New York: McGraw-Hill Book Co.

Watson, Goodwin (1946), *Action for Unity*. Washington, D. C.: Commission on Community Interrelations, American Jewish Congress (pamphlet).

———— (1947), *Action for Unity*. New York: Harper & Bros.

Weschsler, I., and J. Reisel (1959), *Inside a Sensitivity Training Group*, Industrial Relations Monograph No. 4. Los Angeles: Institute of Industrial Relations, U. C. L. A.

Wester, Bernice (1956), "The Student Council as a Class," *School Activities*, 27, 259–260.

Wey, Herbert (1948), "An Experiment in Group Guidance," *Bulletin of the National Association of Secondary School Principals*, 32, 124–129.

Whalen, E. (1946), "English Classes Handle Newcomer's Orientation," *Clearing House*, 21, 27–30.

Whyte, W. F. (1943), *Street Corner Society*. Chicago: University of Chicago Press.

———— (1949), "The Social Structure of the Restaurant," *American Journal of Sociology*, 54, 302–310.

Whyte, W. H. (1956), *The Organization Man*. New York: Simon and Schuster, Inc.

———— (1952), "Groupthink," *Fortune*.

Wilcox, Glenn W. (1958), *Basic Study Skills*. Boston: Allyn and Bacon, Inc.

Willerman, B. (1959), "Changing the Attitudes of Fraternity Members Toward University Control," *Personnel and Guidance Journal*, 37, 542–550.

Williams, H. F. Jr. (1954), "The Town Tells Teens About Jobs," *Personnel and Guidance Journal*, 32, 266–269.

Williamson, E. G. (1955), "The Fusion of Discipline and Counseling in the Educative Process," *Personnel and Guidance Journal*, 34, 74–79.

Williamson, E. G., and J. Foley (1949), *Counseling and Discipline*. New York: McGraw-Hill Book Co.

Wise, William M. (1959), *They Come For The Best of Reasons: College Students Today*. Washington, D. C.: American Council on Education.

Witty, P., J. B. Conant, and R. Strang (1959), *Creativity of Gifted and Talented Children*. New York: Teachers College, Columbia University.

Wolfe, A. (1949), "The Psychoanalysis of Groups: Parts I and II," *American Journal of Psychotherapy*, 3, 525–558, and 4, 16–50.

Wolff, Kurt H. (1950), *The Sociology of Georg Simmel*. Glencoe, Ill.: Free Press.

Wood, Donald I. (1953a), "Current Student Election Practices," *Student Life*, 20, (3), 14–15.

——— (1953b), "The Leadership Class: A Survey of Current Practice," *Student Life*, 20, (1), 20.

Wrenn, C. Gilbert (1951a), "Professors and Professional Membership," *Occupations*, 30, 24–29.

——— (1951b), *Student Personnel Work in College, with Emphasis on Counseling and Group Experiences*. New York: The Ronald Press Co.

——— (1957), "Status and Role of the School Counselor," *Personnel and Guidance Journal*, 36, 175–183.

——— (1959), "Philosophical and Psychological Bases of Personnel Services in Education," in National Society for the Study of Education, *Personnel Services in Education*, Fifty-eighth Yearbook, Part II. Chicago: University of Chicago Press, 41–81.

Wrenn, C. Gilbert, *et al. Report of American Personnel and Guidance Association Commission on Guidance in American Schools*. Washington, D.C.: American Personnel and Guidance Association.

Wright, Barbara (1928), "A Method of Using the Group Conference as a Guidance Device," *Vocational Guidance Magazine* (now *Personnel and Guidance Journal*), 7, 26–33.

Wright, E. W. (1959), "Multiple Counseling: Why? When? How?" *Personnel and Guidance Journal*, 37, 551–557.

Wright, Grace S. (1950), *Core Curriculum in Public High School*. Washington, D. C.: U. S. Office of Education, Bulletin 5.

——— (1952), *Core Curriculum Development: Problems and Practices*. Washington, D. C.: U. S. Office of Education, Bulletin 5.

——— (1956), *The Core Program: Abstracts of Unpublished Research*: 1946–1955. Washington, D. C.: Government Printing Office.

Wright, Ralph E. (1956), "Teaching Occupational Information in Illinois Secondary Schools," 35, 30–33.

Wrightstone, J. W. (1960), "Demonstration Guidance Project in New York City," *Harvard Educational Review*, 30, 237–251.

Yonge, K. A., and N. O'Connor (1954), "Measurable Effects of Group Psychotherapy with Defective Delinquents," *Journal of Mental Science*, 100, 944–952.

Ziller, Robert C. (1957), "Four Techniques of Group Decision-Making Under Uncertainty," *Journal of Applied Psychology*, 41, 384–388.

INDEX OF NAMES

Shaffer, L. F., 106, 107, 115, 360
Sharp, O. L., 208
Shartle, C., 265
Shaw, M. E., 63, 90, 137, 235, 344, 360
Sheldon, W. D., 273, 296, 360
Shepard, A. H., 153, 158, 181, 361
Sherif, C. W., 8, 25, 34, 54, 361
Sherif, M., 8, 25, 34, 54, 240, 361
Shimberg, B., 215, 244, 312, 349
Shoben, E. J., 106, 107, 115, 222, 360, 361
Shosteck, R., 260, 361
Shostrom, E. V., 276, 298, 299, 336
Shriver, B., 64, 337
Siegel, L., 78, 361
Siegel, M., 264, 361
Siegel, S., 34, 139, 361
Simmel, G., 12, 24, 66, 73, 361
Simon, H. A., 57
Singer, S. L., 317, 361
Sinick, D., 309, 361
Skinner, B. F., 28, 105, 361
Slavson, S. R., 15, 240, 267, 294, 299, 361, 362
Small, J. L., 311, 362
Smallenberg, H., 5, 14, 353
Smith, E. E., 183, 362
Smith, G. K., 337
Smith, G. M., 211, 215, 295, 302, 313, 344
Smith, M. R., 16, 182, 205, 345
Snyder, T., 222, 362
Snyder, W. U., 97, 273, 342, 362
Snygg, D., 83, 362
Solem, A. R., 297, 353
Southard, C., 295, 336
Stagner, R., 107, 362
Steese, P. A., 321, 362
Stefflre, B., 317, 346, 361
Stevens, N., 347
Stevens, S. S., 340
Stice, G. F., 64, 69, 338
Stock, D., 123, 165, 362
Stogdill, R. M., 42, 123, 165, 174, 359, 362
Stone, C., 309, 362
Stone, Calvin, 339, 353
Stout, M. W., 179, 362
Strang, R., 14, 16, 19, 171, 177, 225, 235, 236, 250, 268, 362
Strodbeck, F. L., 128, 129, 334
Strong, W. M., 19
Stroup, H., 169, 170, 363
Sullivan, H. S., 148, 363
Summerskill, J., 282, 353
Super, D. E., 253, 255, 259, 260, 266, 363
Swanson, E. O., 231, 363
Symonds, P. M., 363

Taba, H., 45, 241, 242, 243, 250, 253, 363
Taft, R., 83, 103, 363
Tagiuri, R., 28, 85, 103, 139, 140, 141, 186, 342, 347, 363
Talland, G. A., 278, 363
Tannenbaum, R., 24, 57, 69, 80, 138, 363, 364
Taylor, A., 315, 364
Taylor, E. K., 185
Taylor, F. K., 294, 364
Taylor, H. M., 318, 364
Tead, O., 186
Terman, L. M., 12, 24, 364
Thelen, H. A., 14, 19, 34, 43, 48, 50, 57, 76, 123, 142, 165, 362, 364
Thibaut, J. W., 103, 127, 349, 364
Thistlethwaite, D. L., 115, 364
Thompson, A. S., 323, 364
Thompson, G. G., 34, 93, 95, 165, 343
Thompson, L., 97, 112, 364
Thompson, O. G., 207
Thorndike, E. L., 118, 364
Thorndike, R. L., 119, 127, 137, 210, 364
Thorpe, L. P., 103, 364
Thrasher, F. M., 12, 24, 364
Thurstone, T. G., 231
Tiedeman, D. V., 255, 259, 337, 364
Tompkins, E., 186
Torrance, P., 256, 364
Trager, H. G., 167
Trapp, E. P., 281, 364
Triplett, N., 24, 365
Trueblood, D. L., 15, 182, 365
Truman, Harry, 75
Trump, J. L., 253
Tuma, A. H., 211, 345
Turner, C. E., 365

Vinache, W. E., 196, 365
Voeks, V., 208

Wagner, J. A., 80, 176, 365
Walker, L. C., 90, 344
Walston, E. B., 26, 68, 84, 96, 106, 111, 206, 213, 261, 306, 313, 316, 321, 344
Walters, G. F., 365
Warters, J., 19, 274, 314, 365
Watson, G., 44, 57, 365
Wattenberg, W. W., 6, 73, 76, 117, 189, 234, 240, 358, 365
Weaver, A., 124
Wells, H. G., 208
Wells, K. A., 243, 244

INDEX OF SUBJECTS

process observer, 165
training and, 164–166
Expectations, in groups, 32, 33

Faculty members, 29–31 (*see also* Teachers)
Faculty sponsors, 178, 179
Faculty-student relations, 201, 202
Failure in groups, 29
Feedback, 119, 165
Fictions, 67
Field trips, 256, 258, 259
Flexibility, 47
Ford Foundation, 312
Formal groups, 40, 42, 43, 195, 196, 326
Formation of groups, 37–57
Freedom riders, 44
Function, in groups, 9, 10, 58–70, 326
Function of members, 159, 160
Functional leadership, 326

Gangs, 25, 37, 39, 51
General Aptitude Test Battery, 259
General education, 261
Gifted groups:
  educational planning, 235, 236
  flexibility in, 235
  guidance for, 235, 236
Gifted students, 235, 236, 260, 261
Goal achievement, 68
Goal development, 112
Goals in groups, 10–13
  group, 184
  individuals and, 183
"Great Man" theory, 59
Group counseling, 216–218, 267-299
  case studies in, 271
  classifications, 294, 195
  closed groups in, 275
  college, 285–287
  content example, 288, 289
  definition of, 268, 269, 326
  didactic, 294
  ethics in, 271, 272
  examples of, 285–296
  excluding persons from, 274, 275
  group composition in, 274
  "group guidance" and, 270
  growth in, 282, 283
  high school, 287–291
  history of, 267, 268
  hospital, 291–296
  individual and, 267 ff., 296, 297
  instruction sheet for, 275

methodology issues, 273
open groups in, 275
outcomes, 290
phases in, 276–285
  acceptance, 279, 280
  closing, 284, 285
  listening, 280
  problem-solving, 283, 284
  rapport, 278
  understanding, 281, 282
practical problems in, 273–276
pre-counseling groups and, 271–273
process of, 268, 269, 273–296
referral and, 271
role playing in, 282
sociometry in, 289
special applications, 295
therapy and, 268–270
training for, 269, 270
two leaders, 298
types, 285–296
values, 283
Group field, 8, 81
"Group guidance," 13–17, 215, 327
  content in, 215
  counseling and, 270
  history, 5 ff., 13–16
Group maintenance, 68
Group size, 75–78
Group therapy, 326 (*see* Group counseling*)
Groups:
  articulation, 187–190
  climate in, 60
  college, 7, 251, 252
  committee work in, 179
  communication in, 25, 27, 28
  cooperation and competition in, 240
  counseling in, 14–16, 216–218, 267–299
  definition, 7 ff., 326
  democratic, 75
  discussion, 271
  elementary school, 152, 233, 234, 239, 240
  functions of, 58–70
  goals, 112
  growth in, 158–160
  high school, 5, 6
  history, 3 ff., 24, 25, 137
  illustrations:
    college, 29, 30, 155, 175, 182, 198, 201, 202, 204, 262, 263, 272, 285–287
    elementary, 5, 6, 26, 73, 153, 154, 183, 184, 192–194, 203–204, 256
    graduate school, 4

Size, in groups, 9
  effects of, 77
  friendship groups and, 76
  group counseling, 273, 274
  interaction and, 77, 78
  learning and, 78
  participation and, 77, 78
  perception and, 83
  principle, 76
  variables of, 76
Slow learners, 260, 261
Social control, 27, 28 (*see* Control)
Social groups, 199, 200
Social needs, 107, 108
Sociability, 49 ff.
Society and education, 147, 148, 150
Socio-drama, 264, 330
Sociometry, 92–95, 289, 330
Spontaneity in groups, 38–40, 330
Sports Illustrated, 170
Stability in groups, 52, 53, 330
Staff conferences, 225, 226
Statistical concepts, 220, 221
Status, 330
Status needs, 116
Strength of groups, 37, 50–56
Structure in groups, 41, 42, 58–80, 142, 289, 290
Student activities, 163, 164, 168–186
  administration and, 169–172
  committees, 179
  confusion in, 183, 184
  control, 177, 178
  co-ordination, 177–180
  counselors and, 181–182
  democracy and, 171, 172
  faculty sponsors, 178, 179
  goals of 183, 184
  improvement of, 180–184
  involvement in, 170, 171
  learning in, 180
  philosophy of, 169–172
  school government, 176–180
Student centered, 330
Student government, 169, 170, 176–180, 201
Student leaders, 67, 262, 263
Study groups, 41, 191, 330
Supervisory leadership, 65, 330
Syntality, 59, 69, 70, 330

T. groups, 157 ff.
Task groups, 10–13, 126, 219
Tasks, 10, 126, 330
  T. group use, 158
  function, 330

growth and, 158, 159
Teacher centered, 331
Teachers, 29–31 (*see also* Faculty members)
Teachers, elementary:
  climate creators, 235
  effecting growth, 234
  as group leaders, 240
  learning roles, 235
  teams of, 234
Teachers, junior high school:
  challenges to, 241
Teaching:
  test interpretation and, 223, 224
Team training, 113
Team teaching, 206, 330–331
  concepts of, 238
  core courses and, 311
  example of, 238
  results, 239
Test data use, 209–231
Test interpretation, 216–218
  case conferences in, 224–228
  role playing and, 228, 229
  student training, 221, 222
Test score machines, 212
Testing:
  anxiety in, 196, 197
  consumer training, 212–214
  failures of, 209 ff.
  individual differences and, 219, 220
  integrated programs, 229 ff.
  interpretation cases, 227, 228
  interpretation example, 216–218
  orientation, 196, 197
  philosophy of, 210 ff.
  research in, 211
  self-analysis and, 213, 214
  student involvement, 214–216
  student reactions, 213, 221–223
  using groups in, 223-230
Tests:
  counseling and, 211
  interpretation of, 212, 213
Threat, in groups, 31, 97, 98
Traditions, creativity and, 184, 185
Training:
  anxiety in, 152, 153
  casebooks in, 162, 163
  content and, 161–164
  decisions in, 156 ff.
  design of, 155
  emotions in, 152, 153
  evaluation of, 164–166
  example of, 153, 154
  flexibility in, 154–156

24374